D.R.Harris & Co Lᵗᵈ

—ESTABLISHED 1790—

CHEMISTS AND PERFUMERS

SPECIALISTS IN SOAPS, SKINCARE AND SHAVING SINCE 1790

29 St. James's Street
and 52 Piccadilly
020 7930 3915
www.drharris.co.uk

GRANTA

12 Addison Avenue, London W11 4QR | email: editorial@granta.com
To subscribe go to granta.com, or call 020 8955 7011 in the United Kingdom,
845-267-3031 (toll-free 866-438-6150) in the United States

ISSUE 153: AUTUMN 2020

p.55 extract from 'The Garden' by Einstürzende Neubauten used by permission of Blixa Bargeld; p.78 extract from 'The Social Life of Water' by Tony Hoagland from *Application for Release from the Dream*, copyright © 2015 by Tony Hoagland, reprinted with the permission of The Permissions Company, Inc., on behalf of Graywolf Press, Minneapolis, Minnesota, www.graywolfpress.org; p.227 extract from *King Cole* by John Masefield used by permission of the Society of Authors as the Literary Representative of the Estate of John Masefield.

This selection copyright © 2020 Granta Trust.

Granta, ISSN 173231 (USPS 508), is published four times a year by Granta Trust, 12 Addison Avenue, London W11 4QR, United Kingdom.

The US annual subscription price is $48. Airfreight and mailing in the USA by agent named World Container Inc, 150–15, 183RD Street, Jamaica, NY 11434, USA. Periodicals postage paid at Brooklyn, NY 11256.

US Postmaster: Send address changes to *Granta*, World Container Inc, 150–15, 183RD Street, Jamaica, NY 11434, USA.

Subscription records are maintained at *Granta*, c/o Abacus e-Media, 107–111 Fleet Street London, EC4A 2AB.

Air Business Ltd is acting as our mailing agent.

Granta is printed and bound in Italy by Legoprint. This magazine is printed on paper that fulfils the criteria for 'Paper for permanent document' according to ISO 9706 and the American Library Standard ANSI/NIZO Z39.48-1992 and has been certified by the Forest Stewardship Council (FSC). *Granta* is indexed in the American Humanities Index.

ISBN 978-1-909-889-36-1

Charles Bowden's
"Unnatural History of America" Series

"A trademark
hallucinatory tour
of the Southwestern
borderlands by its chief
literary interpreter."

—KIRKUS

$24.95 hardcover

A powerful meditation
on human greed and
bloodlust with razor-
sharp reporting on
Mexican drug cartels at
the US border.

$24.95 hardcover

A kaleidoscopic journey
that penetrates the
senses and redefines the
notion of heartland.

$24.95 hardcover

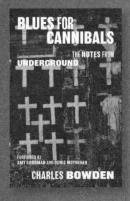

"A thrillingly
good writer."

*—NEW YORK TIMES
BOOK REVIEW*

$17.95 paperback

"Bowden manages to write
about these currently
unfashionable topics with
humor, style, and laconic
compression."

—EDWARD ABBEY

$17.95 paperback

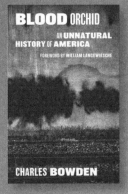

"Bowden's anger
is delicious."

—OUTSIDE

$17.95 paperback

UNIVERSITY OF TEXAS PRESS

[...] Language is also ownership, we describe our thoughts, and by default corral the heart [...]

From *Of ownership* by KAREN McCARTHY WOOLF

Mslexia Poetry & Pamphlet Competition 2020

POETRY JUDGE:
KAREN McCARTHY WOOLF

1st prize £2,000
(plus mentoring and
writing retreat)
2nd prize £500
3rd prize £250
Special prize £250
for best poem by an
unpublished woman poet

PAMPHLET JUDGE:
AMY WACK
Poetry Editor, Seren Books

1st prize £250
plus publication
of the pamphlet
by Seren Books

DEADLINE: 7 DECEMBER 2020

www.mslexia.co.uk/competitions
competitions@mslexia.co.uk
+44 (0)191 204 8860

mslexia

THE WORLD TODAY

CHATHAM HOUSE'S INTERNATIONAL AFFAIRS MAGAZINE

AESTHETICA SHORT FILM FESTIVAL

DISCOVER NEW CINEMA AT HOME

300 FILMS | 100 INDUSTRY EVENTS
50 MASTERCLASSES | 1 ONLINE PLATFORM

3-30 NOVEMBER 2020

BOOK YOUR PASS | ASFF.CO.UK/TICKETS

CONTENTS

Introduction

E very day we wake up to news of environmental catastrophe. Wildfires raging, ice caps melting, oceans warming, species on the brink of extinction, people displaced by natural disasters. During the course of this issue's production, some of our writers found themselves besieged by droughts or storms, some were even forced to flee their homes due to wildfires and floods. Nature is no longer a place of refuge.

It is easy to feel overwhelmed and helpless. But, like all fears, the solution is to face the anxiety head-on. Only by understanding what is happening can we embrace the thought of change; and only by learning from those who are providing solutions can we develop a sense that salvation is possible. Hope is something my husband and I found after embarking on our rewilding project in West Sussex, in southern England. In less than twenty years we've watched wildlife pour back onto our land, drawn like a magnet to rebounding natural resources. Our depleted soil has restored itself, and now acts like a filter, purifying run-off from the polluted land around us. Vegetation cleans the air. The land holds on to heavy rains, preventing flooding downstream, and our wetlands, vegetation and the soil itself suck carbon from the atmosphere.

The great American biologist E.O. Wilson says that if we are to safeguard the systems on which all species – including our own – depend, we must devote half of all available land mass to nature. The evidence is encouraging. Nature is forgiving. It will bounce back – if we let it. And nature, more than anything else, as Judith D. Schwartz describes, holds the answers to the environmental crises we have created.

We still need to eat, of course. And a revolution is afoot – one that has the capacity to reverse soil degradation, pollution, water loss and carbon emissions, and improve food security. Across the planet, farmers are leading the charge into regenerative agriculture, learning how to heal their land by working with nature, rather than fighting against it. Nowhere is this more critical than in the brittle zones at the front line of climate change, as Australian farmer Charles Massy shows us.

We forget, often within a few generations, that our landscapes and seas were recently much richer; the depletions have begun to seem normal – a syndrome known as 'shifting baselines'. Callum Roberts, revisiting a coral reef he knows well, finds that writing about nature today is, fundamentally, about seeing what isn't there. There's a need to peer into the deep past, too. Tim Flannery unveils a world of wondrous Australian megafauna at a time when our planet was at its most biodiverse, before the mass extinctions caused by humans. And this can open up the mind to new ideas, like species reintroductions. Embracing 'novel ecosystems', welcoming plants and animals into places where we might never have considered them before, is the subject of an entertainingly provocative piece by Ken Thompson.

Often the hardest thing is to admit our mistakes. So much of new nature writing, both fiction and non-fiction, is about challenging preconceptions, traditions and cultural biases, changing a mindset. Only when we dare hope for the return of millions of salmon to our rivers and of grey whales to the Atlantic, dare envisage a landscape where vultures might soar and wolves roam once more, will we learn how to become a keystone species ourselves.

Of course, many societies in the world have lived in harmony with nature for millennia. Indigenous voices can teach us about sustainability and the fundamental importance of forging a closer, more respectful relationship with nature; voices like those of Sheila Watt-Cloutier in the Arctic, Manari Ushigua in the Amazon and Rod Mason in Australia. The knowledge is already out there. We just have to listen.

The contributors to this issue all have a deep understanding of how nature works. Some are scientists, experts in their field; others, environmental journalists exploring the latest thinking about ecosystems and how to repair them; or poets, novelists and activists examining our responses – or lack of them – to the current crisis. Never has there been a greater need for writers who can communicate about the environment in such clear, immediate and powerful ways, who can envisage the past as well as the future. The stories in this issue will, I hope, be both enlightening and empowering, transforming the way we look at the planet, and galvanising us to bring about change. ∎

Isabella Tree

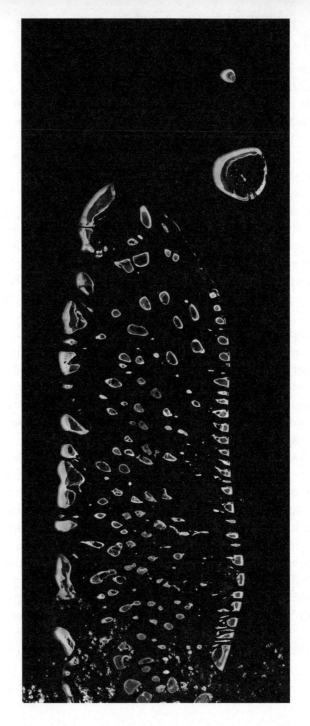

Ari Atoll, The Maldives, 2019

SHIFTING BASELINES

Callum Roberts

It is extremely difficult to divine what is happening below the water from what is visible at the surface. Ghost crab volcanoes rise from the sand beside a lagoon of duck-egg blue. The air is clear and still cool as the first sun touches the palm crowns. Noisy mynahs argue over the contents of a plastic bag stranded on a beach that is smoothed to perfection by the falling tide. Below the glassy surface, stingrays pass like shadows with movements so subtle they seem to glide without propulsion. A little offshore, sudden splashes and arcing cascades of silvered fish give away the primordial interplay of hunters and those hunted.

This coral reef in the Maldives lies at the heart of the Indian Ocean, where the fight for life goes on daily, as it has for countless millennia. But a new struggle is under way against an invisible force that has not been felt for millions of years, upending the relationship that built these reefs, a partnership first formed during the age of the dinosaurs between coral and a microbial seaweed. These seaweeds, called zooxanthellae, somehow evolved to live within the coral animal's tissues. As plants, they gifted corals with abundant food produced by photosynthesis, enabling the corals to grow more rapidly than their predecessors, whose only source of food was passing plankton. In return, living deep within coral tissues cupped inside hard limestone skeletons, zooxanthellae gained protection and used exhaled carbon dioxide to make food. Photosynthetic calories fortified the corals as protein supplements do bodybuilders. Thus endowed, corals could lay down limestone fast enough to outpace the forces of destruction: rasping grazers, burrowing worms, snails and sponges, chemical dissolution and storm waves.

Over tens of thousands of years, corals built structures that criss-cross thousands of kilometres of ocean and descend hundreds of metres into the abyss. It is hard to reconcile the immense geological antiquity of the coral-seaweed partnership with its present susceptibility to disruption. Corals love warmth, basking in tropical seas that rarely dip below swimming-pool temperatures, but equally, they wilt under unusual heat. Although we rarely think of them this way, the oceans are afflicted by heatwaves too, and, just as on land, the frequency and duration of these are on the rise due to global warming. When oceanic temperatures increase just a degree or two above the typical maximum for a region, and stay there for a month or more, the relationship between coral animal and internal zooxanthellae turns nasty, swinging from benefit to cost. In this fevered state, for reasons that are still unclear, the corals must rid themselves of the zooxanthellae quickly or they will die. Because the seaweeds produce most of the colour in coral, when they are expelled the corals turn a deathly bone white in a phenomenon known as mass bleaching. A bleached coral is a starving coral, and since corals store little fat, unless temperatures fall quickly and they can regain more zooxanthellae, they perish.

The Maldives is a nation wholly dependent on coral. It consists of twenty-six atolls built upwards by coral growth over thousands of years as sea levels rose after the last ice age. The reefs are topped by 1,100 islands created from dead coral fragments and sand swept up by Indian Ocean waves and bound together by shrubs and palm trees. From space, the country appears as a double string of bright emerald rings that runs north to south across a thousand kilometres of dark sea. Zoom in closer and, inside the giant circles of reef that make up the main atolls, dozens of ring reefs rise from the bottoms of pale lagoons. This is one of the major coral provinces of the world, comparable to Australia's Great Barrier Reef in size and complexity. The Maldives' profusion of reefs, developed over a period that we know from the geological record, has been one of the most prolific eras of reef construction in planetary history. But in 1998, tragedy struck.

In December 1997, far away from the Maldives, an El Niño – a large-scale disturbance of oceanic and atmospheric circulation – began to spread a pool of warm water across the eastern Pacific. First it scorched the Galapagos Islands, then in early 1998 it spread like a hot tongue along the equator, wrapping around Australia and Indonesia before slipping into the Indian Ocean. By May the hot pool had crossed to the coast of East Africa and entered the southern Red Sea. As the heat engulfed reefs along its journey, the corals bleached before dying en masse. Indian Ocean reefs were devastated, losing between 70 and 95 per cent of their coral. In the Maldives, living coral plunged from covering between half and two-thirds of the reef to less than a twentieth.

With hindsight, we realise that this global mass mortality of coral was an early example of the immense planetary upheaval that is visible everywhere today. The world is changing in ways beyond experience. Places where benign climates have nurtured civilisations into life now see wildfire, drought or tempest in their midst; seas that have lapped the same shores since the end of the last ice age are rising again as glaciers are burned off mountainsides or surge into the ocean, unmoored from their rocky seabed anchors by probing warm water. There is a febrile atmosphere about these times, as the earth's thermostat drifts upwards. Each broken record – each new disaster – is like a gasping whitecap on a steepening wave, the harbinger of a coming crash.

Climate sceptics (and there are still a few weaving fairy tales to explain away the implacable mountain of evidence) love to remind us that the planet has often changed throughout its history. During the early Eocene epoch, 50 million years ago, the climate was over 10°C hotter than now, there was no ice at the poles and the sea above the Arctic Circle was an improbable 20°C. The sceptics' argument implies that today's changing climate is somehow less serious because changes have occurred previously, but there are two crucial differences between past and present. The first is that changes today are happening faster than previously. Four of the past five mass extinction events were marked by a tremendous release of greenhouse gases leading to global warming and ocean acidification (from carbon dioxide dissolved into the sea). The mother of mass extinctions was the end-Permian collapse, brought on by vast reservoirs of lava bubbling up through today's Siberia, vaporising coal measures and carbonate rocks into carbon emissions at a rate of a fifth to a third of a gigaton per year. Today's emissions blow into the atmosphere thirty to forty times more rapidly.

The second vital difference between past and present is us. Past changes had natural causes, like volcanoes or orbital wiggles, but present warming is unequivocally our fault: you can't release aeons of solar energy stored in fossil fuels without disruption. But the heat produced by these fuels is only a tiny part of the warming; it is the greenhouse effect, by which released carbon dioxide and gases like methane trap incoming solar energy, that makes the greatest difference. In the time that it takes you to read this sentence, the world will have trapped additional heat that is equivalent to the explosion of thirty Hiroshima-sized atomic bombs. Read that again, it wasn't a misprint. By the time you have, the total will be sixty atomic bombs.

I first began to take my master's students to the Maldives to experience its marvellous coral reefs in 2014. Sixteen years had passed since the El Niño warming had shrivelled its corals and their renewal was nearly complete. Just as a tree which falls in the forest can offer opportunities to others, space freed up on a reef is soon colonised by seaweeds and a riot of invertebrate life, including new corals. Coral growth is slow, typically ranging from about a centimetre a year for colonies with rounded stony shapes to twenty centimetres for the most vigorous arborescent species. Although visible scars remained, the wounds had more or less healed. Corals tumbled into the depths down slopes half obscured by moving clouds of fish. Table corals spread seaward from the reef front like stepped ledges, around which schools of snapper fish flowed in braided streams, their bodies lined with gold, dark eyes circled in glowing daffodil yellow. Such resilience was uplifting. I began to believe again that coral reefs might outlive today's relentless human destruction.

Then in 2015, history repeated itself. A giant El Niño disturbance erupted in the eastern Pacific and spread towards Australia. By March 2016, the northern Great Barrier Reef had lost 60 per cent of its coral. By May, corals throughout the Maldives had bleached and, by July, 50 to 70 per cent were dead. One particularly exquisite reef near the island my students and I use as a base, a showpiece gem in a richly decorated crown, lost 99 per cent of its coral.

Three years on from this catastrophe, I am back with another class. We slip underwater with our scuba tanks and glide gently down to the reef. It is beginning to look healthier, less damaged. Fish that depend on coral for food or shelter suffered greatly when the corals died, but are coming back. Tiny *Chromis*, newly arrived from their drifting planktonic larval stage, fill the water like emeralds, their scales glinting and sparkling above their coral shelters. Black-and-white humbug fish, neat and rounded like the boiled sweets after which they are named, retreat among the branches of a coral head at our approach, then blossom outward again after we pass. Newly settled corals speckle the bottom, like young plants pushing up from recently thawed soil.

But despite the exuberant colours, the play of light and wondrous forms, I see the absences: animals that should be there but are not. These ghosts haunt me as I pass by towering columns that should be half-living coral but instead are rock spattered by sponges and tufted with hydroids or weed. Within their clefts, giant groupers and spangled emperor fish should be hiding. The occasional encounter with a hulking fish, round-bellied and scarred by age, only serves to remind that there should be more. Most of my students are fresh to the scene and revel in the immediacy of the experience. To them, the blanks are invisible.

I also see things that should not be there. The sponge that covers the bottom like fungus is a pretty turquoise patch to my students. To them, the matted algae that stain the seabed rust brown shiver in the current like waterweed in a summer river. For me, they are a cloak that chokes off recovery, snuffing out tiny corals before their lives have really begun.

The difference in our perceptions illustrates a phenomenon called 'shifting baseline syndrome'. Shifting environmental baselines are intergenerational changes in how we perceive our world. Each generation sets its mental benchmark of normality by how the world looked when first encountered, often in youth, and sees change relative to this. Younger generations accept as normal a world that seems tainted and degraded to older people.

Shifting baselines weave through many aspects of life, usually unnoticed, since that is their power. In 1871, John Ruskin, the English critic and artist, railed in 'The White-Thorn Blossom' against what he saw as the desecration of a small piece of heaven in the Derbyshire hills by a railway viaduct:

> There was a rocky valley between Buxton and Bakewell, once upon a time, divine as the Vale of Tempe; you might have seen the gods there morning and evening – Apollo and all the sweet Muses of the Light – walking in fair procession on the lawns of it, and to and fro among the pinnacles of its crags. You cared neither for gods nor grass, but for cash (which you did not know the way to get). You thought you could get it by what the *Times* calls 'Railroad Enterprise'. You enterprised a railroad through the valley, you blasted its rocks away, heaped thousands of tons of shale into its lovely stream. The valley is gone, and the gods with it; and now, every fool in Buxton can be at Bakewell in half-an-hour, and every fool in Bakewell at Buxton; which you think a lucrative process of exchange, you Fools everywhere!

The twist in this tale is not Ruskin's rage, which many of us feel daily at the destruction by commerce of natural wonders and beauty, but what happened a century later. By the 1960s, the railway had become uneconomical and the line was closed. Instead of taking swift advantage to remove the blight, the Headstone Viaduct was Grade II listed and preserved for its grandeur. Looking at photographs of this softly wooded valley, spanned by five elegant arches of moss-covered stone, I find it hard to agree with Ruskin: my baseline was set in a world where viaducts were admired, not castigated.

Shifting baselines have a darker side. The recent resurgence of right-wing ideology has been blamed on many things, with one view being that immigration and globalisation have placed immense strain on feelings of cultural and national identity, leading to a backlash. Another is that growing inequality breeds resentment and despair that usher the dispossessed into the arms of populist leaders. Such leaders are again spouting the fascist and authoritarian tropes used by Stalin, Mussolini and Hitler. Their words were taboo and almost unspoken by generations of people who lived through the horrors of two world wars or grew up in their aftermath, but younger people today are falling for the rhetoric in part because their personal experiences of peace and stability tell them little, or nothing, of its danger.

These are extraordinary times. The Renaissance heralded in a resurgence of art, literature and technology, expressions of the period's renewed curiosity about how the world worked and our place in the universe. Not even the greatest minds of the day, however, predicted that within a few centuries we would transition from being at the mercy of nature to reshaping it. That headlong growth in understanding and influence – that fevered rebirth of culture between the Middle Ages and modern times – is itself a wonder of nature, but it far outstrips growth in our common sense. We know what we are doing to the world, we know how to stop the harm, but again and again we fall short when it comes to action. Like a teenager, our capacity for calamity has grown faster than our self-restraint, a mismatch that leaves us dangerously exposed.

The question of the age is whether we can adapt from fulfilling our own selfish interests to fulfilling the self-interest of humanity before it is too late. If we let the growing flood of human impact run its course, nature's beauty and abundance will be pruned so savagely that there will be only remnants left. They will hint at past majesty, as a marble torso or shattered face pulled from the earth lets us glimpse the nobility of ancient Greece. Those of us who document nature's struggle, as the boot of human progress presses ever harder upon the earth, look on with feelings of helplessness as the world did when the Taliban destroyed the Bamiyan Buddhas, or when ISIS sacked Palmyra. Each forest cleared is another assault; every coral bleaching, a silent tragedy.

Scientists are trained to record and report dispassionately, distancing themselves from the phenomena observed. But sometimes it is hard not to get caught up by emotion. I once dived off an island in the Arabian Gulf and found the reef pulverised to rubble by anchors thrown from fishing vessels. The anchor of a neighbouring boat had smashed a hole amid the delicate fawn branches of an *Acropora* thicket, lying within the hollow like an iron claw. A fragment-strewn path passed through the coral to the anchor, cut by dragging chain. The loss felt all the more heartbreaking because the destruction was not yet complete. Here and there turrets of living coral emblazoned with the liveries of a hundred species of invertebrates hinted at past glories.

If humanity were to feel the cumulative burden of loss and damage over millennia, it would already be unbearable, but shifting baselines have a protective influence. The patch of bluebell woodland hemmed in by housing can bring as much pleasure as the heavy-timbered wildwood that was once there, perhaps more. Young Singaporeans grow up surrounded by skyscrapers and hanging gardens, and many prefer them to the 'green hell' of jungle they have replaced. For those who have seen pages torn from the book of their experience, or badly overprinted with vulgar development, the story is jarring and incomplete. But for those new to the scene, it's a different tale.

You cannot regret the loss of something you never knew existed, but shifting baselines, while soothing the sting of loss, do not fully protect us from the consequences of today's recklessness. We know what we have done. Unlike the dinosaurs, whose demise was no fault of ours, we rue the loss of the dodo, or great auk, or Atlantic grey whale, because we killed them all. Some of the most threatened species today are among the most iconic: Siberian tigers, Javan rhinoceros, vaquita porpoises, Amsterdam Island albatrosses and a menagerie of others. Imagine a future in which these animals exist only as virtual-reality holograms recreated from old television documentaries.

Losses to nature risk far worse than the impoverishment of human experience; they also threaten our well-being. As ecosystems disintegrate, we are seeing losses of critical functioning upon which life depends. For example, in degraded habitats plants and ocean phytoplankton produce oxygen and extract carbon dioxide less quickly from the atmosphere than in healthy intact habitats, accelerating greenhouse warming. Coastal habitats like coral reefs or mangrove forests, under assault from growing human pressures, protect coasts less strongly, just when rising sea levels mean we need their protection more. In September 2019, the Intergovernmental Panel on Climate Change reported on risks to the oceans and frozen parts of the planet. There is no scenario of greenhouse gas reduction that will stop sea level rise, they concluded. If the world were to shift to carbon-neutral energy production tomorrow, sea levels will carry on rising between one and three metres in the next 200 years. That is bad news for the 880 million people who live on very low-lying coasts. It is terrible news for global food production, which is disproportionately concentrated on fertile, low-lying river deltas and flood plains.

Here shifting baselines represent a clear danger, suppressing perceptions of harm and lowering ambition to reverse human impacts. A good example can be found in European marine protected areas. Many permit the continuation of extractive and damaging activities, like bottom-trawling for fish, dredging or mining for aggregate. The logic applied is that the wildlife present is resilient to these activities because they survive them today. This is often true, but it is because the habitats are a product of the activities, not because the activities are benign. We have mistaken altered and often heavily damaged habitats for the norm. That error seems improbable, but was easily made. Much of the damage occurred long before marine scientists began to look underwater in the second half of the twentieth century, so they assumed the habitats they found were natural and subject primarily to environmental forces. I was hoodwinked myself as a student taking my first, hesitant dives into the North Sea in the 1980s. I thought the monotonous backdrop of shifting sand, gravel and mud I encountered was the outcome of powerful waves and currents that prevented animals and plants from gaining a foothold. It was only decades later that I discovered the richness of life that carpeted the seabed where there was protection from trawling and dredging: moss-like bryozoans, feathery hydroids, lace nets of coralline algae, sponges of gaudy orange, purple and yellow, and the waving tentacles of burrowing anemones covered the bottom, while shoals of juvenile fish sheltered among dark thickets of seaweed.

The premise of present-day naturalness is almost always undone by reference to the past. For example, a report on Irish Sea fisheries from 1836 includes the following descriptions, among many similar, depicting a world in which marine life was far more abundant than today:

Turbot are so abundant in Dundrum Bay, that they are speared close to the dry strand.

The middle of [Carlingford] Loch is deep . . . and the bottom occupied by an immense bed of oysters, of which vast quantities are taken to Dublin and other towns.

[In a season] a Skerries boat may catch Ling to the extent of thirty or forty hundred weight, dried; twelve or fourteen hundred [weight] of Cod, of five score to the hundred [weight]; and thirty hundred [weight] of Skate.

The dense cod shoals, skate the size of tables and rugged oyster beds are all gone from the Irish Sea today.

It is salient also to examine fish catches from when records first began in 1889, as Ruth Thurstan, one of my former students, did. She looked at the productivity of bottom-trawl fisheries in England and Wales and was astonished to find that a fleet powered mainly by wind landed five times more fish annually in the late nineteeth century than the sophisticated modern vessels one hundred years later. When she accounted for the technological advances that made the modern fleets more powerful and efficient, the gulf was even greater: nineteenth-century boats landed seventeen times more fish per unit of fishing power expended than those of the twenty-first century. If a nineteenth-century fisherman could somehow be transported to the present, they would conclude that the sea had been emptied of fish and the bottom left barren.

Some fish have been almost eliminated from their former haunts. Thurstan's figures suggest that halibut, a large and succulent flatfish, have undergone a greater than 99 per cent decline in the southern North Sea since 1889. Historical records from the 1830s show that sailing vessels deploying hook and line often caught a ton of halibut per day on the Dogger Bank alone, a sprawling underwater hill between England and the Continent, while today's entire fishing fleet lands less than two tonnes of halibut in a full year of fishing the Dogger. Yet the conservation objective set for a recently established English marine protected area on the Dogger Bank was to maintain the habitat as it is today. Not only does such low ambition hold back the recovery of nature, it mandates that it should not happen.

As baselines shift across generations, we have forgotten the past so completely that few people question whether a different world is even possible, or desirable, today. There are two antidotes to this complacency. History supplies the first: more and more scientists and historians are disentangling the roles of human and natural causes in long-term environmental change. Their research tells us that the world was generally richer, ecosystems more complex and vibrant, and animals bigger and more abundant in the distant past. The second antidote is provided by protected areas. When areas are fully protected from extractive and damaging uses, remarkable transformations unfold. Fish and shellfish become more prolific, much bigger and more productive. Different habitats emerge, like kelp forests re-establishing on naked reefs, oyster beds scrambling upwards from the bottom, or the seabed blossoming again with the rich crusts of invertebrates that historical accounts describe. Nature has great resilience, and when given respite from human damage, it soon flourishes once more.

Rapid global change supplies an urgent imperative for a rethink of conservation practice. For the last several decades we have been losing on two fronts: as the planet heats up and the human imprint grows, the natural world is on the move and in retreat. Likewise, our efforts to save species and habitats are failing even to reduce the rate of biodiversity loss, let alone reverse it, while greenhouse gas emissions still rise long after we know they should have begun to fall. Like Nero, we fiddle as Rome burns.

What we are beginning to appreciate, belatedly, is that we cannot solve our problems by technology alone or live without nature. Saving biodiversity cannot be achieved by tokenism. At present, the international community has agreed to protect just 10 per cent of the sea and 17 per cent of land for nature. Wildlife needs far more space if it is to keep the planet habitable, and if we give it that space, it can help us out of our present troubles. In photosynthesis, evolution has produced the best means of extracting the greenhouse gas carbon dioxide from the air, releasing at the same time the essential by-product of oxygen. While we wrestle to bring down emissions, nature can slow the speed of warming and adapt to the consequences of climate change.

Again and again I have watched and carefully documented the vigorous resurgence of life given protection from hooks, nets, traps or dredges. Most of the protected areas I have studied are little more than hectares to a few square kilometres in size, like the coral reefs of St Lucia in the Caribbean. But they prove that nature is buoyant and prolific given a chance. These findings, now replicated in hundreds of protected areas scattered across almost all seas and oceans, make a compelling case for greater effort. A large-scale programme of protection, rewilding and habitat restoration is called for, more ambitious than anything attempted so far. Many of the world's foremost scientists are calling for the safeguarding of a third to half the planet, and greatly improved management of the rest. This is not utopian fantasy. The fantasists are those who think we can somehow engineer a replacement environment, or believe we can thrive in a world of megacities and industrial agriculture alone. Our approach must shift rapidly from trying to save nature from ourselves to giving nature the space and freedom from human impact to save us. The draft text of a possible new international agreement for the next ten years of nature conservation sets out a vision for 30 per cent of land and sea to be protected by 2030. If adopted by the Convention on Biological Diversity, it would represent a major advance. But protected areas will need strong protection from extractive and destructive uses to make the difference we need.

I am an optimist at heart – how else could I be an environmentalist if I did not see hope as better than despair? But at some point, optimists must be pragmatists. Global change is racing away from us as the gulf widens between what we should do and what we are doing. The discomforting truth is that regardless of what we do, many of the changes under way today are unstoppable and accelerating, at least for the immediate future. That doesn't mean we should give up. On the contrary, we must redouble our efforts to wean ourselves off fossil fuels, because how fast we do this will dictate how long the damage will endure. If we act decisively, there will be a few centuries of strife before more settled times return. We might even prevent the complete loss of coral reefs, if we're lucky, but if we drag our feet, we condemn our descendants to thousands or tens of thousands of years of loss and turmoil. ■

THE ARD, THE ANT AND THE ANTHROPOCENE

Charles Massy

It is a late September spring morning on our farm: a time of frenetic bird, animal and vegetative activity. Spring/summer migrants – yellow-faced honeyeaters, fan-tailed cuckoos, dusky woodswallows and diamond firetail finches – arrive almost daily. Some stay, others dally briefly before moving on: their exotic calls redolent of urgency, movement. Out in the paddocks, kangaroos and wallabies belly-bulge with pouched joeys, and the bleating of lambs and anxious ewes echoes across the landscape.

But such a vibrant expression of life had not been witnessed for over 150 years here on the Monaro in the Snowy Mountains of New South Wales, Australia. In less than a few decades since the European invasion of our region in the 1820s, introduced livestock had destroyed vibrant, long co-evolved soils and grasslands. The axe and fire then compounded this, helping to decimate woodland and forest. Later still came the eviscerations of the plough, then industrial fertilisers and finally ecocidal chemicals. Such loss remains unrecognised, for no contemporary farmers have ever had even a glimpse of what this landscape once was, or what it could be: spongy soils, hydrated grasslands, lakes and chain-of-ponds streams, all richly diverse and abounding in a variety of fungal-digging small marsupials, birds, insects and various other animals now lost.

Then there was the even greater loss. Within but three decades of the European invasion, a local Indigenous culture that had been thriving for over 25,000 years faded away, initially through massacre and displacement, later via 'relocation' and finally by a 'writing out' of mind and history.

I grew up an only child. My mother died when I was five, and I barely remember her, as little was said about her. Despite my loss, I was gloriously able to roam free across the grasslands and bush of our 4,000 acre farm. I became a keen ornithologist and nature lover. Reflecting on my awakening biophilia, I am sure that this time spent in nature as a child was a significant solace for my early loss.

Then, when I was twenty-two, my father had a heart attack and I returned from university, where I was studying zoology, to manage the farm. I knew little about farming and so I sought the best advice from experts and read widely. The experts included scientists, agronomists, Department of Agriculture advisers and leading local farmers: all fully committed to modern industrial farming. And I became a competent and conventional industrial farmer.

Our farm's operations revolved around merino sheep for wool and breeding other kinds of sheep and cattle for meat. These animals had to be fed, and I took pride in aggressive tillage of our ancient soils and remnant native grasslands, along with the sowing of so-called improved or introduced grasses, legumes as well as forage crops like cereals and brassicas. This meant intensive use of industrial fertilisers. Later still, at the end of my industrial farming phase, came two years of spraying herbicides so I could improve my farmland – or what I had, by that stage, come to regard as an inert substrate or 'soil box': over which I aggressively manipulated my mechanical levers.

My induction into this industrial mindset was reinforced by the almost ubiquitous practices of my district's peers. As I read the literature on 'best practices', browsed the rural press and attended field days, it was as if by osmosis – and certainly by social pressure – that I became cemented into the industrial farming paradigm.

My life had somehow become schizophrenic. I still deeply enjoyed the natural world on our farm as I studied and recorded our native flora and fauna, and I revelled in my bushwalking, rock-climbing and mountaineering. Yet I had somehow compartmentalised my mind: nature and my farm landscape stood either side of a deep chasm.

Propped on the front of my desk is a photo that is, in essence, timeless. Set against the backdrop of a crumbling rock buttress stands a young hill farmer. The photo was taken in 1978, when, aged twenty-six, I was on a mountaineering expedition to the Indian Himalayas. The farmer gazes at me with a shyly proud mien. He wears worn but natty red-and-blue-striped trousers, an old coat and a coloured wool beanie. He is carrying a wooden ard, or scratch plough: the ploughing implement first used by humans in the area known as the Fertile Crescent, where Western agriculture evolved.

The base of the plough is perhaps three feet long, made of a triangular piece of wood and pointed at the front. Two vertical wooden insertions protrude from it. The first piece, slotted midway along the ard's base, bends forty-five degrees forwards and is around six feet long and notched at the end. This is the draft pole, where a primitive harness can be attached to either a bovine or human. The second insertion, slotted near the back, is a vertical piece of around three feet with a thin handle added to the top. This is the stilt, designed for a human to control the plough horizontally, or tilt it as it is dragged through the earth, scratching a single furrow.

Some 10,000 to 12,000 years ago, the forerunner to ploughing or tilling – to the ard – was the domestication of edible seeds from grasslands in the Fertile Crescent of the Middle East. Closely associated was the domestication of sheep and goats. Then, following early slash-and-burn agriculture, tillage technology evolved and the ard was the breakthrough. It was the next step in what was to become an 8,000-year process of technological and cultural revolution leading to modern human civilisation and, eventually, to the Anthropocene.

While modern machines used for tillage, seeding, fertilising and spraying chemicals appear a far cry from the simple ard, they all do something fundamentally destructive. A process of degradation occurs each time the earth is disturbed, turned over and, nowadays, poisoned. Vegetation is disrupted or killed; biota and structure are destroyed; carbon is released; and the living soil is opened to the elements. The soil dries out, and the sun's heat kills further soil biology. Soil particles, loose and friable, blow away in the wind or wash away with the rains. Over time, this leads to desertification.

In the Fertile Crescent, the original grasslands were diverse and grew from healthy, spongy, absorbent soils. The great river valleys of the Tigris and Euphrates contained abundant alluvial soil, and most of the lands around the Mediterranean were forested. Within a few millennia, overgrazing began to simplify, and then destroy, the grasslands. Misguided human irrigation techniques (too much flooding and poor drainage, excessive evaporation of stored water) led to salinisation of the great rivers' soils, and tree felling for shipbuilding, construction and agriculture denuded the forests.

In nations that were once so rich in grasslands, woodlands and forests, all are now largely desert, constantly afflicted by drought and attendant social conflict. All this is because humanity still seems not to have understood that the fundamental resource on which our livelihoods, civilisations and very existence depend is a living soil.

The ard stands for an extraordinary journey of human cultural evolution, but what followed its invention was inexorable destruction. Research shows that over geological time, through natural erosion, soil is produced at the rate of only inches per millennia. But today, across the world, soil erosion caused by humans occurs at a minimum of twenty times the geological rate.

When heavy rains occur or when dust blows, erosion rates become higher still because of bare fallows and overgrazing: inches of soil per decade or two. This is a key reason why the average duration of civilisations (except in such fertile river valleys as the Nile) has only been 800 to 1,000 years: or thirty to thirty-eight human generations.

This 'graveyard of empires' includes those of Mesopotamia, the regions of Lebanon and Syria, Carthage, ancient Greece and Rome, Nabataea, Phoenicia, the Indus Valley, and a number of civilisations in Central and South America. Well over twenty great civilisations through history fell because they lost their soils and could no longer feed their populations. The death of island cultures due to the destruction of soil and its nourishing forests mirrors these in microcosm, such as Easter Island and Mangaia in the South Pacific. Our modern industrial civilisation has soil erosion rates of an order of magnitude greater than any civilisation of the past. The UN Food and Agriculture Organization has confirmed in its 2015 'Report on the Status of the World's Soil Resources' that agriculture has degraded 5 of 13.4 billion hectares (or 37 per cent) available for agriculture globally. Alarmingly, given that soil is the lifeblood of human society, this report confirmed that between 24 and 40 billion tonnes of topsoil are lost globally every year.

However, the accelerating rates of soil erosion in recent centuries have been largely dismissed because they are not as dramatic as ice ages, or comets impacting Earth. They are just as deadly on a planetary scale, but only a handful of people have tried to raise the alarm.

In the early 1970s while mountaineering in New Zealand, I came across large areas of red ice on Aoraki/Mount Cook's Tasman Glacier. The red came from millions of tonnes of soil that, during the drought of the mid 1930s, had become airborne as powerful winds swept across Australia's vast rangelands, drawing the soil up into the jet stream to travel over 4,000 kilometres. Not accidentally, Australia's 'dust bowl' of that time was contemporaneous with that of the United States and occurred for the same reason: inappropriate ploughing of once-vibrant grasslands and woodlands, combined with overgrazing and inconvenient weather.

But we haven't learned. Covering the front page of Melbourne's *Sun Herald* on 8 May 2019 is a photo of a broiling, dark-red dust storm, reaching thousands of feet high into the black of the sky. It is captured advancing like a towering blanket towards the city of Mildura and, beneath the headline WALL OF DUST, the accompanying article implies the drought is to blame.

However, in recent decades there has emerged a bright and hopeful light in the ancient field of agriculture. At this millennial moment of Saharan heat, of Amazonia ablaze and the loss of billions of tonnes of Greenland ice into our briny oceans, new but also ancient forms of agriculture are rapidly emerging. Instead of destroying soil, these practices recreate soil and the natural systems on which it depends. This movement is increasingly recognised as 'regenerative agriculture'. And for me, the realisation, nay epiphany, that there was another way to farm came late in my farming career.

From 1979 to 1983, rainfall on our farm more than halved. Through dry winter months and clear skies, frosts grew until pipes burst in ceilings and water troughs. The wind blew constantly, and dust with it, while sheep walked the fence lines, incessantly bleating.

For me, as a naturalist, the pain was doubled. There were no vibrant grasslands left in which quail could play hide-and-seek; no undisturbed secret nooks for them to swivel in delicately cupped dust hollows late into the evening; no insects to tangle in my hair and around my eyes at night as I rode the motorbike to turn off overworked water pumps; or skylarks singing from invisible perches hovering high above in an empty sky. On our moonscaped paddocks it was as if the natural world had fled in disgust – leaving me, I now realise, with a repressed sense of guilt.

But I doggedly fought on, knowing no other approach. We bought semi-trailer-loads of grain, one after the other, to feed the sheep, as our debt grew ever higher. In the exhaustion of trying to fight a drought, I did not realise I was depressed. But the rains did eventually come, and the world exploded into life – the birds, insects, ants and echidnas returning or re-emerging. With this renewal of life and busyness, the pain of that first big drought quickly faded.

To an outsider it may not seem appreciably difficult, practically, for an individual farmer to switch operations to an alternative, regenerative agricultural approach. But it is. Overthrowing the lifetime habits of mechanical intervention and industrial agriculture, of generations of inherited practice, is extraordinarily hard. I was painfully reminded of this recently when a friend of mine, clearing out his desk, unearthed an old article in the rural paper the *Land* from 1987. It featured me in a piece about another drought just four years after my first experience.

The headline read EIGHT-YEAR CURSE. The article described me feeding grain to our stock during our district's 'thirteenth month of drought declaration' so I could protect my valuable merino sheep genetics. The author records me 'refusing to cut any corners', complaining about ten dry winters, and running up a feed debt as I pinned my hopes on 'a good spring'.

The article speaks volumes. To me at that time, nature, perversely, still seemed to be the enemy. I was going to 'defend' and 'fight' this drought. I would force my land to run the stock, irrespective of damage to ecosystems and bank balance. As environmental writer George Seddon once noted: 'Drought is a problem of perception, applied when Nature has failed to meet our expectations.'

And of course, 'nature' fails to meet our expectations when we expect the impossible from it without understanding how it works. Scores of books and hundreds of scientific papers have been written on this subject – a subject that boils down to the power of paradigms. I would eventually end up doing a PhD and writing a book on the subject, but, in essence, the power of a society's culture and prevailing philosophy is what determines how we manage our landscapes and how we regard 'nature'.

European settlers arriving at the ancient land of Australia brought with them a world view that had evolved following the scientific, industrial and capitalist revolutions of the seventeenth century and later. Incorporated in their prevailing philosophy was the idea that Indigenous peoples were lesser beings; that the ancient, highly leached continent and its soils and systems would behave like the young, rich, post-glacial environments of north-western Europe – and that the weather and climate would behave likewise: soft and safe, with regular rain on rich soils: not dry, harsh and riven by regular droughts. Reinforcing this were the cultural farming habits of untold generations of northern European farmers.

Tragically, these expectations persist today and the cost has been vast landscape degradation, millions of hectares of dryland salinity (the build-up of salt in non-irrigated areas), and hundreds of millions of tonnes of topsoil either washed away or sent into the stratosphere towards New Zealand. In less than 200 years Australia has suffered a 50 per cent loss in forest cover and massive extinction rates of biota. It is now estimated there are 29 million hectares of dryland salinity.

Today, I am aghast at my earlier thinking, but for the vast majority of farmers, the deeply embedded industrial metaphor is reinforced by government policy, societal thinking, university and agricultural college teaching, and constant reinforcement in the media. Added to all this is enormous pressure from agronomists and, of course, the powerful agrichemical and other multinational agricultural companies.

By the time I had come through my first big droughts, I knew things weren't right, but did not yet know how to fix them. I reflected on my earlier farming days in the mid 1970s, and recalled examples of how I had overgrazed my land and ploughed a sandy paddock on a steep hillside, which was subsequently gutted by a storm. For the first time I felt shame and remorse at what was a thoughtless gambler's punt, feelings that grew when I traversed large areas of Australia, visiting clients who bought rams from our merino sheep stud. Over twenty years, working with scientists and leaders in the Italian and British textile industry, our family had evolved a unique strain of merino sheep that was resistant to the savage blowfly that plagued Australian sheep farmers, and they produced a fine wool for the elite fabric market. Needless to say, we weren't welcomed by either the scientists who dominated alternative breeding research, or the extremely conservative and backward-looking merino industry and its strong power base going back 180 years.

Clients who did buy our sheep were of the 'early adopter' variety – innovators and freethinkers – and I noticed a number had begun adopting some regenerative agriculture approaches. In time, I discovered there was a group of ecologically oriented farmers across the nation who had weathered the recent droughts with ease by treasuring their capital base – their landscapes – through sensitive, flexible, ecocentric management. These farmers were landscape managers who sought to heal and empower the natural processes of their landscape. It was then I finally realised – with a shock – that I was landscape illiterate: that I couldn't read, sense or understand how living landscapes functioned.

On these visits to clients I discovered a multitude of new techniques and thinking, some of them refinements of old methods, others, little less than revolutionary. Along with new forms of regenerative cropping – new tillage methods, integrating livestock into the crop rotations and eliminating industrial inputs – I encountered the movement of holistic grazing begun by Zimbabwean ecologist Allan Savory and now adopted all over the world. In simple terms, this practice attempts to mimic the positive impact of creating healthy grasslands that the giant African migratory animal herds exerted in the past. This mimicking is done through the clever use of high-density animal grazing and regular movement and planning by farmers. There is a plethora of new thinking around the use of trees and shrubs, and constantly evolving practices in the regenerative use of water. Approaches that enhance landscape through integrated design include permaculture and permagardening. Permaculture is a worldwide movement that originated in Australia, and which uses the patterns of natural ecosystems to grow healthy food and fibre in sustainable human communities, based around fundamental elements of design. Permagardening is a spin-off of this, and involves sustainable, biointensive agriculture on small areas of land to create gardens that last all year, and that, through high biodiversity, offer high yield and high nutrition.

Some of these techniques had been advocated by luminaries such as Charles Darwin in his 1881 book on earthworms; romantics like Goethe's protégé Rudolf Steiner and his theory of biodynamics; and a group of early-twentieth-century thinkers in organic agriculture, including Albert Howard and Robert McCarrison, who had learned from a culture of Indian subcontinental agriculture going back millennia.

Late one day, I left a farm with my head spinning from what I had just witnessed. Dianne and Ian Haggerty now farmed over 45,000 acres, having begun just twenty years before with a sizeable debt on 1,600 acres. Some 14,000 of these acres comprised diverse native vegetation, chock-full of extraordinary biodiversity, which they farmed according to a radical new form of cropping they called 'Natural Intelligence Farming'. A combination of earthworm juice (vermijuice), which is microbe- and nutrient-rich, and compost extract was applied as fertiliser at planting, with added fertiliser provided by the dung and urine of livestock grazing the cover crops and trampling the residues into the soil. This eliminated the need for chemical inputs and resulted in massive reductions in costs. The abundant microorganisms in the system degraded toxins and provided disease resistance, increasing production and enhanced nutrient-rich and healthy grain quality in even the toughest of landscapes. This system and others like it have the potential to transform agriculture across the planet.

It was to take one more world-view challenge before I finally made the shift to a new regenerative farming approach. A small group of expert ornithologists and native plant botanists from Canberra and other local areas had come for a visit to help catalogue our native birds, animals and plants. Included in their group was a local Aboriginal man whom I had not met before. Of quiet demeanour, he initially said little as we drove up to a large patch of bush atop our farm.

It was only after a couple of hours, which had been dominated by the naturalists' leader expounding on every species we passed, giving the Latin names for each one, that I found myself alone with the Aboriginal man, who had remained on the edge of the group. His name was Rod Mason, and he was a direct descendant of the Ngarigo: the Indigenous Nation which had occupied our region for over 25,000 years. Of gentle manner and humility, he was, I subsequently learned, a senior law man.

We chatted quietly while the others moved off, and I soon discovered that Rod had both a wicked sense of humour and an extraordinary knowledge of the natural world that was radically different from my own and that of the other 'experts' in the visiting group. To Rod, each plant, insect, animal and bird had its unique name, but also a beloved persona. He saw all of them as if they were distinct, personally known individuals, with distinct identities and idiosyncrasies. As our friendship deepened in the ensuing years, I realised he was gently revealing an entirely different world view from that of Western and Linnaean science which reached back millennia, with stories of animals now extinct and of their relationships and connections with one another. For Rod, the rocks, trees, birds and other fauna, along with certain natural spirits, had a place and a story in an existence where each element and creature, through being deeply known and cared for, played a crucial role in sustaining life and the regional ecology.

Occasionally, Rod also shared with me painful stories of early European arrival in the 1820s, 30s and 40s; of the unacknowledged massacres (in one case, he was even able to name a police sergeant who had issued government shells to the white settlers who carried out the murders); of the mustering of Ngarigo people into concentration camps; and then finally their trans-shipment to locations far from their traditional country and ancestral connections.

S ome years after our first meeting, Rod and I sat high on the side of a hill under an old snow gum, gazing down across our landscape to the coastal range. In the middle distance was a 200-acre ephemeral lake, named on European maps 'Buckley's Lake' after an early white settler. At that moment it was typically dry – just a large expanse of black, capped soil. In my lifetime it had rarely been full. Rod quietly told me its ancient name was Bundawindirri, and that it was a sacred lake, where the spirits of his people both arrived and departed from Earth.

As we talked, Rod told me how, in the 1860s, his great-grandfather had speared a jabiru stork on Lake Bundawindirri; that it had been covered in flocks of magpie geese, and that overhead vast mobs of grey-and-yellow budgerigars had swooped about, glinting in the sunlight. The fauna and flora he began to describe now only exist 2,240 kilometres away in the tropical north of Australia.

Drawing on his powerful cultural memory, Rod then carefully described a landscape that, only 170 years before white settlement, was totally different. There had been no incised creeks or steep banks. In their place were spongy, moist grasslands, woodlands, forests and river valleys and lakes, all fully hydrated and connected from top to bottom down our vast continent. On most days in summer and winter, mist and fog would have hung around until near midday. I realised he was painting a picture of massive ecological change, wrought initially over just a few decades, then subsequently and savagely escalated by the mouths and hooves of badly managed sheep and cattle – and by axe, gun, rabbit and plough.

Rod went on to describe how his people overwintered on the coast, then arrived up on our Monaro tableland in spring. The Ngarigo people were the famous moth-hunters who, along with other Indigenous Nations, moved into the Snowy Mountains from November to April to feast on bogongs. These jelly-bean-sized moths, a relic of the ice ages, annually migrate from as far as southern Queensland, over 1,000 kilometres away, to aestivate (the reverse of hibernation) in the cool of summer under granite rocks in the dark. For the Aboriginal peoples they were a rich and nourishing food. Rod said that after burning off the hair and wings, his ancestors then mashed the moths into a rich and delicious paste called Dubbal.

I said to Rod: 'So you came up for the bogong moths?' He just smiled. 'No,' he said. 'They were the final bonus. We came to this country here – Narrawallee, the Big Grass Country – to hunt the big grass birds: the plains bustards, the bush turkeys, emu, the big pigeons, curlew and others. On our way up here and into the mountains, and especially going back before winter, we carefully burned country; and we gardened, to manage our different resources: our orchards, our herbaries and pharmacies, and the special riparian areas around lakes, rivers and swamps. We were always managing, Charlie. We created patterns and mosaics; lovely meadows where we hunted kangaroo and wallaby, and dug for yam daisies. It all needed managing.'

Before us, 1,000 sheep or more were cutting across the pulverised black soil of Lake Bundawindirri, raising a large dust cloud. Rod looked down at his hands, then back at me. The anguish in his eyes caused me to clasp his shoulder, but I felt totally useless.

It was then that I realised I had to change my way of farming. I assiduously researched and visited leading regenerative farmers and adopted their ecologically sympathetic grazing and biodiversity management practices. Within a few years I had dispersed our beloved merino sheep stud and accelerated our native vegetation planting and protection. Rod had shown me not just what was lost, but what was possible.

One Saturday morning, a few years after I had met Rod, our family formalised our change of heart and held a large clearing sale of all our industrial farm machinery: a large tractor, various old ploughs and tillage implements, a range of seeders and combines; our only spray rig; drought feeding carts and grain self-feeders for sheep. All this gear represented the past: domination, poison and harm. I knew some of our neighbours were puzzled at our actions, but I didn't care. Somehow, a weight had been lifted from my shoulders. We had scuttled our boats and were now fully committed to an exciting but as yet uncharted journey. The benefits of shifting to an ecologically simpatico farming approach continued to build. By increasing ground cover and soil health through holistic grazing, and planting over 50,000 mixed native trees and shrubs of local provenance, landscape functionality soon followed. One obvious benefit was the cessation of grasshopper plagues. Since the 1920s, every five to seven years our farm had been denuded by millions of these little wingless grasshoppers who ate everything in their way. They even ate the green paint off veranda posts and green patterns on tablecloths hanging on the clothes line. The cost of these recurring attacks was incalculable because the plagues had regularily plunged us into virtual drought. This meant lost production, increased fodder costs, less environmental resilience.

Now, with good ground cover and a higher soil moisture profile, the adult grasshoppers have no large areas of bare ground in which to lay their eggs, and the in-ground moisture enables nematodes to predate any egg beds. With increased grassland diversity and enhanced native plant corridors and mosaic patches, there has been an appreciable increase in grasshopper predators: reptiles, small and large insectivorous birds, including large mobs of crows, and insects, including a wide variety of praying mantises, parasitic wasps and spiders.

Just the other day I was out at dawn with my sheepdogs, high up on a hill. Spread below me, as the eastern sky began to change from pink to apricot, was a waving grassland bedecked in silk: glistening spiderwebs, virtually one to each plant, dew-dropped in silver and orange.

In 2017 Paul Hawken, one of the world's leading social and environmental activists of the last few decades, edited the publication *Drawdown: The Most Comprehensive Plan Ever Proposed to Reverse Global Warming.* The title is taken from the atmospheric term for 'that point in time at which greenhouse gases peak and begin to decline on a year-to-year basis'. Meticulously researched, *Drawdown* posits one hundred substantive solutions to the challenge of excessive, Anthropocene-linked carbon dioxide in the atmosphere. The book is about hope and remarkable existing solutions to combat the Anthropocene: solutions that, in Hawken's words, 'lead to regenerative economic outcomes that create security, produce jobs, improve health, save money, facilitate mobility, eliminate hunger, prevent pollution, restore soil, clean rivers, and more.'

Drawdown includes eighty methods of pulling carbon out of the atmosphere, each accompanied by calculations, in gigatons, of their impact on total atmospheric CO_2 reduction. Out of the top twenty methods, ten are regenerative agriculture techniques. When I combined these methods, I discovered that regenerative agriculture is the outright leader in sequestering carbon (with far more than double the impact and amount of the next best method, re-engineering refrigeration). The emerging practices of a healthy ecological agriculture can make significant headway in our greatest of all challenges – the environmental and climate change crises of the Anthropocene.

I find it increasingly difficult to grasp the enormity and challenge of these times. When in doubt or turmoil, I walk our farm. Recently I set out to take a mob of sheep down a laneway to our woolshed. Attracted by a splash of green on a hillside, I left my sheepdog to hold the tail of the mob, and climbed the fence to examine a clump of ferns protruding from the crevice of a granite rock. The rock ferns (*Cheilanthes*) are a reminder of a moist Gondwanan history when Australia was still linked to Antarctica and South America, where their ancestors appeared 360 or so million years ago. The granite boulders themselves hark back even earlier. Weathered, knobbly, grey-white and moss-encrusted, these ancient granite tors were laid down somewhere between 390 and 420 million years ago.

I noticed the boulder had a horizontal crevice midway along its northern end. This made the mossy grey rock resemble some antediluvian dinosaur, grinning as it basked in the sun. As I drew closer, miniature dinosaur descendants – Cunningham's skinks – scuttled from their sun-baking and squeezed back into the crevice. Here, I reflected, were the spawn of Jurassic times basking on granite even older.

At the base of the rock, a lone bull ant spied me as he went about his business. Around 2.5 centimetres long, this fearless ant, unfazed by my size, reared up, exposing his sharp pincers and a row of teeth. Anyone who has spent time in the bush will be aware of the excruciatingly painful bite these little blokes inflict with a modified ovipositor sting at the end of their body: a sting that can sometimes kill a human if anaphylactic shock is triggered. A member of the genus *Myrmecia* or bulldog ants (of which Australia contains all but one of the ninety or so known species), this red bull ant was true to his ferocious and aggressive kind as he advanced on me.

We know now that, like the grey scuttling skinks, the bull ant is a Mesozoic creature. He belongs to the most ancient of all ant genuses, his ancestors tracing back to early Cretaceous times, some 112 million years ago in Gondwanan Brazil, and the ant's archaic heritage is revealed in his primitive anatomy and social life. This is because, unlike most modern ants which reside in huge colonies, bull ants not only live in small colonies with no subcastes, but the queen is similar to the female workers or gamergates. But these little guys are not primitive creatures. Their compound eyes enable acute colour vision, and they also possess sophisticated broad-spectrum, antimicrobial glandular secretions. Such complex attributes do not evolve in moments.

It made me think of the fifth and last great extinction event on Earth, which occurred at the end of the Cretaceous epoch, some 65 million years ago, when a massive bolide collided with Earth.

Luckily, the bull ant's ancestors must have been deep underground. And this happenstance saved them from the impact's accompanying shock-wave blast, heat pulse and the killingly high carbon dioxide concentrations, not to mention the resulting earthquakes, volcanic eruptions and massive tsunamis. Somehow, these ancient ants also survived the acid rain caused by the release of gases, as well as the release of mutation-causing chemicals (pyrotoxins).

While North and South America felt the main shock of the impact, the global temperature spike, the poisoned atmosphere and the ensuing decades-long cold darkness ensured a global extinction event. It was not, however, total. Ironically, for Australia, this extinction event marked the phoenix-like rise of distinct Australian land flora, fauna and associated co-evolved ecosystems. While 100 per cent of all non-avian dinosaurs were wiped out, along with 75 per cent of lizards and marsupials, some life survived. Within 5 to 10 million years this life had radiated and diversified, and included in this cohort were the ancestors of the feisty bull ant, with his indomitable 'will to live'.

Our Earth is now experiencing its sixth great extinction. Millions of species are rapidly dying out due to human agency. There is a high chance we ourselves could be collateral damage: that we too may end our days gasping for oxygen, our body systems collapsing under excessive heat and radiation, or from thirst and civil strife. Our inertia in the face of the Anthropocene brings to mind the fabled Icarus: we believe we are immune from natural forces, including an ever-hotter sun.

At this time, I am putting my money on the bull ant as the most likely to survive the next great Earth-systems challenge. For the bull ant knows only how to ferociously fight for life. By contrast, we humans appear maladapted to extended life on this planet, as we continue to exterminate the very ecosystems that sustain us.

But we still have a fighting chance. There are cracks in the dominant, destructive pattern of our presence here on Earth; perhaps the Covid-19 crisis will trigger a more sustainable economy and way of living; and in pockets of the globe, down quiet rural roads, along urban footpaths and in backyards, farmers and city folk alike are finding ways to become nurturers and enablers of nature and its self-organising systems.

By transforming what we think of as 'civilised' agriculture as first furrowed by the ard, through to a new form of regenerative agriculture, we may find a pathway to sustained life that would complete a 10,000 year cycle of redemption: from ard to absolution. ∎

© ROD MASON, Ibai Wumburra
Rod Mason's (Ibai Wumburra's) forefather, Ibai Mullyan, taken in the region of Dalgety in 1881 when he was eighty-one
He was a leader of both the Wolgai and the Ngarigo peoples

HOLDING UP THE SKY

Rod Mason

AS RECOUNTED TO CHARLES MASSY

This piece is the result of a number of years of friendship between myself and Indigenous Ngarigo Senior Law Man Rod Mason, known also as Ibai Wumburra. It is based on notes taken with Rod's consent over a number of years and from an extended interview, recorded with his permission, after what are now termed the 'mega-fires' of eastern Australia in late 2019 and early 2020. Rod has expressed his approval of the result, and of how his words are represented here.

Before the White invasion, Australia comprised around 500 Indigenous Nations, with over 250 distinct languages, each indivisibly married to its particular area of land or Country. Due to his grandparents' familial, clan and totem relationships, Rod is strongly connected to, and responsible for, four Countries, which cover a wide area of Australia, from the central Australian deserts, to the Kimberleys in the north-west, to the top end of Arnhem Land and into western and north-western New South Wales.

Being a senior law man, Rod is a leader in his community, trainer of initiates and upholder of his people's stories and traditions, while also being a custodian of the Country, its sacred places, knowledge, religious ceremonies and cultural belongings.

Charles Massy, 2020

ROD MASON

M y name is Rod Mason or Ibai Wumburra. I am an elder and
community leader. I was bred, trained and taught to be a local
rainmaker or Jillagamberra of the Ngarigo people, known also as
the Manaroo people, of south-eastern New South Wales, and I am a
healer, trained by my grandfather. My totems are the Kaua (echidna)
and Ibai (eagle-hawk), and I am of the Wolgal-Bemmergal clan.

In telling my story here, it's important for the reader or listener to
understand that the information I'm sharing has come down through
my family. It's what I've been taught by uncles, aunties, grandparents
and so on. It's neither 'right' nor 'wrong'. It's my family's information.

I hope this provides Indigenous and non-Indigenous people
with an insight into how we see Country, and perhaps adds another
dimension to their own personal land-management endeavours and
their 'care of Country'.

M y people are the icemakers and rainmakers, underground
water and cave people, keepers of the spirit world. We were
ice-travellers who come out of the central and western desert Country
in the big drought of the ice ages [c.25,000–15,000 years ago]. We are
from the ice dreaming. The last of our people, we are only a few now,
we live down here now, on the coast.

The most important thing is we remember who we are, where
we're from, our link to this Country, our links from one side of
Australia to the other, our Tchulkpa [law, story and ceremony, told
in song and holding the religious and cultural knowledge of Ngarigo
society]. Our story's already written there in the landscape, in the
plants, the rivers, the creeks and the rocks, everything.

It reminds us today that even though we're this side of Australia,
we came when the ice melted. We had no choice. All the animals were
coming this way, so our family's responsibilities was to follow the ice
and the animals that come east; some followed the animals that went
north, like the pigeon, Wobba, and all them other things, the stork,
Jabiru, and them others that went back north where they come from.

The big ice-drought forced us out from our Homelands in the

46

central and western desert, towards Lake Mungo or Muttaringi and across. It's all part of the storyline with us, the songline [songlines or dreaming tracks are the routes that were taken by the ancestral beings during a period known as The Dreaming, when ancestral beings performed heroic deeds, creating, moulding or enhancing key features of the landscape through 'singing up' the Country into life].

Our ancestors didn't have books, but we had good memory. We wrote our journey on the landscape and in the landscape, and even to this day we can read our story backwards from here. We are ice-age travellers, we travelled through the ice age; no clothes. All we had was the three laws: wind, rain and fire.

I chose, in my life, through my grandparents, to make Country. 'Cause Country never go away, it gave birth to us; Country never leaves us; Country is forever – so we are responsible for her. I'm therefore a Marminga, a man of Country.

People say 'How do you make Country?' Well, we light fire first, and we call the rain through the fire, and the wind blows what we need. And anywhere we see red dirt here in eastern Australia, that come from the old Country. We know the wind blew here for us to have ceremony. To put on our bodies that nice red dirt.

See, we got stories going way back to that time. Even earlier. There's one old family story of how we walked across from Indonesia at low tide [when all the lands were connected], and because of that I have Makassan ancestry in me – had a DNA test. All that's in our old Tchulkpa. We've got stories of the ice age, the animals that came, and the animals that went – animals that you never see no more. So we're part of that extinction world.

We even got cultural memory, down the lower Snowy, of ambushing diprotodons, old Jummalung [giant wombats, about the size of a rhinoceros]. Around Buchan there. They had very old pathway traps. These big things, two, three times bigger than a cow, would fall down and then you got 'em, spears, stones, you know. Those diprotodons, 20,000 years and the rest.

Old Jummalung, they used to hunt us too – old Nanny used to say these big things would come outta the bush there and chase all the old grandparents – chase 'em to the rocks, and, 'cause the Jummalungs couldn't climb, then they'd throw rocks and spears down at 'em.

We also got stories of giant goannas [lizards, larger than the Komodo dragon, long extinct] and others, stories of being chased by them – hear the bushes breaking and they'd take off. Warwagga – big goanna, scary. So you see, our stories go back thousands of years. We didn't have years and calendars then, but by'n'by.

We still got stories of when them White fellas, the Berimba, arrived in our Country. Country we had managed for thousands of years. We still have stories down here on Wallaga, the coastal Country, of the day the giant pelican came. It was Captain Cook's ship, all white sails, looked like a giant pelican slowly cruising up the coast, no effort, but giant. 'Musta been made by Dimboola?' they thought – that bloke, our creator, the All-Fatherer, who made all the birds up there on one of his campgrounds on the Monaro high plains, Bobundara there; where he gave them all different beaks, different legs. But this big white pelican, he turned out to be greedy, him and his giant beak and gullet for scooping everything up, and soon began to eat all the Country, fish, animals up – including us.

There was massacres. We still know the sites. Can tell you the name of the police sergeant who led one, using government-issued shells. I can still show you those shells, and the bones. Then later come the blankets, infected with smallpox from Sydney, the Rocks there, and the poisoned waterholes, strychnine, and arsenic too, in the flour they doled out. Finally they sent my people into a concentration camp, there near Delegate, and later shipped 'em off to the coast, until they dumped 'em into Sydney, La Perouse there. Took 'em off Country. They died like flies, heartbroken, taken off Country.

And even before that the sheep and cattle had come. No time flat they ate the heart outta the Country. Eroded. She dried up, the spongy valleys, our herbaries, our pharmacies, our fruit orchards, our hunting nooks, butterfly gardens and crannies, our camps. All carefully managed. Didn't understand it, and most important they didn't know how to burn and care for Country. All my people gone, except a few of us come back and settled down the coast here.

I grew up mainly in desert Country. That's where I learned how to burn Country, the desert, and then down here, the coast and forest Country. And I learned how to burn from both my grandfathers and the other old men, and from my grandmothers.

There are little secrets when you're taken out on Country and taught by elders, you know. How to watch a fire burn through an area; watch a wind swing around at a certain time of the day; and back-burn on itself. It will clean itself up and you don't need anything. So it's just patience and living with that thing, you know? Otherwise, do the wrong thing, and someone from our family or friends will be taken.

I started learning when I was a little toddler, two or three, something like that. They wrap you up, put you in the bushes; you smell the smoke; you know something's going on there. Might get your leg burned, or forehead burned. That's all right, that's how it was. That was in New South Wales, on my grandfather's Country, west of Coonamble.

So using fire, we make Country. We still make Country now. We go into a small swamp, burn about half a mile of it there, go back the next year there, all is brand new – you got things popping up you didn't ever see. The first time done, it's magic. Like at Lake Mungo before we went back to burn. Nothing there, just sand. But then we burned it and now you see all the wild flowers. We got wild-flower gardens growing under local gum trees they didn't even know existed there and casuarina trees – which used to grow along the edge of the waterways. So everything was in its natural patterns: just need fire at the right time, charcoal, to spark up, some rain to come – just through fire.

I began learning too when ten, eleven, twelve in the long grass Country on the Monaro, in Nullica and in Narrawallee. I started burning near the camps; created nice soft ground there, charcoal in the ground there, you know, to keep it cool on a hot day. You can feel it, walking into it. Nice and cool on a hot day under trees. Like a big fridge. It was that charcoal, and moisture in the ground. And when a fire went through there, it was protected by the charcoal. You can't burn through charcoal, you know that, eh? You try and burn charcoal? Then you're there forever. So that's the little blanket we put down in our campgrounds – keep us cool on a hot day, warm on cool days.

We had our own air-conditioners, our own fans – it's just that all these things have eroded away through poor management, through exclusion – we weren't allowed back to these areas. We understand air currents, pressure, breezes. My Nanny used to pick up a little feather, just like that, and on its own it would just fly up. We sit there, lying down and watch it. How'd she know that? She'd know exactly where to put that feather. Just let her go, and it would spin around on its own – go up and down; up and down. See, we was taught things there: patience; observation; understanding. That's all it is.

You know, the original burning patterns are still in the ground. We need to burn open ground again, we need charcoal. She's a filter; helps water quality, and we know the different charcoals from gums to ti-tree shrubs which give a finer ash. We know how to burn to nourish and create our fruit orchards for pigeons, our herb gardens, yam gardens, our ferneries, our wild-flower havens for butterflies, wattle thickets for possums and tucker for [marsupial] gliders.

Part of the problem too is we lost all the little fellas in the grasslands and forests – the bandicoots, the woylies, the bettongs, the bilbies, pottoroos, the desert hopping mouse. Their favourite tucker was mushrooms, fungus. They spread 'em round, and fungus kept the Country moist. Those little fellas, it was their favourite tucker, but we've lost 'em nearly all – the sheep, cattle destroyed the Country, and the plough drained it, turned it into desert some places, and the foxes and cats destroyed 'em – still do, especially after these fires. That fungus, nearly all gone now. So the Country dried, and dry Country, well, she burns more and hotter – lotta damage. Yeah, that's a big part of it.

You see, it's just like a wet piece of carpet drying out, taking the fungus away. Becomes that dry that part eventually dies, and one day you'll walk over it and put a tear in it. That's what's happening. Like old newspaper. Spill your tea on it, and it turns brown, yellow, and one day it rips. That's what's happening to the Country. That's why these fires were so bad. Most of it – the drying – is unintentional, because of lifestyles, you know, and lack of listening, learning and understanding. Needs patience, eh? So that's what happens when you're impatient. And that's why we say: listen to us and learn from us, you know. It all starts there . . . our personal life experience is critical.

But time's running out now. If we don't come up with something we can do together, instead of one leaving the other behind, then it's never gonna work. This place'll turn into more desert. And this summer was a sign of what will happen: drought, then big fires.

This Cobargo fire? She started up on the coastal range, on Nullica, the scarp range up there, maybe sixty, seventy kilometres away direct – got here in a flash, less than an hour or two I guess. Dry forest, big heat, big wind, making its own wind, then turned into a Warrawaddy, a fire tornado. I have Country halfway up there, near the Tuross River, our old Country. Over a few years I been rescuing young koalas from forestry clearing, up on the range – they was getting run over on the road. Caught 'em, one by one, put the little fellas in me truck, brought 'em down onto my Country. Looked after 'em. I had a colony of forty or so, all ages: happy, breeding. The fire killed 'em all. I went up there. Dead koalas, charred, lying on the ground. I sat down and I cried. Left the bodies there to feed other animals. Just cried and cried. That's the Big Scorch. Not Natural. Big worry.

This summer here, this year, she's been a big warning, see. In our culture, our stories, we talk about the big fire tornadoes, the Warrawaddys. We're on the edge of Cobargo, which got hit this summer by that fire tornado. That was a Warrawaddy, and it was a warning. A very severe warning, that one. Fire tornado. Only reason our home was saved was I'd burned properly around it over the previous five months, but I lost my shed and hundreds of cultural belongings – many you can't replace, old, spiritually valuable, important for ceremony. Embers blasted in through a gap under the door. Then I realised it was a proper Warrawaddy. I thought the house was gonna burn, so I took the stuff; was prepared to die defending it, saving it.

The Warrawaddy, it's big fire, and we're very scared of them. When you see them, that's danger, and that's what happened here at Cobargo. To tell anyone that's not Indigenous, they wouldn't understand. They would say 'Oh, that's just a hurricane,' a fire hurricane, or whatever they want to make it. But to us that's the Warrawaddy. He's been sent for a reason. He's telling us 'Danger, danger! Someone broke the law; Country's not good.' That Warrawaddy put the fear right up us, it did, especially when people see a tornado, say a wind tornado: what'll they do? When that happened to us in the old days, we ran into the caves.

In a way all this is because of what we've done to the Country, drying it out, degrading it, no proper burning, losing all the fungus and little digging animals and such. And after the White people come, and their animals, then later come the steam engine. There was sawmills, ships, and the steam engines just ate the trees, real quick. Ate 'em up.

There's a lotta stories I can't tell – and including about fires. But this summer, including this one here, it's a big, big warning. Fire, wind, rain. We're gonna meet all them three one day, all together, fire, wind and rain, all together one day very soon if we don't do something about what's happened and happening. Three at once and no one's gonna run anywhere, and that's when this world starts all over again. Some people might call it 'end of the world'; to us that's our explanation of when it comes to that time to say goodbye to everyone and everything and this world will start again.

See this picture? That healthy man with initiation scars? That's my forefather, a senior law man of the Ngarigo, born 1800 – Ibai Mullyan, also called Murray Jack 'cause he worked for old Murray over on the Indi or Murray River. The photo's taken at his camp, late 1880s or so, between Matong and Ironmungie, near Dalgety on the Snowy River there – Bumangee. He died at ninety-four. Looks like a young fella, eh?

Ibai Mullyan, him and my ancestors, every year they were given gifts of rare greenstone axes, hatchets by people from other tribes, from all across eastern Australia, some further. These people would come, and when they looked up from a distance, they saw the giant trees in Gippsland, to our south, in Gungoona, and they knew these big, giant trees were holding the sky up.

We were the people who held the sky up from a distance. My people. That's why we were given greenstone hatchets from all over the place, some coming huge distances. It was a very important task, caring for Country under these forests. Those gifts was for us to look after the Country and to keep the sky held up. Keep them big tall trees there. People come from all around the southern areas and east, all came up to the Snowies there, the high Bogongs, and corroboree with us because we were the ones who held the sky up in the distance.

If we didn't do that, they believed we'd let the sky fall on 'em. Was a real ancient responsibility. People'd travel hundreds of miles to give us gifts, and when they came, some from the desert, and saw the size of the trees, 'Whoo! No wonder they hold the sky up!' And when they looked up they'd see the clouds at the top of the trees, the trees holding up that sky. That blew 'em away when they realised where they were – nothing but gratitude. 'Cause those trees were the only ones left to tell the story, just like my people. When the trees are gone, no story.

Ours is the voice from the land, through us. We gotta listen to it. And I always say, as my grandfather said, Australia's still young yet. We're still young in this Country – even though we've been more than 60,000 years. And we've gotta get ready for our responsibilities – we've got a lot of new people coming out, lotta humans, come to Australia, and now the balance's changed, one person's going faster than the other.

We always say 'We've got all the time in the world.' We'll watch this come and we'll watch it go. But this year's a warning, 'cause what the White invaders done to our land, well, look at this year: drought, fire, and down here and in the forest, giant Warrawaddys, fire tornadoes; a Big Scorch that's off the charts. The two're connected. I'll argue that with anyone. Anyone on this planet. I don't care how many degrees they got on their walls, but just through personal life experience I'll challenge 'em with their personal life experience. Because I'm the bloke who's been out there lighting all this stuff in the past. Teaching young ones to watch, listen and learn.

Today, no management, no care of Country, and the government still allowing the logging. Well, there goes that story. The sky's falling on us. It's getting closer and closer. We was highly respected for holding the sky up, not letting it fall on anyone or thing. That'll go one day.

All we ask is to first listen to each other, and understand each other. So that's all it is. We will accept non-Indigenous, but the key to it all is understanding – listen to each other, very, very important – and understand each other. That's where it all starts. ∎

John Kinsella

Third Eclogue of the Vegetable Garden

'you will find me if you want me in the garden
unless it's pouring down with rain'
– Blixa Bargeld

Garden

It has rained overnight – not a lot,
but enough to touch below the surface layer,
tempt or taunt or soothe the subsoil. A deeper
quenching than any the gardener
has been able to give us. His giving voice
is a ploy as we are prepped to his end,
an end in which only some of us will see
our way through to seed, the gestural
hibernation, the activism of prayer-time.
Ask yourself what you are doing
to the collective body and soul
as well as each angle of sustenance,
each propagation towards an organic
            cosmology, that before and during
the first instant, it was all root, rhizome, tendril.

Gardener

What leaves the bounds of protection –
the fence against foragers and diggers –
is to be celebrated, and I wish it well
where it doesn't choke out others.

This puts me in a position of responsibility
and sunders your agency, which is either
hypocrisy or paradox of physiology.

Garden

I fool you – I only want growth
to maximal effect, and growth isn't
necessarily what you desire, what
you have in mind. I throw up so many
deceptions which ethics says you can't
be thought of as such – I taunt you
with plants you can't possibly
let run their course. Dilemma?

And that rain shower, what are
its implications beyond a day or two?
Many, I tell you. Different birds
have arrived and certain insects
have switched into next stages,
different predations and ingestions.
But it's also the optimism of rise,
of stretch, of loving the sun
you have so come to fear
when it works on a different
timescale from your despoliations.
You have refocussed it, but I – we –
search it out through the lens
of cloud tracking its halo,

find heat in gravity
nurturing. We're not
giving up the code yet,
no matter how much the esurient
'knowledge seekers' try to unravel
us, reduce us to nuts and bolts.
At least you admit none of them
by choice. At least. We share
            that resistance,
but what do we *apportion* in austerity?

Gardener

I have a report of potatoes
reaching up from their hollows,
waiting to be covered layer by layer,
but not here, not yet. Too dry.
This little rain won't reach
them in their heart of hearts.
Not yet. But as you say, optimism!

Garden

We can feel the diggings – the vibrations
of tunnelling and flicking out sand and clay –
they find the softer places we aren't given
access to – they dig into your 'forbidden',
these rabbits edgy with drought, furiously
searching for places to birth under trees
that are drought-tolerant dying dying.

All those schemes you have – the cayenne
and vinegar, the disturbing entries and exits –
put to the test at a time of stress. You'd expect
us to support your vision, but for all your
veganics, we'd add lustre to our growth
if our roots tapped blood and bone
like your grandfather spread in sackloads.

Gardener

He did. And he told me as a child to smell it,
all that growth, he said, that goodness, but
I knew it a haunting from the family tales
of his falling into the offal pit at Benny's Bone Mill,
and that he couldn't stand the site of the uncooked,
and wanted his dead flesh burnt to a crisp.
He counteracted his anxiety with blood and bone –
death outside of recognition, ebullient growth,
garden in raptures to the strains of piano,
violin, euphonium, the brass band he played in,
green thumbs on the brass valves, 'sweet-voiced'.
But you, dear garden, in your dusty realm,
your sensitivity to subterranean acts,
will grow from the sheddings of your own,
unless a bird perches, eats and shits – fine, fine!

Garden

Constraint and restraint and dependence.
Not GM or hybridising or messing with our

essence, but we are variables and beholden
to your whims and needs. Even our celerity
if fed and watered is pulled back, to grow
at a pace of your desiring. It's you messing
with 'nature's gap' to play out your drama.

Gardener

See the female red-capped robin curving
its wings – run, curve wings out as if to wrap,
then flock and run, gather materials for a nest –
early if so, very early, but dry is compulsion
and seasonal switch – six – four – two –
one blow of dried leaves of *Acacia acuminata*
to catch in a beak and run arch run. Not display.
Not antics. Ritual and knowledge and more.
Not mutually exclusive, and alongside the garden.

Garden

The garden. An article. Property per the denial
of property? Slipshod. Winds lifting and smoke
building, smothering – the degenerative burn-offs.
The fixed point of the recidivists at a time of crisis
is to keep the demi-old Euro farming ways in full
swing – fire meets fire and quenches the lack?
I see you choking up – it's not me alone
that . . . precipitates . . . your hay fever, the failure
of etymology because it sounds like a plague
of insects sweeping in before I have risen.

Gardener

It is dusk and yet the fantails unmask
themselves along with red-capped robin
to pick mosquitoes and gnats and late
flying ants from your troposphere,
to change with specificity that which you
encourage. I see this, and vicinage
works propinquity and I allow
that I am almost a plaything
and not. This elevation
to catch the sun halo the hills.

Garden

Last words, requiems, elegies.
What you don't know set
against all you want to know –
your records, your maps, your
declarations against secrecy;
but at least this is not
the fallout zone of many
of our confrères, consœurs . . .
colleagues. This open secrets act,
this defiance *if not breaking*
of drought, our folioles of doubt.

SYMBIOTIC ROOTSCAPES

Merlin Sheldrake

In the rainforests of Central America lives a small gentian flower, *Voyria tenella*. Their flowers are a vivid blue, and their stalks pale white. These 'ghost plants' have no leaves, nor any trace of green. In the place of branching, exploratory root systems they have clusters of fleshy fingers that sit like small fists in the shallow soil. With no leaves and no green pigment, *Voyria* plants are unable to eat light and carbon dioxide in the process of photosynthesis. Their stubby rootlets are ill-suited to absorb water or nutrients from the soil. How, then, can *Voyria* survive?

A few years ago, I travelled to Panama to study the symbiotic relationships that form between plants and the fungi that live in their roots, known as mycorrhizal fungi (from the Greek *mykes*, meaning fungus, and *rhiza*, meaning root). More than 90 per cent of terrestrial plants depend on these partnerships. They are a more fundamental part of planthood than flowers, fruit, leaves, wood or roots, and lie at the base of the food chains that sustain nearly all terrestrial life. Fine threads of tubular fungal cells – known as mycelium –

emanate from plant roots into the surrounding soil. These cells can link different plants in shared networks that have come to be known as the Wood Wide Web. This is how *Voyria* are able to make a living. Through shared fungal networks, nutrients and energy-containing sugars pass into *Voyria* from neighbouring plants. Mycorrhizal associations are so prolific that between a third and a half of the living mass of soils is made up of mycorrhizal fungi; their mycelium is a living seam that helps to hold the soil together. Globally, the total length of mycorrhizal mycelium in the top ten centimetres of soil is around half the width of our galaxy. In 1845, Alexander von Humboldt described the 'living whole' of the natural world using the metaphor of a 'net-like, entangled fabric'. Mycorrhizal fungi make the net and fabric real.

Thinking about fungi makes the world look different. The longer I've studied their behaviours and remarkable abilities, the more fungi have loosened the grip of my certainties about how the world works. Over time, as the familiar has grown increasingly unfamiliar, many of the well-worn concepts that I use to organise my experience – including notions of identity, autonomy and individuality – have become questions rather than answers known in advance. *Voyria* have helped me pursue some of these questions. In Panama, I wanted to find out more about how mycorrhizal networks behaved, and spent weeks scrambling through the jungle searching for these charismatic flowers in the hope that they might tell me something about what was taking place underground.

Symbiosis – the intimate association formed between different species – is a fundamental feature of life and enables new biological possibilities. Mycorrhizal fungi are some of the more striking examples. These ancient associations gave rise to one of the pivotal transitions in the history of the planet: the movement of plants' ancestors out of the water and onto the land. These algae had no roots and were ill-equipped to scavenge for water and nutrients in the open air. They struck up a relationship with fungi, accomplished foragers that served as their root systems for the first 50 million years of their life on land until early plants could evolve their own. This makes mycorrhizal associations the foundation of all recognisable life on land. To this day, plants' fungal partners help them cope with drought, heat and the many stresses that life on land has presented since the beginning. Plants supply their fungal associates with as much as 30 per cent of the energy they produce in photosynthesis. Mycorrhizal fungi supply their plant partners with nutrients, such as phosphorus and nitrogen, and defend plants from disease. Their association is literally radical.

Ecology is the study of the relationships between organisms. Networks of mycorrhizal fungi embody these relationships and help lead us out of reductive stories about self-contained individuals locked in a competition for resources. I like to imagine the bewilderment of an extraterrestrial anthropologist who discovered only yesterday, after several decades of studying modern humanity, that we had something called the internet. It's a bit like that for contemporary ecologists, grappling with the many ways that mycorrhizal fungi change our understanding of how organisms interact. As *Voyria* demonstrate, nutrients can move between plants via shared fungal connections. They are not exceptions. 'Normal' green plants in the shaded understorey might be sustained by resources acquired from their more amply provided neighbours. It isn't only nutrients that pass through these networks. A plant attacked by aphids can release signals that alert neighbouring plants to the imminent threat. Bacteria use fungal networks as highways to travel through the bustling obstacle course of the soil. Even if plants don't share the very same network, mycorrhizal fungi regulate plant coexistence, in some cases intensifying the competition between plants and in some cases relaxing it.

Whether in agriculture, forestry or in our attempts to restore degraded ecosystems, we depend entirely on the healthy functioning of mycorrhizal relationships. But they are hard for us to see, hidden within plant roots and underground. In this photoessay, I use laser scans of roots to explore the astonishing intercourse between plants and their fungal partners, subterranean worlds of intimacies within intimacies. All of these images are scans of non-photosynthetic ghost plants, whether the blue-flowered *Voyria* or otherwise. The roots of these plants are densely inhabited by fungi and the resulting rootscapes are particularly spectacular. I collected the samples while in Panama, where I conducted research at the Smithsonian Tropical Research Institute, and imaged them using a novel technique developed by Magnus Rath and colleagues at the Philipps University of Marburg in Germany. With a watchmaker's precision, Magnus prepared the roots for scanning. I then used a laser microscope to scan 'slices' of a sample ('confocal laser scanning microscopy'), and from stacks of these images reconstructed three-dimensional projections. By using different coloured lasers it was possible to render the plant and fungi separately. In all of the images that follow, plant tissue is artificially coloured in blue-green, and fungal tissue in red. Many consist of three panels showing the same section of root with the plant tissue made increasingly transparent. These techniques provide extraordinary new vantage on the entangled flourishing that underlies our past, present and future. ∎

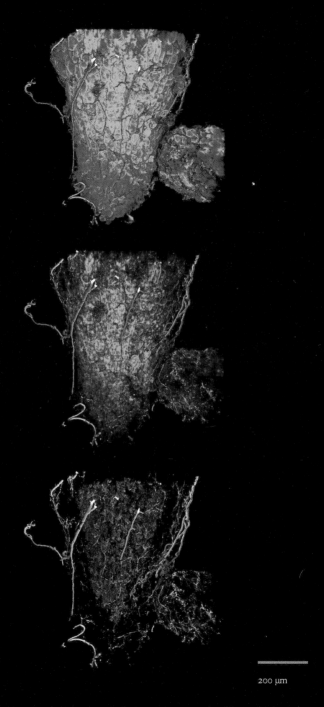

200 μm

Root tip of *Voyria tenella*. The root systems of *Voyria* have evolved into fleshy fingers that serve as fungal 'gardens' or 'farms'. Most of these roots are about half a millimetre, or 500 micrometres (μm) in diameter.

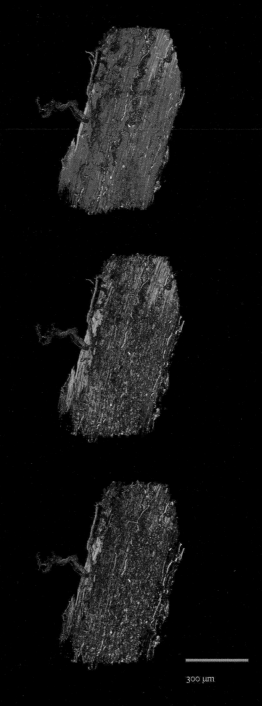

300 µm

Root of *Voyria corymbosa*. You can see tubular fungal cells, or hyphae, extending out from the root into the space around the root, known as the rhizosphere. This is a rare glimpse of the connections that link plant roots with their surroundings.

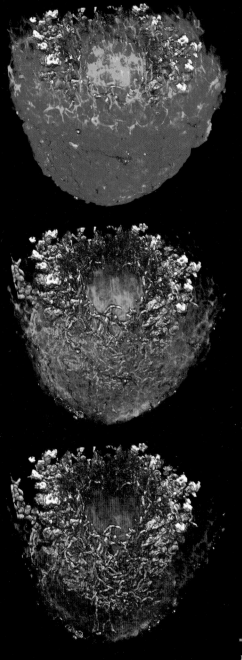

100 μm

Root of *Voyria tenella*. Mycorrhizal relationships must be intricately managed. Fungi are confined to certain areas where the transfer of nutrients takes place.

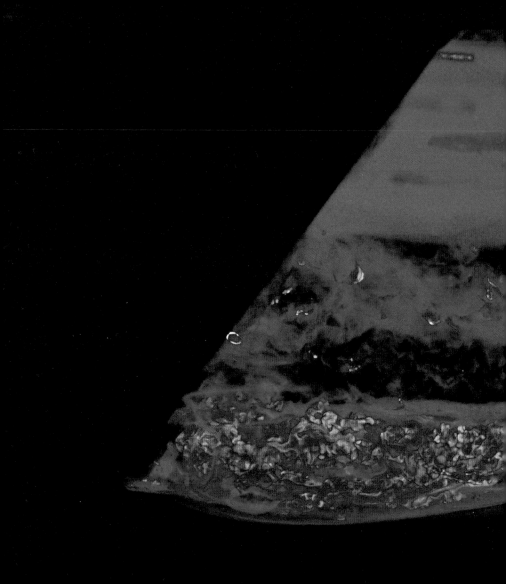

Section of *Gymnosiphon suaveolens* root. The organ of exchange between the fungus and *Gymnosiphon* is a branched structure, formed by the fungus, known as an arbuscule.

50 μm

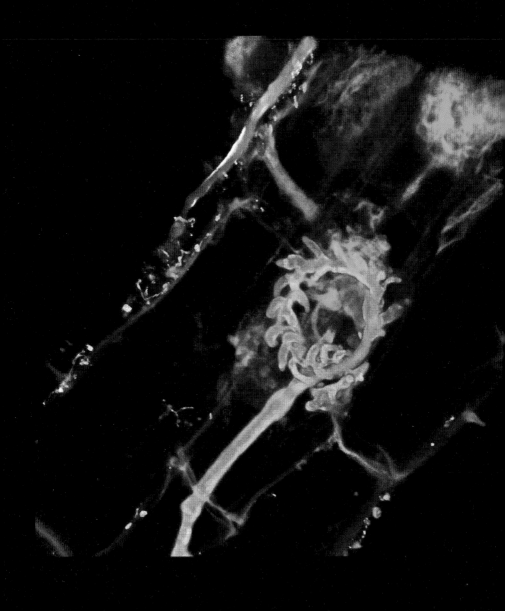

Section of *Gymnosiphon suaveolens* root. This crown-like structure has never before been reported and its role is unknown.

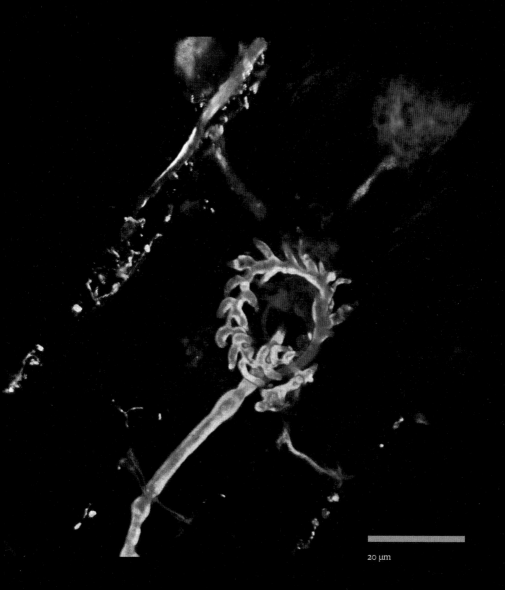

20 μm

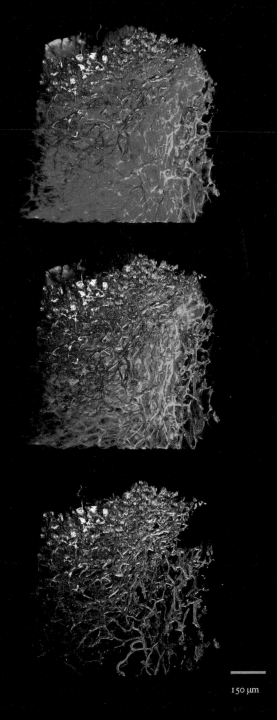

150 μm

Section of *Voyria tenella* root. The different forms of the fungus within the root are clearly visible.

WATER IS NEVER LONELY

Judith D. Schwartz

T he first thing I notice about the cloud forest is its lovely, gentle
sound. I walk along a path narrowed by trees and moss-covered
rock and hear the light whisper of water, faint but constant. It is a
soothing sound, but rather than white noise, I'd say it's more like
silver, or crystal, such is its brightness and fragility. Indeed, this
high-montane forest preserve has a crystal-like name: Joya del Hielo,
which roughly translates to Jewel of Ice. 'Ice' because the temperature
is always cool. Here, in central Mexico's eastern Sierra Madre
Mountains, the mist and the high altitude guard the chill. At least
they do for the time being. Alas, nearby logging and land clearances
making way for farms and pastures are altering the humidity up in
the hills.

My guide today is Roberto Pedraza Ruiz, a naturalist and prize-
winning photographer. In 1987 his mother, Martha 'Pati' Ruiz Corzo,
co-founded the Grupo Ecológico Sierra Gorda, a conservation and
education organization that protects the cloud forest enclave. Pati,
once a high-heel-wearing music teacher during her city years, lives
in a small mountain cabin surrounded by ancient sweet gum trees.
She is short and stout and fierce; she is driven by a passion for the
earth and its 'beauty-ness'. I have watched her stand before legislators
at the Mexican Senate in a drab brown tunic and rubber-treaded

sandals and move the formally attired officials to tears, laughter and song. In 1997, through sheer determination and a refusal to keep quiet, she managed to convince the state of Querétaro to declare one third of its land – some 383,567 hectares – a biodiversity reserve.

The headquarters of the Sierra Gorda alliance is an education and training center in the town of Jalpan de Serra, a three-hour-plus drive from Querétaro airport where Roberto picks me up. The last stretch rising into the hills is one of the most dizzying experiences found outside an amusement park: switchback after switchback, swerving away and then driving directly at the sun. (Roberto had recommended Dramamine.) At some point we start passing over and through the clouds. Sometimes the mist thins out, revealing purple and red mountain flowers and bushes with yellow blooms. Sometimes I can see only the ghostly silhouettes of trees.

The road glistens and the leaves on the trees are wet; pines droop under the weight of moisture clinging to needles. It is early March and the rainy season doesn't start until June, Roberto says, emphasizing that the dampness is from the humidity alone. Roberto, who is now in his mid-forties, says that when he was growing up the rain was soft and light, but in recent years it has come in heavy and sudden downpours. Today Roberto is happy to be driving amid clouds. 'The cloud forests have been stressed,' he says. 'It's been a dry winter.'

The route to Joya del Hielo the next morning is also zigzagging, but not vertiginous like the airport run. Roberto watches out the window for birds and reports on what he sees: clay-colored thrush, oriole, woodpecker, kestrel. 'This area is a stronghold for bearded wood partridge,' he says, referring to a long-tailed forest fowl with a red beak and breast the color of cinnamon. 'I haven't been able to photograph it – that's a big frustration in life. I saw one with chicks and made a call, but they were too quick.' On another occasion he and a film team finally gave up on one and left the site at 2 a.m., only to return the next day to find it had shat on their equipment. Roberto frequently arranges for photographers and film crews to visit Joya del Hielo. A few years ago the BBC came to get footage of the bumblebee hummingbird, the world's second-smallest hummingbird, which weighs less than a penny.

After bumping along a dirt road for a few minutes we arrive at the edge of the cloud forest reserve and are greeted by a fallen tree crossing and obstructing our way into Joya del Hielo. It proves too heavy to move. Roberto dispatches his chainsaw, and after getting through and driving for another kilometer, we get out and leave the car. I grab a notebook and my water bottle. Roberto shrugs. 'I don't need water in the cloud forest,' he says. He grabs his camera and a machete.

As we walk, Roberto points out jaguar scat and the spot where a puma and jaguar had a fight; the forest is home to all six of Mexico's feline species. Life appears in layers. Spiky bromeliads – in Roberto's words, 'flats for frogs and salamanders' – jut out from the trunks of hardwoods, while cacti are growing in the nooks of trees. Flowering carnivorous plants, with sticky leaves able to catch and digest insects, grow on limestone. Roberto peers up at a large oak tree where various orchids reside. 'There's a whole ecosystem on that one,' he says. Further on we pause at another large, grand oak, clothed in mist. 'This is the king of the forest,' says Roberto. 'His "brother" passed away six years ago in a storm. The former owner of the land said, "How much charcoal can be made from that?"'

The abundance of life in the cloud forest is stunning. Everywhere you look life is dripping, climbing, crawling, dangling, hiding, sprouting from, nesting on, nestled in. 'Those are 500- to 600-year-old cedars,' Roberto says. 'I don't know why they spared them.' He notes that the previous owner was known to log with impunity.

Some 200 meters past the cedars, we reach an area where Roberto has identified three previously unknown species of magnolia, two of which have been found only in this forest. (One variety is named for him: *Magnolia pedrazae*.) He calls magnolia 'living fossils', since they are considered earth's first flowering plants. This section of the cloud forest, at 2,000 meters above sea level, is a nursery for rare magnolia trees. Now that they are known to be here, and are protected from chainsaws and browsing cattle, the magnolia population is rebounding. When they bloom, the fragrance suffuses the whole forest, Roberto says. 'Here's a young one. There is hope for the species. When you look closely, nothing here is alone.'

The thing about water is that it depends upon water. When land in the area below Joya del Hielo is cleared of vegetation for farming and firewood, this means less water circulating in the vicinity, a key aspect of what Roberto calls stressors to the cloud forest. If the lowland dries out, it becomes that much more difficult for a higher-altitude forest to make a cloud. Moisture in one place informs moisture elsewhere. As the late poet Tony Hoagland wrote in 'The Social Life of Water', 'All water is part of other water. / Cloud talks to lake; mist / speaks quietly to creek.' Similarly, the loss of water in one location can have the effect of drying out another. For example, depleting an aquifer for irrigation wells, as is happening across North America's agricultural lands, lowers the water table so that nearby streams and wetlands dry out and wildlife has no place to go. As many of us who've seen these patterns playing out have realized, aridity is contagious.

When rain soaks in and is held in the soil, the area stays moist and covered in plants. When the surface is exposed, water evaporates or runs off, leaving the land parched and, in certain environments, prone to fire. Climatic conditions are largely determined by how water circulates, how it moves across the landscape and through the air. Water problems like floods and droughts are often symptoms of climate change, but supporting the water cycle can help regulate and moderate temperature. To a large extent, the story of climate is the story of water.

Plants, particularly trees, are central to the wetting or drying of a landscape. For one, trees embody water. According to Andy Lipkis of TreePeople, an NGO in Los Angeles, the root system of a mature tree can retain tens of thousands of liters of rainwater. Bill Mollison, the late Australian scientist and early teacher of permaculture, which applies insights from nature to farming and design, said 'a tree stands there as a barrel of water'. Trees are also continuously putting moisture back into the environment. With their vast green surface area, they hold and evaporate water. More significantly, they transpire, as water moves up from the roots and out through the leafy canopy. A good-sized tree can transpire 400 liters of water each day.

You can think of a plant as a water pump, pulling moisture from the surrounding soil and releasing it as vapor. From the plant's perspective, this process is vital for regulating its own temperature because transpiration is a cooling mechanism, in that it consumes energy. Turning liquid water into a gas not only uses energy, it also dissipates the heat beaming down from the sun. Solar energy hitting a bare surface – think midsummer tarmac – creates 'sensible heat', or heat you can feel. If instead that radiation falls on vegetation, thanks to transpiration it becomes 'latent heat', suspended in the water vapor through space and through time. This is one reason Joya del Hielo feels so cool: those plants that fill every available niche are busy transpiring, which postpones the unleashing of heat and ensures it remains in the realm of potential.

In the aggregate, as forests, trees are moving around tremendous amounts of moisture, and therefore energy. In 2015 I spoke with Brazilian scientist Antonio Donato Nobre, who described forest-driven 'aerial rivers': bodies of moisture that sail, unnoticed, through the sky. He said airborne waterways above the Amazon rainforest contain more water than the mighty Amazon River below, as twenty metric tonnes of water flow out from the trees and into the air. The notion of water continuously floating above the earth reminds me of the Hebrew word for sky, which is *shamayim*, or 'there is water'. I had always found this curious. Likewise, in her essay 'Clouds', Rachel Carson writes: 'Up there is another ocean – the air ocean that envelops the whole globe.'

Antonio Nobre likes to say, 'Every tree is a geyser.' To a large extent weather comes down to the agency of trees. Trees cast out moisture, but they also pull it in. According to a theory called the biotic pump, the cumulative transpiration of trees in a forest forms a low-pressure zone which creates a vacuum that draws in moisture. This laden air cools and condenses over the forest, and we have rain. A healthy forest is at once generating its own rain – that soft, crystalline song in Mexico – sending water abroad and tugging water in from elsewhere. It is a dynamic system, as moisture both rides the current and creates it. Trees and clouds are talking to each other.

Past a certain threshold, however, tree loss interrupts the dialogue. This worries Roberto Pedraza Ruiz, who says that a patchwork of small, protected forests does not function in the same way as a large wooded expanse. Meanwhile, it has been four years since I interviewed Antonio Nobre and encountered his poetics of the rainforest: seeing thick, extensive forest as a 'green ocean', with waves of humidity lofting over and across. What seemed eternal now feels unnervingly provisional since the world has, with appropriate horror, witnessed the relentless felling of trees in the Amazon basin in the last two years.

That deforestation leads to drought and even ecological collapse should be news to no one. The demise of civilizations like the Mayans, Anasazi, Easter Islanders and (at least in part) of Rome offer a cautionary tale. Alexander von Humboldt, a naturalist and adventurer born in 1769, wrote that cutting trees on hillsides 'seem[s] to bring upon future generations two calamities at once; want of fuel and a scarcity of water.' In his 1864 book *Man and Nature* – original title: *Man the Disturber of Nature's Harmonies* – George Perkins Marsh, the nineteenth-century diplomat and scholar whom many consider America's first environmentalist, wrote of the need to restore forests to 'devise means for maintaining the permanence of its relation to the fields, the meadows and the pastures, to the rain and the dews of heaven, to the springs and rivulets with which it waters the earth'.

Back to the Amazon basin: at what point will the trees and the clouds stop communicating? How many more blows of the ax before the great, damp inhalations and exhalations, the sources of moisture for so much of the hemisphere, are stilled?

I live in a watery part of the world. South-western Vermont, which spans the Taconic and Green Mountain ranges, is richly forested and is part of the United States' 'wet belt'. We receive various forms of precipitation throughout the year, sometimes the whole repertoire – rain, hail, sleet, snow and mist – all in the same day.

They say every snowflake is unique. I would venture every snowfall has its own signature as well. Today's is coming down in clumps, as if some prankster were tossing dampened wads of tissue from a great height. Sodden November snow like this creates definition: it clings to surfaces, so as to add an outline to every limb and vine it lands on. The effect is something like the Japanese woodblock style called *ukiyo-e*, also known as 'pictures of the floating world'. By mid-morning the temperature is above freezing. The air is so thick with white that it's hard to pinpoint exactly when the snow stops.

My friend Jim Laurie, a sort of freelance ecologist and educator based near Boston, likes to come up to Vermont and walk in the snow. He'll point out tiny snow fleas – a kind of springtail – and where the beavers have been. For many years Jim had a job at a Texas chemical plant. There he experimented with ways to remediate water with sunlight, air and microorganisms: the effluent moves through a series of tanks seeded with microbes from different ecosystems and emerges pristine. He later worked with ecological designer John Todd to develop the Eco-Machine, a ballroom-sized installation that mimics natural environments like streams, ponds and marshes, to yield clean water. Through the 1970s and 1980s Todd was associated with the New Alchemy Institute, known for pioneering research into biological models for energy, farming and shelter. While using plants, aquatic creatures and sunlight to purify water sounds like a kind of alchemical magic, this is what nature does.

On a recent visit Jim explained to me that water, by its very nature, has a tendency to affiliate. This is because H_2O, the water molecule, is polar: with one end positive and the other negative (the hydrogen and oxygen sides, respectively), one water molecule is drawn to another, as with a magnet. He referred me to Nobel laureate Richard

P. Feynman's observations on how atoms 'jiggle' and interact. In a 1983 interview, the theoretical physicist said that within a drop of water 'the atoms attract each other. They like to be next to each other. They want as many partners as they can get.' Even on a microscopic level, water seeks company.

S panish meteorologist Millán M. Millán has a saying: 'Water begets water, soil is the womb, and vegetation the midwife.' Millán, who was director of the Center for Environmental Studies of the Mediterranean, documents the change in precipitation patterns in the western Mediterranean region. Specifically, his focus is the loss of the summer storms that dependably wafted in from the sea each afternoon, cleansing the air and providing water for the farms north of Valencia. Starting in the 1990s, at the behest of the European Union, he has been researching the rains, with methods ranging from the latest mapping and measurement instruments and simulation models to the small observatory in his thirteenth-floor apartment in Valencia, from where he watches the clouds advance and retreat. Millán's conclusion: the once-regular rains have stalled because the connection among key water sources has been severed.

According to Millán, the missing rains have a lot to do with what's been done to the land – much in the name of development. Over many decades, marshes along Spain's eastern coast have been drained for agriculture, housing and tourism. Wetlands, too, have become sites for construction. Throughout the area, soil has been covered up with buildings, asphalt and concrete, replacing natural vegetation. We can add to this a long legacy of deforestation. The Spanish Civil War in the late 1930s was especially brutal for trees: as George Orwell wrote in *Homage to Catalonia*, up in the hills 'everything thicker than one's finger' was burned to keep militiamen from freezing.

The trouble is that those trees, shrubs and grasses played a crucial role in recycling water along the Mediterranean coast, and that without the collective work of those plants – transpiring moisture that is carried along by sea breezes – the mechanism stalls. The result of removing trees, sealing soils and replacing wetlands with farms or hotels, is a landscape with far fewer plants. This means forfeiting not simply the plants themselves, but all that the plants do, including emitting moisture. And so here in Spain, the would-be rain is cut off from its source.

Millán says the vapor lifting from the sea was never enough to make it rain; rather, the light wind picked up additional moisture from the soils and plants as it drifted across the landscape. In this environment, Millán says, the moisture concentration required to generate rain is twenty-one grams per kilogram of air. The typical summer sea breeze is fourteen grams per kilogram of air. Without that critical seven grams per kilogram taken up over land, the rains don't come.

To borrow Millán's own aphorism, the scenario in the western Mediterranean is like this: with the 'womb' and the 'midwife' either under stress or absent, water can no longer beget water the way it once had. Much of the moisture borne along the winds goes back to the sea, while some vapor accumulates and drifts to where the conditions are conducive to rainfall. Millán's research has linked this moisture to heavy rains and flooding in central Europe. In his words: 'Basically, you're cutting a tree in Almería and getting a storm in Düsseldorf.' When it does rain near the shore it comes down in torrents, triggering floods, mudslides and erosion.

In November 2019 I travel to Valencia. One day Millán drives my husband and me from the coast into Aragon province, up to the edge of where mist from the Mediterranean Sea provides moisture. This is the continental divide, beyond which the land derives moisture from the Atlantic. We stop in Teruel, where Orwell sustained wounds during the Spanish Civil War. Millán offers ongoing commentary about the meteorological present – when the weather will turn, as foretold by the movement of clouds – and the ecological sins of the past. 'Two thousand years of bad management and wars,' he laments as he points out the sites of doomed irrigation schemes, monocultures of fast-growing but flammable pine and derelict, deserted farms.

One reason he brought us here, Millán says, is to highlight the importance of observation as opposed to relying solely on models and projections. Weather anomalies like altered rain patterns are often explained as the result of climate change – a term that is itself an abstraction, he says. He wants us to see that our actions upon the land play a significant role, particularly as this alters the fate of water. I ask: 'What if vegetation returns to these areas? Might the return of transpired moisture bring back the summer rains?' He says yes – and that he advocates for this – but the rain wouldn't necessarily arrive where reforesting happens, and could be sixty to eighty kilometers away. This water isn't irredeemably lost, after all. It has merely been waiting for companionship.

Given that there's always moisture up in the atmosphere, what brings it back to earth? This happens thanks to condensation, the inverse of transpiration: once the air cools beyond a particular threshold – the dew point – the water molecules gather, or condense, to form clouds, fog or dew. This releases heat that has been held in vapor, high up at cloud level or, as in early morning dew, where the air is cool. The falling raindrop requires another element, some tiny speck to condense around, so that they become partners in rain.

Nature provides a variety of 'precipitation nuclei': ice crystals, bacteria, fungal spores, pollen, scented compounds emitted from trees. (The last of these Antonio Nobre calls 'scents of the forest' or 'fairy dust'.) In the 1970s David Sands, a biologist at Montana State University, studied a pest that seemed to provoke frost damage in cash crops like wheat: a bacterium that prompted ice crystals to form at temperatures that would not typically cause freezing. He flew a small plane over farm fields and held a petri dish out the window to collect samples amid the clouds. When he found the same microbe – *Pseudomonas syringae*, which Sands and others who do research on 'bio-precipitation' affectionately call 'Sue' – he surmised that in promoting ice nucleation, the bacterium also played a role in making rain.

Bacteria like Sue are very light, and winds often lift them into the sky. From the microbe's point of view, promoting ice formation and catching a ride with the crystal assure its descent to the ground, where, presumably, it can infest another crop and perpetuate itself.

When it comes to rainmaking, not just any old particle will do. Walter Jehne, a soil microbiologist in Australia, says all the stuff we humans have been putting up into the air – industrial pollutants and the '3–5 billion tonnes of fine dust aerosols that are added annually due to our land degradation and desertification' – is not conducive to precipitation. Rather, the pieces are too small and not 'hygroscopic', or water-attracting. Instead of serving as scaffolding for raindrops, they linger around the atmosphere and form hazes, which, according to Jehne, absorb heat and suppress rain.

Jehne is sure we can help that humidity become rain by restoring the natural systems that facilitate it. Where we have dusty, eroding soil, we can rebuild that soil so that it holds on to water and sustains plant life. Where we are losing tree cover we can replant ecologically, based on native polycultures. For we need those trees to transpire and pull in moisture, and to emit the volatile compounds – the 'scents' – that sow the rain. And where we have a landscape that is thriving water-wise, that is green and lush and diverse, we must protect it with all the strength we've got, which may involve resisting political or economic forces as well as questioning notions of 'development'.

As a scientist in the world's driest and most fire-prone continent, Jehne is attuned to the nuances of moisture, and explains that the fate of our landscapes comes down to 'fire or fungi'. In every setting, plant matter needs to be broken down as part of the life cycle. Where there's moisture, material is decomposed by fungi and bacteria, helped along by leaf-eating insects and animal life. (He refers to koalas as 'aerial alimentary canals'.) When it's dry, fire swoops in to do the job. In terms of retaining moisture, Jehne says we shouldn't worry about rain per se, but rather what happens to the rain that falls. His point is that we have a choice: we can manage land to support fungi and all the creatures that consume and break down plant matter, or in a way that beckons fire. It all hinges on how we work with water.

Which brings us back to the Joya del Hielo. What would happen to that sonorous mist – not to mention the jaguar, bearded wood partridge, orchids and magnolia – if the Grupo Ecológico Sierra Gorda were not able to garner the funds to preserve this beautiful cloud forest? Then again, what if Pati, Roberto and their colleagues were able to keep a larger area safe from development? The jaguar and its wild feline brethren would have that much more forest to roam, and the recently discovered *Magnolia pedrazae* that much more ground upon which to become established. One way the group helps protect the region is by providing local communities with means of earning income that don't entail cutting down forests, by providing aid to those establishing traditional eateries, making crafts and offering ecotourism. This way not every standing tree looks like firewood or charcoal.

We just had a big snowfall, the broad, white, skiable kind. The local newspaper ran the requisite photos of children in hats and puffy jackets sledding on the hills. Once our mountain road is plowed, I walk our elderly beagle, Tsotsi, to a waterfall about a kilometer away. It is just above freezing, but I hear the waterfall well before I reach it: a rushing sound. Compared to the soft dripping in the cloud forest, the sound is fuller, even a bit raspy. I watch the water stream down through thick piles of snow and columns of icicles that melt ever so slowly into the flow.

In the early 1800s much of southern Vermont, including this mountain, was cleared for sheep farms. The Northeast's wool industry quickly went bust, and trees grew once again. Our second-growth forests stabilize soil and make sure water doesn't rush down and erode hillsides. As is the case in the Sierra Gorda, the Amazon rainforest and everywhere else, these trees are an integral part of how water moves through the landscape. Along the slope are the oaks, maples, poplars and birch that keep us company up here. They stand like sentries aside the rocky crevice where cool, fresh water runs down through the ice and snow. ■

Bosque musgoso, 2018

Nigel Mott passing up the salmon putchers, Lydney, the Severn Estuary, 2002

SURVIVORS

Adam Weymouth

I cannot tell you the names of the rivers that I speak of. Their mussel beds are now so rare that few people beyond those that study them are permitted to know of their existence at all.

The freshwater pearl mussel has a life that is longer than our own. In Britain and Ireland they live up to 120 years; in latitudes closer to the Arctic, in Finland or in Norway, up to 300. Individual specimens have been around since the invention of the steam engine. One can count their growth lines, much like tree rings, beneath a microscope. They have been on this planet for 120 million years, and they came to British and Irish waters at the end of the last ice age. 'You fall in love with them,' Evelyn Moorkens, who has devoted decades to their research, confides in me. 'I have given my life to them.'

Male mussels release sperm through their siphons. Female mussels inhale the sperm and retain the fertilised eggs within their bodies, incubating them, each female with up to 4 million larvae clinging to her gills. By late summer the female mussel can no longer breathe for offspring. She releases them through her own siphon into the river's flow. But for a sedentary species to hold their position in a fast-flowing river demands a plan. If not, over the millennia they would ultimately be swept into the ocean, even if only by a few metres' drift each generation. The plan they have is salmon.

Juvenile salmon, hatched in the same pools that the mussels inhabit, inhale the larvae as they pass. There they remain, encysted on the fishes' gills until the end of the following spring. They do not harm the salmon. Some studies suggest that they confer a benefit, that the antibodies the salmon develop when the larvae attach protect them from the sea lice and other parasites that they may acquire during their lives. Before the salmon depart for the oceans, the mussels, now grown large enough, detach from their hosts and burrow down into the river's bed. In five years they return to the surface, where they remain for the next century or so.

When they were abundant, pearl fishers would decimate mussel beds, ripping shells apart in search of the occasional gem. That has long since been made illegal, but agriculture, the draining of the bogs surrounding rivers and the silting up of riverbeds all continue to decimate stocks. Like salmon, mussels require their environment pristine. They filter their own water, but they cannot keep up with modern practices. Their young are dying, their populations ageing. They need only breed twice in a hundred years, but even that is a challenge these days.

And then there are the salmon, as integral to the mussels' life cycle as the mussels are themselves. Wild salmon in Ireland are at their lowest levels since records began. Once, 30 per cent of adult salmon returned to the rivers of their birth to spawn; today it is more like 3 per cent. The story is the same in Scotland. That country's last commercial operation, a single man netting on the River Esk, was shut down in 2018. Salmon runs in England and Wales hover on the verge of extinction. If the salmon go, so do the mussels.

For now, they cling on.

I hear of Nigel Mott on the news one morning. A fisherman, one of the last commercial fishermen of wild salmon on the River Severn, has won a landmark case against the Environment Agency (EA). For several years I have been travelling in Alaska, documenting the decline of salmon and Indigenous salmon fishing there, and there are strong echoes with the court cases I have been following on the Yukon River, 4,000 miles away. I give him a call.

Nigel collects me from the coach station in Bristol. His car is full of rope and bits of beehive. We leave the city, cross the Severn and drive up the north bank of the river towards Lydney. At the edge of town he pulls off the road and steps out to unlock a five-bar gate. Nigel is in his mid-seventies, his hair thin and grey, and he walks stiffly, bent forward at the waist, but he has a tough energy to him, thick arms, a life carved from hard work. We head across rutted fields, lurching, much faster than I would drive them, but this was Nigel's commute for more than forty years, and besides, we are chasing the tide. We run parallel to an embankment, and then we crest the rise and plough through an ungrazed field and Nigel brings the car to a sudden stop.

We get out. The song of skylarks. And before us, stretching away, is the Severn. I am accustomed to seeing it from the bridge, but from here it is shocking and vast, at least a mile, maybe two, from bank to bank. In the near distance, the first of the bridges; behind it, further, the other. The sky is grey, the river brown, and flowing on the tide at quite a pace. The wind is cold. Across the water one of the world's first commercial nuclear power stations, Berkeley, now decommissioned, sits solid in the gloom.

Piles of discarded putcher baskets are abandoned on the bank like the remains of shopping trolleys, in the weeds of the shoreline and on the rocks that prop the shore up and which prevent the banks from sloughing away into the mud. Nigel built his putchers from stainless steel – once they were woven from two-year-old willow – and they won't be going anywhere any time soon. Quite possibly they will outlast the salmon. Some of the fish weir remains as well, long timbers of larch stretching out from the bank, crosswise to the river's flow, now slumped at angles and beyond any sense of repair. The putchers, each of them longer than a person, would have been stacked in the weir, four tiers of them, pushing out over a hundred metres into the river. Six-hundred-and-fifty baskets. Six-hundred welds on each one. There is evidence here of fishing weirs that goes back several centuries at least, though it is likely they have existed for millennia. The Severn has the third-highest tide in the world, at thirty-one and a half feet, and for sloshing salmon through baskets you could hope to find nowhere better; nowhere else caught fish like this. Sited in the swiftest channel, their wide mouths pointing upriver and funnelling to a point, the four ranks of baskets would be set on a low tide at the beginning of the season and entirely covered by the river on each high. The salmon would be caught on the ebb of the tide and trapped as they flowed downstream, unable to turn back against the force of the river. 'Like a pig in a passage,' Nigel says.

The season ran from 16 April to 16 August. He and his partner checked and cleaned the baskets twice a day, sharing the work two tides on, two tides off. Crows followed the ebb tide so you had to get to the fish quick, before they plucked the eyes out. There were perhaps ten operations on this stretch. Everyone knew everyone. Nigel had a twenty-year lease here, and a permit for 600 salmon in the season. That made £60,000 or so, shared between the two of them. But things had been getting tougher for some time.

'The summer of 1990 was the best season we ever had,' he says. 'The river was absolutely stuffed with fish. And we haven't had a decent season since.' Numbers had been dwindling for years, but around 2000 they collapsed. In 2010, to protect the run on the Wye, the EA halted fishing. Nigel argued that the mouth to the Wye was downstream of their operation, and that a few small-time fishermen could not be responsible for the collapse of the Wye's run. In 2012 the fishing was reopened and the EA issued them with new permits – for thirty salmon in a season. 'I might have gone on in a minor capacity for quite a number of years,' says Nigel. But with the catch limit set so low there was no living to be made, and no sense in carrying on.

A man passes us, walking his dog. They know each other, in the easy way that people out here do, no real surprise to find each other on a forgotten piece of riverbank. Nigel greets him, though not by name.

'Does it bring back memories?' the man asks, gesturing to the putchers.

Nigel waves the memories away. 'Best not think about it,' he says. The man nods. He whistles his dog and walks on.

Nigel pulls two lave nets from out the boot of the car. If there was a method of fishing more ancient, more basic, than the putchers, then I am looking at it. Such nets do not come from tackle shops; Nigel makes them himself. Three poles of wood of similar length, each six feet long, one a handle, the other two hinging open into a V, held apart by a chock of wood, and a handmade net strung between them, so that the whole apparatus is like a vast shovel. The handle of Nigel's net is ash, the rimes hazel, although black willow, he says, is best. The crosspiece is elm, a piece of wood which has still not settled and found its shape in the fifty years since he fitted it. In this it is like the river, with its sandbars skulking about beneath the surface, its banks forever on the move. Plenty of ships have run aground through here. It is a good net, it has served him well. But there's no point in a good net, he mutters, if there are no fish to catch. Nigel's £60 lave licence permits him to catch a single salmon in a season. One.

We pick our way down the sludge of the bank, leaning heavily on the nets. Lean forward, weight on the toes, keep moving, or the mud begins to suck you downward. At any moment I expect Nigel to tell me that all this is a joke, the very gullibility of what a city boy will believe of country life. But then we are in the shallows, the water up to our thighs, and with a warning not to drift too far downriver or I'll be heading out to sea, Nigel sinks onto his front, his head directed downstream, and holding the net before him as a float he sculls out into the channel. I watch him go, and then I follow.

The water is warmer than I expected. We move along at quite a pace. I watch Nigel ahead of me, ferrying out into the middle of the river. It makes me think of otters. For a time I drift on my back and watch the sky. If I pull level with Nigel we can chat. Without him here this would feel insane. Plenty of folk have drowned in these waters, not least those who used to work the putchers. In his forty years of fishing Nigel has learned the Severn's ways and moods, although he insists only across this stretch. Take him a few miles upriver, he says, and he'd be lost. We are nearing the bridge, angling directly for the middle of the estuary now, and up ahead the water has a subtly different quality to it, with small riffles upon its surface, and it is for here that Nigel points his net.

Suddenly he stands, and wades downstream, emerging from the river. By the time I reach him he is standing with the water around his thighs, his net unfurled, and I stand up beside him. The bridge, the older of the two, is almost directly above us. The tide whipping around its enormous stanchions. I can make out people in the cars, and from up there we must look biblical. Two miles of water, and two men with ancient instruments balanced in the centre upon its surface.

The way it works is this. We are on the outgoing tide, and salmon, guided by deep-flowing channels, will be pushed towards the sandbar we are walking. When they realise they are running out of river they will turn and swim back upstream, and where they force against the river's flow their wake, or loom, will give them away. At that point we'll hustle over and scoop them up. In comparison with the delicacy of fly fishing, this feels like the use of a blunt instrument. But it is effective. Not so long ago there was a six-man team operating lave nets out of Lydney, making a living. Those days are gone. Yet as we make our way upriver it is increasingly clear that the catching of the fish itself is not really the point. The point is to find a reason still to be here.

The Court of Appeal upheld the EA's decision to curtail Nigel's permit on grounds of sustainability. They found that the 10,000 to 15,000 salmon that enter the Wye each year needed all the help they could get. But the court also found that the EA had given no consideration to the impact on Nigel's life and livelihood, and that his human rights had been breached. Nigel fought the case up to the Supreme Court, where the judge ordered the EA to pay him £187,278 for loss of earnings for the years 2012–14. He is now chasing payment for lost earnings from 2015 up to the present day. So far, the proceedings have cost £400,000. It is, he says, a strain on the finances. But I can see that he gets a great satisfaction from taking on these powers.

'What happened to the fish?' I ask.

'The salmon are in trouble in the whole North Atlantic,' he says over the river and the outrushing tide. 'Our rivers, on the whole, are cleaner than they've been in a long time. It's very hard to understand why the salmon are in such decline if it's not for something new, like salmon farming.' There are no salmon farms this far south: most are concentrated off the west coasts of Scotland and Ireland. Sea lice occur naturally in the wild, but in the confined spaces of a fish farm, where a single cage can house 70,000 salmon, they thrive. It does not take many lice to kill a young salmon. The detrimental impact caused by lice from these salmon farms, when they transfer to wild stocks leaving Scottish and Irish rivers, has been well documented, but Nigel believes that on their migration routes north the Severn's salmon are also becoming infested.

'I don't resent the fact that they farm fish,' says Nigel. 'I don't even resent that there's side effects. What I really resent is that they won't admit there's side effects.' A new business with better prices, pushing out an old business, he says, is simply the way of the world. But he believes the EA has unfairly targeted commercial fishermen for the declines, and has not been transparent about the damage done by salmon farms. 'If other people suffer as a result, in a perfect world, you would pay compensation. You would use some of that success to compensate those who have suffered. And they have done exactly the opposite. They have persecuted us.' Nigel trots to the far side of the shoal where a wake is breaking the surface, but it is only a submerged branch.

We walk for the rest of the afternoon, making our way along the sandbar. We see no salmon. It means, at least, that he can come back another day. After some hours we draw level with the car. Nigel shoulders his net. The sandbar is almost exposed now, the river round our ankles. There is one deep channel we must swim across to get back to the bank. I am beginning to wade in, balancing with my net, when Nigel pauses, looking back. 'I can never resist turning round for one last look,' he says. 'In case one's got stuck on the shoal.'

The following year, the lave net licence is reduced from a single fish to zero.

A laska is one place that is still renowned for salmon. The grizzly standing in the torrent, plucking salmon from the flow. It supports a multimillion-dollar wild-fishing industry, is on every angler's bucket list. Its Indigenous populations harvest salmon for their subsistence every summer, smoking and drying them in fish camps along the banks. The fish are said to run so thick up some rivers that those on the outside are forced onto the banks. Bristol Bay, on Alaska's western coast, is home to the world's largest salmon run and is its most important fishery, providing 75 per cent of local jobs and in 2019 generating over $300 million from salmon alone. But Alaska is iconic because it is the only place like this that's left. Europe once had the greatest density of salmon rivers in the world. In Anglo-Saxon times, rent was sometimes paid in salmon. Daniel Defoe, on a walkabout of Scotland, wrote in 1724 of 'salmon in such plenty as is scarce credible'. At the beginning of the nineteenth century, the salmon sold in Billingsgate were taken in the Thames. Yet the last salmon in London was caught in 1833. Today it is extinct from most European rivers, including the River Salm in Germany, after which the salmon is said to be named.

In 2013, I began travelling in Alaska, researching the sudden decline of king salmon on the Yukon. I wanted to see how the collapse was altering the lives of the many people, and the ecosystems, that depend on them for survival. A fish with such an extravagant life cycle, one that bridges the river and the ocean, that migrates many thousands of miles both inland and at sea, and that has done so for 20 million years, has become entangled in many lives, both human and non-human. I was unprepared for how tangled it would become in my own.

I am drawn to such places as Alaska; I think many of us are. Places hanging in the balance, where we can still conjure a notion of an idealised wilderness without too much of a mental leap. Since I began writing about salmon, I have started to meet people like Nigel much closer to home whose lives and passions are equally wrapped up in a fish that few of us even consider any more. It took documenting an unfolding story on the Yukon for me to understand that a similar story has already unfolded here. Where the ecosystems have been hollowed out for centuries, the trees so long gone that we romanticise denuded landscapes. Where the culture of salmon is no longer upheld by tribes fighting for their identity, but only by isolated and ageing individuals. Where the battle to save the fish is no longer a rallying cry but a weary shrug, a fight for compensation for a vanished way of life. What did we lose as these myriad, entangled connections were replaced by something thin and simple?

When Edwin Third began work at the Dee District Salmon Fishery Board in Scotland twenty years ago, you could drive for hours along the catchment of the Dee and never see a tree. In the past five years the Board have planted 250,000 on its upper stretches, and they are planning for another million within the next fifteen years. Edwin looks at them sometimes on Google Earth, a haze that once was barren, and the sight gives him great satisfaction. Whatever problems salmon are facing today, and there are many, he thinks that their mighty runs collapsed centuries ago. 'There's a missing story,' he says to me down the phone. 'That the huge declines in salmon happened long before living memory. I strongly believe we had a big reduction in salmon abundance when we cleared the forests.' Scotland's degraded habitat simply cannot support salmon in the numbers it once did. Trees encourage the insects that the salmon feed on. Fallen leaves increase the nutrients in the water. Logjams – 'one of the rarest habitats we have in Scotland' – slow the water's flow, forming the pools that the salmon need to spawn and hatch. Now the climate is changing and many of the upland streams are already so warm that without the shade from trees they will not survive at all. Historically, the estates have kept their lands bare, the preferred habitat for hunting grouse and for stalking deer. But fly fishing is also a large chunk of their income and their identity. Minds are changing, and trees are being planted.

It was in Alaska that I saw how conjoined the lives of trees and salmon are. Not only in how trees nourished the salmon, but in how the salmon nourished the trees. Biologists can gauge the state of a salmon run by observing how well the trees are growing along the banks. The half-eaten, spawned-out carcasses of the fish break down into the earth, and the minerals harvested from the oceans during their adult lives leach out into the soil, so that the concentrations of carbon and nitrogen and phosphorus in the surrounding land can be higher than that of commercial-grade fertiliser. Trees draw up these nutrients; the years when runs are bad are echoed in their tree rings. Up to 70 per cent of the nitrogen in these riparian forests has its origin in the sea. Imagine, if you like, the salmon swimming up the capillaries of the spruce and birch; this is not so far from the truth. Fallen leaves make the waters more acidic, which drives the growth of plankton in the oceans. More leaves, more plankton, more salmon, and the cycle turns again. Salmon in great numbers are so long since gone from Britain, and so long since forgotten, that it is hard to know just how impoverished the land is for their lack. But in Alaska trees can grow up to three times faster along rich salmon streams, and over fifty different mammals take nourishment from them, as well as raptors and other birds, amphibians and insects. Kneeling angelica coincides its flowering to align with the salmon runs, dependent on the blowflies that come in to feast on the salmon carcasses to act as their pollinators, their maggots breaking the salmon down into the soil. Just how significant are the missing salmon to the barren landscapes and the poor soils of the Highlands? A 2016 paper estimated that the vast and global declines in anadromous fish (those fish that migrate up rivers from the sea to spawn) had led to 96 per cent less phosphorus being transferred between the oceans and the land in this way.

There are other signs in Scotland that landscapes can be restored. Forty miles to the south of the Dee, on the River Tay, the beaver, hunted to extinction in the sixteenth century, has returned. Their provenance is unknown – some say escaped, some say illegally reintroduced – but wherever they have come from, they are here to stay. By the time the Scottish government agreed not to remove them they had become so well established – around 550 at last count – that getting rid of them entirely would have been far from simple.

Most of the evidence suggests that beavers produce ideal habitat for salmon by felling trees and forming the deep cool pools they thrive in, and that their dams create nurseries for juvenile salmon and hold back the silt that otherwise clogs the gravel beds that the salmon need to spawn. When the new trees along the banks of the Dee reach maturity, they may lure the beavers northwards.

'We're looking at landscape-scale change,' says Edwin. 'That's what you need to save a species. If the salmon are good and healthy, the whole catchment is good and healthy, including all the other wildlife, and the people that live in that catchment. The salmon is a proxy for everything.'

Several hours south and west of Dublin, about as far as you can drive, is the home and work of Sally Barnes. I find Woodcock Smokery in the fading afternoon, a couple miles outside the small village of Castletownshend, off a lane, up a track churned by the cattle of the dairy farm next door. A sheepdog runs in circles, snapping at the wheels as I park. On the ridge above, where an ancient ring fort sits, you can look out over West Cork's frayed edge at the wild Atlantic Ocean, glinting and swelling in the February chill.

I find Sally in the smokery, pulling fillets of mackerel from a brine in one of the stainless-steel sinks and arranging them on racks. She hugs me, her hands red with cold. She is dressed in a white coat with layers beneath and a thick felt hat holding her white hair in, and her breath comes out in puffs. The air smells of fish and beechwood. Mounted on the wall are wooden chopping boards, concave with age, and fillet knives on a magnetic strip, half the width they once were from several decades of sharpening.

In 2006, the year before drift netting for salmon was banned at sea, Sally won Supreme Champion at the Great Taste Awards, one of the highest accolades in the food world, for her wild, cold-smoked Atlantic salmon. That salmon is still the mainstay of her business, the pinnacle of her craft. Smoked fish is a synthesis of flavours that speaks to both need and craft: a need for food to last the winter and a craft so ancient it has been refined to perfection. A harmony of smoke and salt and fish unique to each smoker, but all intended to preserve that annual glut of protein that came flooding up a river, at once the most joyful, nutritious and essential of foods. But unlike the native families that I met on the Yukon, Sally does not stand at the end of a long line of smokers. She stumbled into it quite by accident.

She spent her early twenties at a teacher training college in London, but she didn't like London, and she didn't like an educational style that to her felt dictatorial. She fled to West Cork and married a fisherman. Having learned to quash her Scottish accent when she moved to a well-to-do English secondary school, she now had to rough up its edges again. But the place suited her. Land was cheap, people were moving in from all over and the scenery was stunning. The fishing was good, too.

The best year they ever had was 1979. In one day they took 249 salmon. The fishing was so good that the men would sleep aboard in harbour, no time to squander on the journey home. 'I'd go down in the evenings with Holly in the car seat,' Sally tells me as she moves the racks of mackerel across to the ancient smoker that takes up one wall, its metal scrubbed to a sheen. 'Take the car down this very steep slip to the harbour, supper in the back, and bring these salmon back up this impossible incline in the back of our Renault 4. My foot nearly pushing through the floor, and there's me and the baby and the baby in my belly, and I'm just thinking what if it all goes pear-shaped and we slide back down into the tide?' Yet their buyer never paid up. More than a year later he gave them a smoker to clear some of the debt, but Sally refused to let her husband sell it. '"I'd quite like to play with it," I said to him. "I'm stuck at home. I could do this at home. Mind the kids, school, look after you, the boat." And so I taught myself how to use it.'

For forty years she has been refining her work. Forty years working with salmon, building relationships with fishermen, building relationships with fish. She buys now from boats on the Blackwater, which meets the sea at Youghal, east of Cork, some eighty miles away, and many years it can be hard to get enough. Fish are frozen within three hours of being caught. At the smokery they are filleted, the scales scraped, the blood massaged through them from the tail to the head. Salted. Washed. Smoked. Sally has grown a deep instinct for the humidity in the room, for the particularities of each fish, their fat content, the weight of them, the pressure in the air outside, which all go to determine the length and the heat of the smoke, the balance of fish and salt. It is an instinct poorly replicated by dials and instruments. She closes the door on the mackerel and packs beechwood chippings into the tray, damping them down and then firing them up with a blowtorch aimed through the inspection hole.

'Perhaps I'm a bit nuts,' she says. 'But the physical contact with these creatures is really fundamental. You think about its life and where it's been. That it's made this incredible journey.'

Her fish have migrated several thousand miles before arriving in this room. Sally believes herself to be the last smoker of wild salmon left in Ireland, and she refuses to touch anything farmed. Farmed fish are flaccid and fatty from confinement; they are prone to heart disease. Their flesh is dyed red with canthaxanthin and astaxanthin, because otherwise they would be an unpalatable grey. Often the smoked salmon in the supermarkets is not smoked at all, but injected with brine and sprayed with liquid smoke like a fake tan. For Sally it is not an inferior product but an entirely different species, so distant has it become from its wild twin.

That night we sit in the kitchen, the Aga pumping out heat. Dinner is mash from the garden, sea spinach picked this morning at the beach, some piece of sheep roughly carved off a much larger piece of sheep, given to her by a neighbour. The kitchen is ramshackle with the legacy of Sally's life, chaotic strata of honeys and oils, pickles and spices and salts, many of them gifts from visitors who have travelled across the world to learn from her. There are tapestries of fish, paintings of fish, photographs of fishermen. While the lamb roasts, Sally slices a piece of a cold-smoked salmon and drizzles it with honey. It is incomparable, so juicy, so rich and meaty, so *red*.

Its crisp membrane, the pellicle, where the smoke has been on it, the succulent, delicate inside, its oils forming a sheen on the inside of the mouth. The taste is, instantaneously, the most direct connection I have made between the salmon on these islands and my time spent on the Yukon.

'I'd just be so thrilled if I thought my neighbours would be able to have their feed of wild salmon again and not think about how it's half a year's income,' Sally says to me over her shoulder from the stove.

When her kids went off to secondary she enrolled in the Open University – first Food Production Systems, then Oceanography. She had been noticing changes in the salmon for some time, hearing the anecdotes from fishermen of low runs and starving fish. She would find undigested food in their bellies when she sliced them open, something unusual and deeply wrong. As her knowledge grew, her interest grew and she became, she says, somewhat politicised. She went to conferences, sat on panels investigating safety in the fishing industry. She formed ties with the Slow Food movement, promoting local, traditional food over agribusiness and mass production. It was fifteen years ago, at the Slow Fish conference, held biennially in Genoa, that she found herself at dinner with salmon fishermen from Kamchatka, in the Russian Far East. 'One of the men said to me: "Are your fish running late?"' she says. 'And oh, my blood stopped coursing. It just went totally cold. I thought Christ, if they're running late on the other side of the planet, in the Pacific, then this is not a local problem. This is a global change.'

When a fish straddles worlds and travels oceans, it is easy to be persuaded that when things go wrong it is someone else's fault. Is the problem with salmon happening out at sea, in the coastal waters or in the rivers? Is it a result of run-off from crop spraying or a lack of food in the oceans? Is it the anglers, the commercial fishermen or the salmon farms? Is it by-catch on ocean trawlers or poachers working the rivers? Is it warming waters, or disease, or a lack of food, or habitat destruction? There is no smoking gun. And there is a lot of money riding on the industries involved, which only obfuscates the issue further. Researching the lives of fish that travel thousands of miles is difficult and expensive. And reform can always be deferred when 'more research is needed'.

After dinner we carry the wine through to the lounge. I stoke the wood stove, she rolls a cigarette. The wind outside is wild, a winter storm passing through.

Sally tells me that she needs 500 fish a year to pay the bills, to get by for the next twelve months. I ask her why not take more, be a little more comfortable?

'Maybe I'm lacking something in my greed,' she says. 'I'm prepared to do the salmon thing, and struggle against the prevailing currents, because it's such a precious creature. What is enough for a human being? For me, enough is a roof, a dry bed, food in my belly, clean water, good company. When I finish my day's work, I walk up to the ring fort and it just blows my mind every time.'

Sally thinks that the people who live in these remote communities should be allowed to make their living on their doorsteps. These places have been decimated as fishing collapsed: people forced out to find work; the arrival of Airbnb. 'Then you get the tourists coming in and buying their properties and coming for two weeks, two or three times a year. That's devastating for these areas. There's no restaurants any more, your post office is closed. Social infrastructure collapses.' Seen this way, the salmon is integral not just to natural ecosystems, but to the very existence of human communities. These wild animals that enable human lives. My thoughts turn back, as they often do, to the mussels.

'Do you think you'll see a day when you won't get your five hundred fish?'

Sally puffs on her fag. The fire crackles. 'I don't like to think that that day will come in my lifetime,' she says. 'But I don't know what it's going to take to change it. Salmon are the ultimate survivor. They've survived ice ages and cataclysms. But are they going to survive humans? It's dubious, isn't it?' ∎

White Creep, 1995–6
Courtesy of the Saatchi Gallery, London

CREEP

Caoilinn Hughes

I t's an autumnal December, one month into the hibernation of lesser horseshoe bats. They would breathe just once an hour, but for the balmy air troubling their sleep. Their eyelids quiver. Ears twitch for the pacifying fizz and pat of first snow; failing that, for the thawing stalactite drip of the new season, begun already? Perhaps the cold has been and gone. Perhaps they missed it, having tucked themselves too far inside the cave's oblivion.

Fiadh had stared out the conference window at the Pyrenees mountains, barely confectioned in snow, trying to block out her co-panellist expounding on subglacial water flows and multivalued sliding laws. *We compared this rapid stream development in the Vavilov ice cap, averaging over three kilometres of movement annually, 3,000 times faster than the surrounding glacial ice, to the unprecedented acceleration observed in* – Unable to enter a hibernate state, Fiadh would slip out of the conference far more easily than she will her field of research. She'll forfeit her tenure-track position at Queen's, as well as a decade's worth of collaborative potential. But there were peaks beyond the window that would, with luck, be snow-blanketed, where she could benumb herself for a time. She hadn't been skiing since her master's in Iceland, back when glaciers had some heft to them, though slackened and fast-diminishing as the legs of a retired cyclist.

Back when the archival wealth of ice was giddying. She fled the room ahead even of her own predictive computations. Before hearing her co-panellist's devastating findings. She closed the door on partial answers to absolute questions.

Not an inch of the horizon is flat. A country not much larger than Northern Ireland's big lake, Andorra has sixty-five mountains, all glacierless but rife with erosional features – cirques, arêtes, roches moutonnées, and no sales tax – so, fair field for a glaciology conference pre-Christmas. Now, the sky is smokily clouded and a warm Mediterranean air flows north. When they come into view, the glistening white summits are as inviting to Fiadh as a wedding cake to a blade. The lower slopes are jungled with school groups, but they'll stick to the groomed pistes, snow-machine-pillowed. The quietest off-piste aspects farther up will be icy, shaded from the afternoon sun. Nothing Iceland's wind-blasted volcanos hadn't accustomed her to. She scans the shadows for a groggy throng of bats.

Garrett smells faintly of bath curtain in his rental ski gear. It wafts with his jerking motions forward and drunken slides back, skiing uphill to the first chairlift. He could be auditioning for the part of a rehabilitating crash victim. A rep from GeoScience Solutions' Dublin office, Garrett had manned a stand at the conference, demoing models of their newest hypersensitive seismological instruments. He'd been outside smoking when he caught Fiadh fleeing. Somehow – in a method available only to men and unreproducible in a lab – he'd invited himself into her solitude. *Jesus. Sly. I hadn't thought of an afternoon sesh. And they rent gear at the lift?* Fiadh had tried to threaten him off with boredom: *I've not skied in nine years. Not since my daughter was born.*

Ah, it's like riding a bicycle. He'd pestled his fag into the ground and smiled so that smoke sluiced out between his widely gapped, blackly delineated teeth.

I know how to ski, but! It's just rare I'm alone, I wouldn't mind . . . Fiadh didn't know this person! A moment's friendliness at his trade stand earlier surely hadn't indebted her to him. *It's a long time coming, just, the chance to go. In Belfast, there's Black Mountain, it's good for a sled, my wee Holly loves it, but, on skis, it's thirty seconds and you're down skirting traffic on the A55.*

Heh. That's class, Garrett had said, *sledding with your kid.* The edges of his eyes pinched, as if he were about to name his own kid, but instead he said: *I'd say the lads on the Shankill have gas craic on it. Or is it not a hill?* He peered up at the sky, as if God was the only one who could answer that: someone by the name of Fiadh wouldn't have a notion.

What I meant was . . . Fiadh carried on, with less subtlety. *I'd part ways once we're up, if that's alright.*

Ah sure, look. We'll form splinter groups. Garrett gave her a look of consternation, to plaster over the one-Ulster-jibe-too-many. *I'm all done here anyway.* He cocked his head to the building. *I'll get my coat.* Then he glanced at Fiadh's lanyard. *I'm sorry I missed your talk, Fi-ad, since you're clearly a genius.* He meant it like a clap on the shoulder, but she felt it as a pat on the crown of her head.

Fay-yah, she'd corrected him, in her concertinaing Belfast accent; now open, now closed.

It's Irish.

Ah yeah, he'd said. *That makes two of us, so. We'll do our best not to walk into a bar, will we?*

Fiadh holds her pass to the turnstile whose arms silently open, then glances back to see that Garrett won't make this lift, but his steady chatter hitches him to her, so she lets the chair swing emptily past. *It's like riding a bicycle,* he calls out, shuffling through the queue just in time for the next lift to knock him in the back of the knees. Fiadh draws down the safety bar and Garrett's skis windscreen-wipe as he hoists them onto the footrests. *I just saw, this jacket . . . has a pocket in the wrist! Will you hold this?* He hands her his sticks and goes about stuffing his lift pass into the rented jacket's wrist-pocket. *Would you* look *at the convenience of that! What?* Fiadh observes the arm he's thrusting out as if to milk something, and the ecstatic expression on his goggled face. (He'd forgone a helmet, claiming he hadn't a great sense of sight or smell so being able to hear came in handy. The shop didn't rent gloves or goggles, so he'd bought himself new ones without glancing at a price tag, orating on the duty to support local economies.) Fiadh smiles with closed lips, partly to establish quietness and partly from associative habit: skiing had once meant toothaching cold. These days are temperate enough to smile recklessly.

The lift ascends smoothly, only shimmying past support towers. The scene below them is berserk: snowboarders slicing directly down the too-mild gradient, obstacles be damned; groups huddled around instructors whose faces are puffy with hangover, their instructees in toilet-desperate squats; others aggressively snowploughing or standing still, twisted back to find the luminous X shape of a friend, poles oaring through the air. It's the same scene on countless peaks across the Continent – even on ones so bare snow is dropped from helicopters like aid.

It's a kick in the nuts, Garrett says, observing a parent skiing wide-stanced, a toddler between their legs. *Nifty little fecks, slaloming around ya . . . doing jumps and racing their shadows, easy as you like. They're not in their heads. They've no expectations. Just . . . happy to be moving on the magic carpet.*

Do you have kids? Fiadh asks.

No, I don't, no. I'd love to.

He goes quiet then. Though the comment had sounded like a set-up, he doesn't weaken its candour with anything. The higher the lift takes them, the less apparent the chaos. Wet air freshens their cheeks as they hush up the velvety landscape, over Scots pines, firs clustered in the shade. There is enough time for the surreal privilege of the situation to decant.

I'm actually infertile.

Fiadh huffs a small laugh out her nose, then glances at him.

Yeah, he huffs back, kindly. *The only infertile inch of the country. Well . . . eight, ten . . . you know, a fair few inches anyway.*

Fiadh lets out a nervous laugh now, grateful for the chance to reset her expectations – or, like the kids, never to have had them in the first place.

My ex, girlfriend of nine years . . . left me over it. He gazes at his gloved hands, poles held parallel like a steering wheel. *She actually, sort of, ghosted me. Went to 'visit' her cousin in Pasadena, and kept, just, staying longer . . . praising the weather, blaming the time difference. If I managed to get through, she'd put me on speakerphone with someone always in the background. D'you ever feel yourself being multitasked?* He glances at Fiadh and his lips wrinkle tight. *Feels kinda . . . violent.* He straightens his posture. *I've never in my life been afraid of myself. I've always been . . . conciliatory. But then? It totally and utterly destroyed me. Was in hospital and all that. I could barely form words. It was like, I felt like . . . concrete, drying. If anyone got close, I'd scream . . . just to protect them. But now, sure, I'm grand. Brilliant. They're only pockets on my wrists, don't you know! I've a girlfriend too, nearly six months. We're going slow. I haven't dropped the L bomb or anything. But she told me from day one she doesn't want kids. She's forty-four anyway. But. So. Nah, she's the absolute business.* He clicks his tongue. *I'll just have to act the seven year old myself for the minute, till it passes.*

Fiadh hears herself saying the words *in all honesty* aloud when she had only meant to think them. Garrett latches on to their promise: if she has regrets, he doesn't mind hearing them. She shakes her head, flustered. It's not what he's thinking: that kids are work, or that you give so much of yourself. No. It's impossible: to tell a man who can't have a child that he's better off without one . . . so he can live without the pain of his child's safety's improbability; so he can give up, if needs must. Trapped sweat tickles her scalp, nauseating. Lifting her helmet to let air in, an image strikes her of Holly opening a drawer to find her mother's mask lain there: her Brave Face, like a front page emblazoned with calls to action. Blood rages in her temples. What was all that evolution for? So that children would be good at dodging embers?

Garrett's gaze on her is a phone, ringing. Finally, she admits that when she dropped Holly off to her father's – who recently surfaced in their lives like a body thrown up by the sea after a localised storm; miraculously sober, sea-foam drying on his lips – he'd kept repeating the word *whereabouts* rather than just asking if Andorra was a city in Latvia or an African country or what. *Neal only vaguely understands what I do,* Fiadh tells Garrett. *He asked what the conference was on, and I told him the usual – glacial melt, chronic underestimation of our general doom, and the tenure-track requirements of documenting it, in real time. The doom. There's loads of data on the drowning part, I told him.* Fiadh tongues blood blisters on the insides of her cheeks, now permanent as moles. *I don't know why I joked. But I held my hand level over Holly, as if to measure her, and I said: We best hope she has your tall genes, Neal.* She glances at the stranger beside her and lifts her chin, just as Holly had done at the doorway, for air . . . or to see the adults better. *Holly looked at me as if . . . I was an ice-cream scoop tipping off its cone.*

The chair lift slows. Fiadh puts on her goggles and slides her skis off the footrests. They're approaching the lift's end. Raising the safety bar, Garrett asks what Holly's dad made of all that. *Would you not be worried he'd get a lawyer?*

Fiadh sounds out a deadpan *Ha!* and shifts her bum to the edge, ready to ski down the off-ramp. She raises her voice over the reggaeton pumping onto the deck of a lift-side restaurant, where the injured and the tired and the functioning alcoholics sink their faces into huge sudsy beers, having called it a day. Already scanning for the route to the next lift that will take her closer to magnet-silver altitudes, Fiadh shouts: *With Holly stood between us – our daughter who can explain the slowing of the Gulf Stream – Neal asked me, dead serious: So you think the Venice thing is part of something bigger?*

They were quiet on the second lift, as Garrett had to get an email off lest phone reception cut out. He only paused to look up and say – *What's above the hill? Another hill!* – and to ask if the conference was any use to her. Fiadh said that she was leaving her field of research, so not really, no. But that someone from the Swiss Federal Institute had phoned her to sound her out about contracting work, adapting her neural network approach to develop algorithms for military detection systems. There were many avenues of doom she could help chart.

Garrett has a piste map up his sleeve. Fiadh doesn't need one, or doesn't want to need one. She'll take the black run east, then go off-piste through a wooded section to connect to an Olympic trail in the adjacent park, where all routes tributary down to a single point. There should be time for a few sheer unknowns before the lifts close. Waving goodbye to Garrett has the effect of opening curtains in the morning: the lightened feeling is gratefulness for this swift intimacy with a stranger, who has reasonably left before breakfast.

As cumulous clouds lust up against the slopes, the few people on these black runs dissolve and reappear like magic ink calligraphy. Fiadh's muscle memory kicks in the moment she goes, though a decade's worth of cell renewal should have nulled it. Leaning her knees uphill and her torso downhill, she shifts her weight from leg to leg, taking wide, swooping fighter-jet turns to feel out the icy surface. She only realises she's smiling when her cheeks push at the base of her goggles. Her girlish self is still there, lingering: the younger self that had been so assured of her equipment, that had moved through the world so free and defiant.

Ice sprays from her skis like sparks from a flint edge as she halts to the side of the trail. Her goggles have fogged up, and she pulls at them to cop herself on with cold air. Stop this. She had come here *not* to think . . . for half a day . . . Her goggles are still mottled, but it's just weather. The *tsshhhhhhhhhh* of TV channel snow harshly cuts in, and Fiadh twists around, expecting an avalanche, but places the sound as the scrape of blade on ice. As he slides past like scree, Garrett is recognisable by his woollen cap held on by his goggles. Fiadh rushes to catch him up, shouting instructions to push off his poles . . . but he's bicycling his legs, scrabbling for grip any which way until a powdery bluff catches him, net-like.

Stay there! Fiadh skis down to collect his stray pole, and she cuts steps into the snow with the edges of her skis to get back up to him.

If you're in pain, Garrett, don't move, and I'll flag someone down to –

Don't! he barks. *Don't call anyone. I don't need* . . . He leans on one elbow and feels for his hat and goggles with his other hand. Then he takes the pole Fiadh's extending. *Fuck's sake. Why the hell is this run open? It's like plastic!*

Aye, there's a fair coat of ice, but no fear of breaking through it, so if you just really carve your turns –

I know how to ski, doctor. Circular breathing in curses, he pushes himself upright, then slides a few inches before getting a grip. He's panting and flushed.

Fiadh doesn't need this. *Well* . . . *if nothing's broke?* She wishes him luck and goes. Despite herself, her exaggerated carving is a demonstration: the line she takes, turning at the margins where snow is deposited from trees. She hears him follow. A patroller weaves past, giving a questioning thumbs up to Fiadh, calling out that they're closing the track. She smiles, but her cheeks don't press her goggles. By the time she hears another scouring slide and rupture of fucks, the patroller's red jacket is out of sight. She should have pre-ordered a gurney. This time, he's lost a ski. His poles ribbon behind him. He's quieter and paler when she reaches him, and maybe there is some self-scrutiny in the question: *It is like wax, right? Like, what the* . . . *?* He looks around, baffled.

You wouldn't bake a cake with it. She waits for him to get up and click his boot into the binding. He shouldn't have rented the platinum package. He keeps clipping the ends of the long skis. If she had a hex key to adjust the sizes, she'd offer to swap. Logistics, logistics. No matter how she dedicates her life to them, preparedness is impossible.

Sorry for snapping . . . Garrett shakes his head in self-reproach. *I'm sorry, I forgot your name.*

Fiadh. That's okay, Garrett. It's rotten, falling.

Yeah, I'm . . . *My legs are going ninety.* He holds his gloved hand flat, as if to measure a child, or a high-water mark, and watches it tremble.

It's adrenaline.

He looks at the trail ahead, clocking its 5 p.m. incline. As if explaining something to a police officer, he says, *I've done runs like this a thousand times with the lads. I just* . . . He looks uphill now, to see if it had been steeper, maybe. *You know when you lose your confidence?*

Fiadh tongues the red sea anemones inside her cheeks, out of Holly's sight. She had just wanted to remember what it was like . . . to *expect* the snow to be thick . . . for the season to turn, normally. She had wanted to feel something else, even if it had to be mourning. It's not just getting older, or knowing all that she knows. It's that – no matter where she searches or how long she closes her eyes – *that* life isn't here any more, if it ever was. She could tell Holly a bedtime story of the halcyon: a mythical bird that calms the sea for a fortnight to lay its eggs on a floating nest . . . and myth has no trouble hibernating . . . only Holly would ask: *Which sea, Mummy?*

He projects his voice barely enough for her to know if he's confessing to himself or pleading:

I don't know if I can do it. It's mad, but I just –

Try breathing once for every turn, she says firmly.

Garrett looks at her doubtfully, air whistling through his teeth. A flake of snow quivers on his lip.

It'll either calm you, or make you turn more. Both are good. She nods downhill then, to say: I'm right behind you. Or: you first. ∎

A giant sphinx moth drinks the nectar from a ghost orchid, 2018
Corkscrew Swamp Sanctuary, Naples, Florida, USA

THE SECRET LOVES
OF FLOWERS

Dino J. Martins

I'm kneeling quietly, staying as still as possible, before a mass of luxuriant white flowers at the edge of a gorge in a distant, hidden corner in the highlands of Kenya. It is 5.45 a.m. Sunrise is still some thirty-seven minutes away. The eastern edges of the horizon are laced with saffron and drunken crickets rasp intermittently. Larks and robin-chats start warming up and in the distance is the forlorn, territorial sawing of a lonely leopard.

A furtive and whirring sighing rustles through the cool, crisp air. Swiftly it moves amid the shadows, more heard than seen, a blurred suggestion of form in the blue-grey stillness before dawn. Then ever so stealthily, with proboscis unfurled, she probes the heart of her unsuspecting, but patient, evolutionary match and is rewarded with a millilitre's measure of nectar. A cute floral nod and it's all over. Millions of years of evolution reduced to just a millisecond of mutual pleasure and benefit.

And like all naturalists who have borne witness to nature's myriad mysteries many times before, I have come to learn and have been blessed with a small discovery.

For the past ten years, I have been studying the intimate interactions between hawkmoths and the flowers they pollinate. Hawkmoths, also known as sphinx moths, are an intriguing and incredible group of insects. They are fast-flying, long-lived and feed actively from many different kinds of flowers, a fair number of which they alone can pollinate. Despite their relatively high diversity, little is known about their actual role as pollinators and in particular as specialised pollinators of highly adapted plants, though it is widely estimated that about 10 per cent of all tropical flowering plant species are pollinated by hawkmoths. Among naturalists, they are known as the quintessential phantoms of the dusk because they emerge, to approach flowers, just as darkness gathers. After hundreds of hours spent waiting to see them, and many thousands of fleeting glimpses of these enigmatic creatures, I've learned to avoid looking for them on cold or misty mornings, to stay still, to move slowly and to watch very, very closely, as their flower feeds can last less than a few seconds.

I grew up in Eldoret, a small, sleepy and rural town in western Kenya, and some of my earliest memories are of watching insects. As a child who suffered from the trauma of a broken home, I found refuge in nature. Later on, my love of insects connected me with the most wonderful foster parents who had come to Eldoret to help establish a new teaching hospital and training programme for Kenyan doctors. Along the way, our lives came together. My foster mother always says we 'met through a moth'. I had been raising giant moths, which all hatched out and fluttered about the day she first visited me at home. Caring for the caterpillars had provided many hours of joy, and had kept me focused and away from thinking too much about what was happening at home, and when they hatched, we were both enchanted. My late mother, my foster parents and many wonderful teachers encouraged, nurtured and indulged my love of natural history, and after finishing school, I won a scholarship to Indiana University. Routine class and campus life, however, was not my cup of tea, but – thanks to some sympathetic professors – I was able to spend time in the Amazon rainforest and the wilds of Kenya, working on independent study and earning a degree in anthropology and biology.

Having finished my degree, I returned to Kenya, determined to use my training to make a difference in the field of conservation, and to understand more about the incredible natural resources that Kenya is blessed with. My work saw me writing, drawing and exploring different parts of the country, learning from insects and plants and sharing these lessons where I could. But after a few years of feeling beaten down by a corrupt culture of patronage, and finding that it was increasingly difficult to get a footing in conservation without the necessary 'connections', I wanted to give up. In addition to these disappointments, I realised that no one really paid much attention to insects, in Kenya or anywhere else, and in conservation circles, most of the funding and attention went to those working on big 'charismatic' animals. Once again the wisdom of my foster parents prevailed. 'Do what you love,' they said. And I did. I undertook my master's degree with a world expert in pollination at the University of KwaZulu-Natal. This allowed me to continue making the kinds of observations about plants and insects that I had loved as a child, and to forge a scientific career with the foundations I had in natural history. After my master's I spent a few years working as a freelance writer, helping out on research projects, falling in love and making all sorts of mistakes, and then, to my utter amazement, I won a scholarship to Harvard University, where I completed my PhD, looking at the evolution of cooperation and interactions between plants and insects on the African savannah.

My journey to this particular moment of discovery on the edge of a gorge in the Kenyan highlands had, in fact, begun the night before.

On an evening walk with the dogs, I had followed a sweet, musky perfume towards the edge of the gorge. Suddenly, the fragrant dusk is filled with sounds and shadows. Crickets, strumming their wings, utter chirps and whistles. A high-pitched silvery squeak, barely within the range of human hearing, punctuates the erratic course of a bat overhead. Leaves rustle and branches creak as gentle gusts of breeze move through the forest. Pinpoints of light – courting fireflies – flash in the damp depths.

The fragrance grows more powerful with each passing minute and, clustered close in the gnarled arms of a dying tree, a spray of white stars, is the source of the delicious scent.

The white stars, softly bright against the dark mottled tree trunk, are orchid flowers: the comet orchid (*Rangaeris amaniensis*), a widespread and abundant species found throughout the highland forests of East Africa. Each flower, crisp and pure white, is a fantastic, marvellous sexual structure.

As with all orchids, three petals and three sepals are arranged to form the flower. One of the petals – the 'lip' of the orchid – is larger and more complicated than the others and sits between the two lower sepals, pointed and curved, completing the symmetry of the star.

Projecting from behind the orchid's lip is a long, tubular and tapering spur which contains a precious store of nectar. The spur itself is six inches long and the nectar level, measured from the bottom end of the spur, comes up to barely half the spur's length. This means that whatever visits this flower – whatever sips the nectar and hopefully transports the pollen – must be able to reach down at least four inches into it with a proboscis, a long, narrow tongue.

In the final moments of dusk, when the far western skies are a pale line of fading burnt sienna, a whirring of wings rustles the air above the flowering orchid and, lured closer by the sweet, heady scent, homes in on the white flowers. This is the convolvulus hawkmoth.

With its attenuated tongue uncoiled and dangling, quivering, the convolvulus hawkmoth hovers in front of the spray of orchids. It probes gently with its extended proboscis and, guided by the symmetrical shape, it reaches effortlessly into the orchid. Its tongue travels down into the spur, drawing the hawkmoth itself closer and closer to the flower. As the tip of its proboscis finds the nectar it drinks deeply.

As the nectar level falls from being swiftly sucked out, the hawkmoth presses itself against the flower. Now the base of its proboscis rubs against a special structure hidden just inside the middle of the flower. Here, waiting patiently, are two pollen masses, known as pollinia, with sticky strands attached to them. The mechanism works perfectly. As the base of the hawkmoth's proboscis presses against the inside of the flower, the pressure forces the sticky strands onto the hawkmoth's tongue.

With no more nectar within reach, the hawkmoth pulls away and in so doing brushes up against a sticky strand, known as a viscidium, which holds fast to its proboscis and pulls out the bundle of pollen. The moth hovers backwards, perhaps surprised by the unexpected addition to its long tongue. The pollen masses of the orchid are now firmly fastened to its tongue.

The convolvulus hawkmoth probes two more open flowers, then, startled by a flitting bat overhead, swiftly flies off deep into the forest bearing the orchid's genes with it. This brief and remarkable incident represents an ancient evolutionary relationship between hawkmoth and orchid, successfully played out over millennia in short, three-second acts, time and time again.

Insects and flowers have been intimately involved for hundreds of millions of years. Much of the food that we eat, and much of the food that we most enjoy, is a result of their synergy. 'One in three bites of food is thanks to a pollinator' is an oft-quoted refrain today, and some 80 per cent of flowering plants rely on pollinators to reproduce and survive. Without them and their symbiosis, our world would be unimaginably poorer.

Insects almost everywhere in our fragile world are under threat. Bees, butterflies and other pollinators are disappearing at unprecedented rates, in many cases before we even fully understand how important they are. Most research has been done in temperate, highly industrialised countries of Europe and North America, but most of the earth's diversity is located in the tropics, and relatively few scientific lifetimes have been dedicated to understanding the vast, complex web of life still here.

Sadly, now even the remote reaches of wild Africa are being tainted by poisons designed to kill insects, spread through global trade and the growth of intensive agriculture. For many decades, rural farming systems across East Africa had been relatively free of toxic pesticides, but in recent years access and use have been increasing. While managing pests is important, and farmers should have access to agricultural inputs and technology, how, where and when these are used do matter. One of the most alarming trends is the dumping across Africa of highly toxic pesticides that have been banned elsewhere, but are shipped and 'donated' to unsuspecting farmers and government agencies across the continent. Exact data is hard to come by, given the skulking, shady deals that make up these transactions, but the UN estimates that many tens of thousands of tonnes of chemical pesticides are being disposed of in the region.

Anyone who slurps down coffee or nibbles on chocolate needs to be grateful to insect pollinators. Nuts, fruits, seeds, vegetables, spices and many other kinds of nutritious foodstuffs from around the world are on our tables thanks to the tireless efforts of these creatures, and we all benefit from learning more about how this works. In farmers' fields across the world I have had the immense joy of learning to see, and helping others learn to see, the importance of pollinators. Over the past decade that I've spent back in Kenya following the completion of my PhD, I've been working directly with rural farming communities as part of my role with Nature Kenya, a scientific society that works 'Connecting Nature and People for a Sustainable Future'. Many farmers are understandably sceptical when I start waxing about the importance of insects. For those who will indulge me, I ask that we look at their crops in flower together. Often, even when many hours and years have been spent tilling and toiling with plants, the essentials of plant sex have gone unnoticed.

This is no fault of the farmers. The flirtations of insects and plants are furtive, hidden and often so brief that if you literally blink you might miss what exactly is going on. But when we stand together, sometimes even holding just a single flower, there is a constant, deep, ancient magic that I can summon. In a moment, when we are watching, an insect will appear. We watch it perch, wriggle, probe, prod and nibble. And the spell is cast. And it is a revelation that this humble act is what puts food on the table, money in the bank, taste and flavour into each meal and, indeed, succour for each and every life. One of the truly greatest joys of my life has been returning to farms where farmers have learned to cherish these humble insects, marvelling at hundreds of happy bees and butterflies dancing in the sunlight and the air genuinely humming with joy. When I see the smiles on the faces of farmers with higher yields and healthier farms and families, I get the satisfaction of knowing that as a mere scientist I can make a small difference in the world for both people and pollinators.

For tens of millions of years hawkmoths and orchids have been choreographing their own co-evolutionary dance. The hawkmoth is rewarded with nectar, potent fuel for its fast-paced, high-energy lifestyle, while the orchid gets a chance to send its pollen off to another orchid. Somewhere distant in the forest, when deposited on the sticky stigma of another flower, it will lead to the production of a seed pod and the perpetuation of the species.

A frica and its islands have a unique abundance of hawkmoth-pollinated plants, and if hawkmoths disappear, then so will the plant species that they pollinate. Indeed, moths are among the most important pollinators in the insect world, with a recent study showing that in the United Kingdom moths move more pollen around at night between different plants than bees and butterflies during the day. To date, some 1,450 species of hawkmoths have been described across the world, with about a hundred species known from Kenya alone. One African/Madagascan hawkmoth, Morgan's sphinx moth (*Xanthopan morganii*) is legendary among students of evolution.

In the 1850s Charles Darwin, observing flowers growing in an English hothouse, puzzled over the magnificent Malagasy star orchid, with an incredible spur that measures up to twelve inches long! Darwin predicted that a hawkmoth, with a similarly attenuated proboscis, would most likely be the pollinator of this extraordinary flower. Of course, this was dismissed as improbable as no one could imagine the existence of such a fabulously endowed creature. Some decades later, a hawkmoth with just such a proboscis was discovered – a subspecies of Morgan's sphinx moth which was named *Xanthopan morganii praedicta,* the subspecies epithet *praedicta* honouring Darwin's remarkable foresight.

Darwin made extensive observations around the mysteries of orchid flowers, and wrote an entire book about them with an apt, if lengthy, title: *On the Various Contrivances by Which British and Foreign Orchids Are Fertilised by Insects, and on the Good Effects of Intercrossing,* which was published in 1862. In it, and in great and delightful detail, he dissects and philosophises around the intriguing structure of orchid flowers.

Darwin's astute, detailed observations, keen naturalist's eye and sense of reverence for nature and the world around him are things that all naturalists have shared. However, this is not something unusual or special: we are all naturally naturalists – a fact that Indigenous peoples and those who live close to nature the world over have known for ages – and anyone who takes the time to humbly, quietly and consistently watch the world around them shares in this purposed gift. It is absolutely essential that, as we work to save species and habitats, we also cherish and celebrate the knowledge that we do already have, handed down through time in song, dance, poetry, legend and stories.

However, in the century and a half since Darwin's initial observations, still remarkably few people have actually observed long-tongued hawkmoths pollinating orchids, especially the very long-spurred species. This makes every observation of mine during my studies slightly dizzying and I sometimes find myself holding my breath when a moth drifts close to a flower that I've been watching. I stand aching with hope that it will fulfil its evolutionary dharma.

The furtive pollinating visits are brief and take place in the dark, and often the orchid flowers are located on plants dangling high on trees in remote, inaccessible and dangerous places. For instance, in some areas the plants survive, clinging to rocks or a lone tree, but the forest and its citizens around them have been hacked, burned, boiled, snared, logged and looted and have disappeared. In others, decades of floods and long, hot droughts have disrupted flowering cycles, and so some years the flowers appear but there are no moths; in others, an abundance of moths but, alas, no suitable flowers.

O ver the forty-plus years I've spent watching insects and plants, this I have learned: our minds are made for natural history; our souls are sculpted for nature's wonders.

Today I live in the vast, wild landscape of the Laikipia Plateau, north of Mount Kenya. As part of the Mpala Research Centre, I work with hundreds of students and scientists from around the world, and one of the key things that unite their many different ways of looking at nature is the first and humble step of recognising what they are looking at, and where and when. Seeing the details and the backdrop both together and separately is essential for science, and crucial for students of ecology and evolution.

To some it seems remarkable that I can name hundreds of different species and understand intricate, intimate details of their lives from just a few minutes of observations. But truly, it *isn't* really that remarkable. Evolution and natural selection have gifted us all with the ability to see details, to tell different species apart, over many millennia. We Absolutely Needed To Know To Survive. Colour Matters. Shapes Matter. Scent Matters. We are shaped by time and many generations to see, feel, think, connect and be part of the world around us. Even though we entered this play late, with just a few million years of adaptation behind us, we are nonetheless part of the script. ■

Manari Kaji Ushigua Santi

OF THE FOREST

Manari Ushigua

TRANSLATED FROM THE SPANISH BY NICK CAISTOR

I first met Manari Kaji Ushigua Santi in Quito in 2014 on the front line of the fight to protect the Amazon rainforest of Ecuador, marching against oil development in his ancestral territory. I had heard about him and knew he was a deeply committed activist who defended the rights of the Sápara Nation (also known as Zápara or Záparo), and their ancestral land. In addition, he is a renowned and erudite speaker who has been involved in the COP21 UN Climate Conference and the UN's Universal Periodic Review of human rights, and has also given TED Talks and visited many colleges and universities. Regardless of the platform, he is always the same. There is a calmness about him. He speaks softly and everyone stops to listen to his profound wisdom, yet he is quick to giggle, and has a boy-like delight in life. His passionate adoration of, and devotion to, the protection of rivers, creatures and ancient forests are both palpable and deeply infectious.

Ushigua's ancestors were powerful shamans of the Sápara Nation who live in the Amazon rainforest along the border of Ecuador and Peru, and he was designated as the successor to his father, his grandfather and his great-grandfather, taking on the role of healer and leader of the nation – the *akameno* (authority).

In the early twentieth century, there were 200,000 Sápara people.

Due to enslavement during the rubber boom, land grabs and intermarriage with neighbouring tribes, their numbers have dwindled precipitously to around 535. Today only four people, all of whom are over the age of seventy, speak their native language fluently.

Zoë Tryon, 2020

I

My name is Manari Ushigua. I am a political and spiritual leader of the Sápara Nation in the Ecuadorian Amazon. I am a protector of the forest and also a healer; some people call me a shaman.

I was born in the rainforest. My mother told me we never lived in one place, we were always travelling up and down the river by canoe, learning from nature and the energies of different places in our territory. I am the ninth-born of twelve children. When the time came for my mother to give birth, we were travelling on the River Conambo, so they stopped and built a fire and I was born on the beach on a bend in the river. Once my mother had rested for seven days and washed me with *tzigta* (a protective herb used seven days after childbirth, to cleanse and mark the return to normal life) they continued on their journey. Sometime later when they returned to the same place the beach had disappeared. Because my placenta was buried there and was then swept away, the elders say I will be searching for it always and only settle when I find it, that is the tale they tell. So my *tsawanu*, my spirit, is searching for my placenta and it is close to finding it.

My father, grandfather and great-grandfather were powerful shamans. My parents knew that I would continue this lineage soon after my birth. When I was born, my father started to blow on me (how shamans transmit knowledge and healing) and feed me some medicinal plants so that when I was older I would have visions and clearer dreams. He prepared me to become a person who understood the jungle but who could also relate to the world outside. When I was a child, I began special *dietas* (fasts) and training to connect with the spirits of the forest and our ancestors.

As I was growing I was always learning from my father and the forest. At that time I really felt that the jungle was so immense and that nothing and no one would be able to destroy it. My father's teachings about the forest made me feel that surety all the more; from the perspective of the spiritual world the security of the forest was assured. I would walk long distances with my father to go hunting deep in the forest, and with my mother to collect wood and gather food from the forest and that she had grown in her gardens. I felt so free being in the jungle, in that space. I had so many questions and I would ask my parents: How did humans appear in this world? How did the plants appear? How did life begin here? My father would answer me with stories and I would repeat them to the other children. I was very interested in learning these stories because as I listened they gave my body life, and spirit.

As a child I dreamed of very ancient things, sometimes I dreamed of my grandparents, my great-grandparents. They would teach me things about how we should love our life, to appreciate all that we have and walk a good path. My grandfather would tell me that life could end very quickly so to love each moment. As a child I would always see spirits. It was completely normal to me. My father told me that we need to study and do *dietas* to become accustomed to understanding these different worlds, that there were other beings and we didn't need to fear them and we could learn from them.

II

When I was about ten my father taught us how to use a blowpipe and we did an initiation for hunting that involved seven days of fasting, without eating anything or drinking any water – we only ate a little bit of squashed plantain. It was a really hard thing for me to do because my father and my mother, all of them, were eating meat and drinking *chicha* (a fermented cassava brew made by the women). But this experience really formed my personality and my ability to overcome feelings of fear or inadequacy.

After the fast I drank tobacco and I had a vision. I found myself far, far away when the world didn't exist – there was just a space. I was with my father, and I went back in time until there was no Earth. I was in the universe and there was a space and there was a force, an energy but with the character of a human being. My father told me: 'This is a spirit, it is a person but it is invisible.'

In this way my father taught me how to be. He opened up a path that connected to the spiritual world and told me to keep dreaming and little by little I would see and learn more. The first spirit I met in my life was the spirit of the birds. I knew about the spiritual world but I didn't know how real it was until I left for the city. It was very curious to me to see the exact birds from my dreams and visions in the material world, that I had only seen in the spiritual world before. These birds never lived in the jungle, only in the city. I would say: 'What am I seeing now? What are these birds doing here?' That was a great surprise for me and very special.

My father was somebody who never left our territory in his life. He never went to other countries, but he knew exactly what kinds of people and what kinds of animals lived in each part of the world, and he told us stories. It was a big shock for me when my father used to say: 'Crossing the sea, where the earth ends, there are *sajinos* (collared peccaries) as small as *huanganas* (white-lipped peccaries).' So when I arrived in South Africa, where I was attending a conference, and I saw those tiny *sajinos*, that was a huge surprise for me. I said to myself: 'How did my father know that those animals lived there, who told him that?' So from where he was he knew about the whole planet. He would explain: this happens here, this happens there, in great detail. That means he had capacity of knowledge, flying, travelling to those places to know them.

Early mornings my father would ask us about our dreams and he would teach us their meanings. He spoke of *arao*, which is a species of parrot. He would say that within its flock, there is a spirit, with very red eyes, and that this lord of all the species of *arao* would be guarded and tended to. The parrots would look after him when he went from one mountain to another mountain in the spiritual world, accompanied by thousands, thousands and thousands of birds, thousands and thousands of parrots. My father told me that's how each animal species that lives in the jungle looks after itself, accompanied by its spirit guardian. When I would hear the songs of these birds I would say: 'Ah, they're looking after the spirit of *arao*!'

My father taught me the ways of plant medicine. We used tobacco and *chiricaspi* (*Brunfelsia chiricaspi*). He would tell us about the medicinal plants, what each plant was used for, how it was used, how it was prepared. For example, if you couldn't use the blowpipe, and the dart starts moving in a circle, he would tell us: 'That's when you have to drink *leima*.' *Leima* is a plant which can be used if a snake bites you. You pick this plant, and cook the root and drink it and that helps to stop the poison, and with that you can continue walking in the jungle until you get home.

He taught us all those things while walking in the jungle. We had to pay great attention when we walked in order to hunt. Walking in the jungle, there were times when a hummingbird came and it made a sound like this: *tium-tium-tium*. That meant that on that path there were lots of animals that could be hunted, but if that same hummingbird changed its sound to: *pis-pis*, that signified that on the path there were animals but that they were dangerous, like a snake or a jaguar, so he said that if that happened in the jungle to walk very carefully and look far ahead, calmly and relaxed, so that nothing would happen.

Once I had a funny experience when I was hunting pigeons with my brother. He hit five with his blowgun and *curare* (poison) and told me to go and pick up the birds, and I ran straight into a herd of *huanganas* who were eating the pigeons. Then they ran at me. My brother climbed a tree and tried to pull me up, but I fell down right into the middle of them and they wanted to bite me and eat me. But I started laughing. There was nothing else I could do. The peccaries just stood in front of me and wanted to bite me, but they saw by my laughter that I wasn't scared of them. If I had shown fear they would have eaten me.

When we were older, all the learning that our father left us, each lesson that he left us, we started to put into practice in every space that we moved in. When he died in 1996 it was very hard for me, but then he began to teach me through my dreams.

III

The big question I always had was: where do we come from? How did we appear here in this world? In my dream I had a vision that my father picked me up and told me: 'I'm going to take you up to where the world disappears.' We went backwards and backwards up into space and there was nothing. From there he made us listen to lots of stories. Someone said: 'It's possible that on this planet there can be life.' I looked but it was invisible, it couldn't be seen. It was just an idea. Then Earth fell like a clap of thunder, and that clap of thunder was so strong it split something and sand and water appeared, the Earth started to form, ah yes that's how the Earth was formed, but that happened many years ago. Then a place of wisdom and knowledge appeared. My father used to say that the people who reach that place are the people who think about the world, how life started in the world, or how the earth was formed. We saw it was a difficult space to get to, it is the jungle in Amazonia. My father says that that's why all who live here in the forest can truly think, we have this wisdom about the Earth, about the forest, because this space for thinking exists, it is here in this physical world.

When we look at the natural world, we see the trees standing there, the insects flying, the birds, the animals, the rivers. If we can see that same reality from the spiritual world, we see these things as people like us: they walk, they move about, we can converse with them, with all the insects, the plants, the water, the air we breathe, it's a person.

We know many, many things. I have told you we have a deep understanding about medicinal plants, about nature, about many different worlds outside of this one. And we know how to connect with different worlds, the world of nature, of spirits. We have always hidden and protected this knowledge, but now we have decided to share this with other cultures. To invite friends into our territory, and teach them so that they can understand us, and learn not to destroy nature. Many other cultures don't understand how to do this, so when we have visitors to our territory the first thing we have to do is a *limpia* (ritual cleansing). We use medicinal plants (*chiricaspi*) and *haoneca* (jungle tobacco) and using these plants we open a window for them to connect with nature and the spiritual world. These plants neutralise and clean the contamination and smell of the city, and the contaminated thinking, so they can be connected to the scent of the forest. Once they are balanced the people can begin to recognise nature and it can begin to communicate with them, but they can't do that when they are contaminated. Then when they sleep that night they will begin to dream, and in the morning we will ask them about their dreams and help them to understand the messages that nature is giving to them. So many people ask about how we connect with nature and this is how we answer: in our dreams and visions, nature spirits teach us.

In our ancestral land, the natural world, everything is clean, uncontaminated and healthy, the land is respected, the earth is in perfect equilibrium. When we ourselves are sick we understand that we must drink tobacco and ask ourselves how we are relating with the energy of the natural world. We use our dreams to understand how the body is, and how our connection with nature has weakened or broken. Using bad words or thoughts can affect our health, but we can reorient ourselves and cure our sickness with the plants.

It's wonderful when you walk in the jungle. You stand and look up where there are thousands and thousands of trees, and if you think how many lives are there you can connect with them, because you are also a living being. By connecting with them they can teach you many things. Stand among the trees and look at them, see how they are connected with each other. From there come all the pure air, pure smells, all the things we humans like, so that's why we say that the jungle is alive. Like us, it has life, it needs to be there, because we also need it in order to be, to practise *sumak kawsay* (living well). (And yes, the Kichwa of Sarayaku, who are relatives and neighbours of the Sápara, have spearheaded the concept of *sumak kawsay* to the general population in Ecuador.) There are lots of people who when they talk of living well talk of having a house, a spear, a wife, babies and a jungle with lots of animals, they say that's living well. But it's not about that, it's about you as a person being content inside yourself, at one with nature – it's there you will discover how to live well. Not in the material world, only in the spiritual world, that is living well. Because the term *sumak kawsay* is from the spiritual world, and not from the material world. It's even included in our Ecuadorian constitution, and our Indigenous concept has inspired many people – politicians, intellectuals, students, activists all over the world – to change the way they see the world. But now the concept is also misinterpreted: somebody builds a hundred-mile motorway and they say that they are carrying out a public policy to put into practice 'living well'. It's not about that, it's about being a good person, a person who is aware – that's what *sumak kawsay* is about.

IV

In a space where a species appears in the jungle, there will always be a change because if there is a species that exists alone in nature, it has a strength, a way of relating, and its presence is special for that place. If we put another species there, it must align with that existing strength, that energy, for nature to continue to function in the same way. If, in that same vein, humans arrive, we have another energy, another smell. Everything changes with our presence when we arrive in a place, the space already starts to change. If in that change our presence is very calm, a complete balance, the change will be similarly balanced. That is how humans first appeared on this earth, but our presence and evolution are changing. We're beginning to abandon the spiritual part of our relationship and connection with nature when we become more material. That is what has caused a negative impact on the earth, because we have created a structure of life that is not good for the earth. For example, to say gold is valuable sounds like a joke because how can it be possible for a metal to have monetary value? It doesn't make sense. But for other cultures – in your world, perhaps – it is considered very valuable and people's need for it has taken us along a path that leads to being very lost.

We Indigenous peoples know how nature works, how water, mountains, trees function and relate to each other, how stars in space are connected with the earth. So I am an advocate for the Rights of Nature. In 2008 the new Ecuadorian constitution included a chapter on the 'Rights of Nature', so now nature is not to be treated as property under the law but nature in all its forms has the 'right to exist, maintain and regenerate its vital cycles'. We people can now legally defend nature and ecosystems, and they can also be the named defendant. We are talking here about a fundamental change in how we humans see our role on the planet: a change from seeing ourselves as rulers and exploiters to contributing to the health, beauty and well-being of nature. Non-Indigenous peoples are beginning to understand that nature has the right to exist, thrive and regenerate just like humans.

Every being that appears on the earth comes with an objective: to leave a good story, a good experience, a good piece of knowledge. We come here because thousands and millions of people come to earth. But if they don't come with the correct objective or aim – when they no longer take the earth into consideration – that's when an earthquake comes. Nature moves and eliminates, because it is a living thing.

We are living in an era where we must be on high alert to protect our lives, the lives of our spirits and the Rights of Nature. We must look after the jungle, making sure it is not destroyed quickly, keeping the spirits alive, keeping the rivers clean with their own spirits, keeping the medicinal trees, big trees, small trees, alive so that they can continue to educate and help us.

Within the earth we know that there are other minerals – petroleum, gold, uranium, copper – and we know that the earth needs all these minerals, that you call 'resources', to continue to function naturally and in a balanced way. These 'natural resources' that are under the ground are the veins of our body – veins of the earth – and through them circulates strength, energy, water, everything, just like the blood in our bodies. They give life to the spirits of the mountains and where there are mountains there are the houses of the spirits. If we look from the material world we only see mountains, but if we look from the spiritual world we see how they are giant cities of the spirits, that is where they live.

V

This is why we Sápara people will not accept oil companies in our ancestral territories. We will fight always for the rainforest and the spirits of the jungle. We are few, but we are strong in our fight and as we are defending nature, we are given much strength.

In 2011 the government of Ecuador divided our ancestral land into oil blocks and in January 2016 they sold the rights to blocks 79 and 83 to Andes Petroleum (a state-owned consortium of the Chinese National Petroleum Corporation (CNPC) and the China Petrochemical Corporation (Sinopec)). Our prophecies foretold that the day would come when foreigners would try to invade our territory and we would have to resist or be wiped out. Two great spirits clashed: the Chinese dragon and our *Piatsaw,* the spirit of our people. We successfully fought them with the help of allies in North America and we succeeded in keeping the oil in the ground.

I was organising with a group of women to travel to meet with the Chilean president as a Chilean oil company wanted to come into our territory to mine for oil. The president of Ecuador brought a lawsuit against us, ten of us, stating we were going to attack the Chilean president, which was not our intention at all, we were going there to defend nature. We were going on behalf of the rainforest and the spirits of the jungle.

But right now the Ecuadorian government is pressuring us strongly to agree to oil exploration on our lands. Under Ecuadorian law we own the land on the surface of our territory but they own everything under the ground. As is stipulated by the Ecuadorian Constitution, international instruments on human rights and the UN Guiding Principles on Business and Human Rights, we must grant our 'free, prior and informed consent' for extractive industry to operate on our ancestral land, and we did not. We knew that any oil extraction would gravely hurt our integrity and existence as a nation, including the existence of our language, which was declared by UNESCO to be 'a Masterpiece of the Oral and Intangible Heritage of Humanity' in 2001. And they still want to look for oil in our rainforest.

The Constitution says the government needs to consult with the legitimate owners of the land to authorise the exploitation. But when we say 'no' they do not accept our answer and keep pressuring us. Now more than ever we need to all come together to defend the rainforest and keep the oil in the ground. We will never give up defending our forests, our waters and our earth.

We say no to any form of extractive industry, we do not agree with it and we will not allow it. We want to encourage a new form of living, of relating to the earth. In this land our ancestors hunted and performed rituals and ceremonies. There is a rich history here in this land, a rich life; our message is that human beings and nature must come together to protect life, and the life of planet Earth.

With all the changes we are facing now, you can see clearly in the jungle how there are species of plants that are transforming into animals, larvae transforming into plants, some larvae into snakes and snakes disappearing to change into fish. Species are transforming in order to survive very slowly, subtly and calmly. That is what is happening now and so our role as Sápara people is to look after the jungle, because if we look after the jungle the changes will happen slowly.

For the Sápara world there is no future, there's a past and there's a present. We are in imminent danger of disappearing. The hope of staying as humans on earth does not exist for us: there are only 535 of us left. We are resisting with our presence, and that resistance has a limit: soon we are going to reach that point when we will disappear. Until we disappear from the earth, from this world, we want to spread our message, so that other cultures who have already forgotten can start to understand and connect with the spiritual world through dreams. We hope that other human cultures will listen to our message and use the wisdom we share or they too will disappear like us. They must instead transform as the forest does.

People will have their connection or link with the natural world again, the jungle, water, air, mountains, with space, the stars, with *yanukua* (the sun), with *kashikua* (the moon), and they can teach the people directly. The natural world is what gives us the best foods and medicines without using chemicals; the best results when we sow with a full moon. That is the knowledge we want to leave behind and to share with other people.

We shouldn't use that term 'connected to nature', it is a concept from your world – we already are nature, we just need to be aware of it. We are living on something that is alive, we are living among many living beings that are around us. We need to be conscious of that in order to be able to feel that we are here, with our good health and good intentions to keep fighting to give more life to the earth, to guarantee the safety of all lives on earth.

I want every one of you, whoever you are and whatever you are doing, to please help protect this earth, this land which gives us wisdom and from where we came. Please learn to dream. We as a culture are going to disappear, but we want to leave this knowledge so other cultures can continue to exist in this world, respecting and understanding nature. And when they are curing cancer using the techniques we speak about, maybe they will say: 'This wisdom was left behind for us by the Sápara Nation, who lived in Amazonia.' So we are working to leave this behind. We are excited and content to do this work. ∎

Sápara women and community members gather in Jandiayacu to discuss the impact of oil and the future of their territory

Ravana and Sita sitting in the beak of Jatayu, opaque watercolour on paper, Kalighat, Kolkata, *c.*1855–60

VULTURES

Samanth Subramanian

The second most famous vulture in the lore of the Hindu epics is Sampati. We run into him midway through the *Ramayana*, after the demon king Ravana has made off with Lord Rama's wife Sita, and when Rama has sent a search party down the spine of peninsular India. The searchers, discovering no trace of Sita anywhere, decide they'd rather starve to death than return in failure, so they settle down in a cave to waste away. Drawn by the prospect of an easy meal, Sampati arrives. He is aged and wingless, but he can still watch, with the plentiful patience of his species, as living bodies turn into carcasses. In principle, vultures have the surest source of food on the planet, because death is inevitable. To find it, all they have to do is look for life and wait.

But then the searchers tell Sampati about their quest, and about Rama's grief, and Sampati realises he has seen what they seek. With his astute vision, he has spotted Ravana in a celestial chariot, carrying Sita across the southern sea to Lanka. And so he tells them about it, even though, in doing so, he is giving them a reason to live again. The nature of Sampati's heroism lies here: not just in an old bird sacrificing food, but in a vulture acting against its most elemental instinct. Vultures appear in such neat lockstep with death that they seem to practically usher it in. Sampati has done the opposite. He has prolonged life. He has driven death away.

The *Ramayana* doesn't describe Sampati at length, but since he resided in a cave, we might presume that he was a long-billed vulture, a *Gyps indicus*. Ranging over central India, the long-billed vulture nests not in trees but on the crags and ledges of rocky cliffs. The cliffs grow so stained with their droppings that, in 1867, the British ornithologist Allan Octavian Hume had a hard time climbing a hill in Rajasthan in search of a long-billed vulture's nest. Having removed his boots, the reason for which he left unexplained, he 'crept to the lowest ledge, a work of extreme difficulty, owing to the excessive slipperiness of the white crusted rocks.' Hume measured the vultures whenever he could and jotted down their dimensions in his scrapbook. The long-billed is not a massive bird. Its wings rarely span more than two metres, and even the plumpest specimens weigh only about five or six kilograms, half the heft of American condors. Its covert feathers – the feathers on the surface of its torso – are a pale buff, but the feathers just beneath are darker. Its head is bare and coloured like wet sand, but its throat has a smattering of thin down, and around its neck, it wears a ruff of soft white feathers. Standing near a carcass, the long-billed vulture looks like a morose undertaker who has doffed his hat but refuses to take off his two-tone overcoat.

Even the doyens of India's vulture community sometimes have a tricky time telling the long-billed vulture apart from its two cousins: the slender-billed, which nests in solitary pairs in trees just south of the Himalayas, and which for decades was mistaken for the long-billed; and the white-rumped, which lives in tight colonies distributed through small groves of ficus or arjuna trees. Together, these species once prevailed in thick abundance in India, a country that provided generous feasts of wildlife and livestock carcasses. No nationwide census was ever taken, but the accepted figure among experts seems to be that there were once 40 million vultures in India. When Vibhu Prakash, a raptor scientist, was working at the Keoladeo National Park in Rajasthan in the 1980s, he'd see vultures lifting into the air at around nine o'clock in the morning, just when the day was heating up. 'We'd watch them disappearing very high in the sky, soaring on one thermal and then another with great speed, and we'd try to estimate how fast they were going,' he said. When an especially big flock flew by, the land darkened as if a raincloud had passed overhead.

India's vultures scout for food by eyesight alone – eyesight so fierce that, for a long time, ornithologists assumed that the birds must have a powerful sense of smell as well. One British army lieutenant, in 1833, killed a dog, wrapped its body in canvas and stuffed it up a tree. Over the next few days, he saw vultures perch directly above the parcel and concluded they must have been attracted by the odour of putrefaction. He skimmed too lightly over the detail that vultures had been roosting on that particular tree even before he'd lodged his dog into its branches, or that the ability to smell out a dead dog from a few feet away was no indication that the birds could pick up the scent of carrion from lofty heights. 'When they actually descended on a carcass,' Vibhu Prakash said, 'it was like an airplane cutting through the air: *whooooosh!* Suddenly they were all around you.' Vultures in mid-feed take the most perfect collective noun: a wake. In sufficient numbers, a wake of vultures can make very short work of a carcass. Skin a cow and throw it into the open, Prakash said, and it will have been divested of its flesh within half an hour.

In South Asia, a land of many devoutly followed faiths, a bird so closely associated with carcasses inevitably becomes entangled in the cultural practice of death itself. Every religion is, after all, a fixation with the notion of death – a way to come to terms with the truth that life always ends. Buddhists in Tibet follow a ritual of sky burial, in which a corpse is formally deposited in a sacred area, to be consumed by vultures and other carrion birds; the Zoroastrians, who migrated from Iran to India more than a millennium ago, have a similar custom. In Hinduism, the venerated cow is never eaten; even the skinning of dead cattle is regarded as necessary but unholy work, to be foisted upon an oppressed lower caste. Until not very long ago in rural India, the cow's remains, once flayed, were tipped into a dump outside the village where vultures had their fill. By sustaining themselves on corpses the vultures were almost reanimating them, using their dead flesh to produce new, young birds. It was a strange, elegant version of an afterlife.

The vultures were here first, of course – present in this part of the world a few million years before any glimmer of human faith came into being. Relatively speaking, we're transients to them. It wasn't that we were folding them into our culture; rather, the vultures were accommodating our whimsical religious habits into their old ways of feeding. And they might have outlived our species handily, had we not been so skilled at poisoning our planet. For, in the 1990s, scientists noticed a bewildering and alarming decline in the population of vultures across India. From the bygone 40 million, the numbers dropped to around 10,000 in 2013 – an annihilation, by any measure. It feels like a doubled extinction. The death of the vulture is also the death of how we cope with death itself.

This isn't a mystery story – or at least, not any more. In 2003, scientists working across Britain and India found that the culprit behind the great vulture die-off was not a pathogen but a man-made drug. Diclofenac, a chemical patented in 1965 by a Swiss pharmaceutical company, began to be used widely in arthritis medication in the late 1980s. It eased stiff joints and reduced inflammation; even non-arthritic patients could use it to relieve the pain of a toothache or a migraine. After the patent expired, diclofenac became cheap: in India, just a few cents per tablet. It was made up into a veterinary product as well, so that farmers could buy it for cows or buffaloes suffering from some wound or illness. With diclofenac, the animals could be kept out of pain for a few more weeks of milking or perhaps even to birth calves – valuable revenue for the Indian farmer – before they died and were carted to the dump. But when vultures fed on these carcasses, the diclofenac residues damaged their kidneys and gave them visceral gout; chalky clots of uric acid built up in their organs, eventually killing them. In this too, diclofenac was astoundingly effective. If we'd set out deliberately to wipe the country clean of vultures, we couldn't have done any better.

The cull of Indian vultures happened just when we were realising, with fresh urgency, that we had to repair a number of other ruptures in the natural order that we'd perpetrated. The smoke in our skies, which warmed the earth; the plastic in our oceans, which killed the fish; the terraforming of our jungles, which evicted their wildlife. When the vultures died off, they stopped eating the bodies of Zoroastrians and Tibetan Buddhists, and of farmed cattle. Their extinction, and their sudden absence from our lives and our deaths, marked the severance of yet another human tie with nature.

In 2006, the Indian government outlawed diclofenac for veterinary use. It helped that there was another drug on the market, called meloxicam, that was just as cheap and effective as diclofenac, and that wasn't toxic for vultures, said Chris Bowden. Bowden is the programme manager of SAVE – Saving Asia's Vultures from Extinction – an alliance that includes the Royal Society for the Protection of Birds as well as the Bombay Natural History Society. Since 2004, he has spent most of his time in India. When I spoke to him on Skype this past May, he was in his apartment in Bengaluru, wearing a T-shirt with the caption: UNTOUCHED PARADISE. A summer storm grumbled outside his window.

For SAVE, lobbying the government to ban diclofenac was, in relative terms, a straightforward process. Building India's vulture population back into even a fraction of its former strength has been another matter altogether. 'The problem was, no one had bred Indian vultures in captivity before,' Bowden said. 'It was just unknown. And so, back in the mid-2000s, we had a lot of people who were very sceptical, and thought that we didn't know what we were doing.' From the absolute shallows a decade or so ago, numbers in the wild have staggered back up to around 30,000 today. And in SAVE's four breeding centres, 'we have so many vultures in there that we don't know what to do with them,' Bowden said. 'Now we're dying to send some of them back into the wild.'

The first few months of 2020 were a torrid time for SAVE's breeding centres. The four facilities are spread across India's northern half: one in the state of Haryana, not far from Delhi; one in the state of Madhya Pradesh, in India's solar plexus; and two in the eastern states of Assam and West Bengal. During the Covid-19 pandemic, every centre found itself in a red zone – a coronavirus hotspot that was strictly battened down. Travel was practically out of the question, and boundaries between districts were sealed.

In the breeding centre in Haryana, near the town of Pinjore, Vibhu Prakash needs a hundred goats a day to feed his 360 vultures. Ordinarily, Prakash buys old, infirm goats, since vultures prefer lean meat to fatty meat. But his usual markets were shut, and the only goats he managed to find during the pandemic had been plumped up on farms. Still, they had to suffice. To source even these goats with any regularity, Prakash and his colleagues had to work until they wilted. 'Our supplier went out to get them from Rajasthan or other states,' he said. 'Then the cops wouldn't let him travel, so we had to get him passes from the government.'

In late May, even as the pandemic burned on, a cyclone hit West Bengal, flattening electricity and telephone lines. The breeding centre in Rajabhat Khawa, located in a wildlife park near the border with Bhutan, lost power. In addition to figuring out meals for its vultures, the staff had to find diesel for their generators – not just to switch on the lights and charge the mobile phones, but also to electrify the fence that keeps the park's elephants out.

Of the four, the Pinjore centre is the oldest. It was founded in 2001, as a partnership between the Royal Society for the Protection of Birds, the Bombay Natural History Society and the state government. Formally, it is called the Jatayu Conservation Breeding Centre – another throwback to the *Ramayana*. Jatayu, the most renowned vulture in Hindu mythology, is Sampati's younger brother, and his heroism ends in spectacular tragedy. When Ravana first kidnaps Sita, Jatayu flies to her rescue and attacks the demon king's chariot. In a mid-air battle, Ravana slices off Jatayu's wings, and the grand bird plummets to his death. Far south of Pinjore, on a rocky hilltop in the state of Kerala, a sculptor has built a colossal concrete statue of Jatayu where he is said to have fallen to Earth. The statue is ludicrously literal but also strangely moving. Its head might resemble the logo of a fried-chicken chain, but one side of its body has been sheared off. Its remaining wing unfurls to the side, and its sole talon claws the air. Jatayu isn't dead yet, but he is already helpless and beyond preservation.

Given the end of Jatayu, calling the Pinjore centre after the slain bird sounds like an odd move, but perhaps the name serves as an ever-present reminder of a fate to be avoided. The first of the aviaries in Pinjore was built in 2004, to designs drawn up by Jemima Parry-Jones, a raptor breeder who directs the International Centre for Birds of Prey in Gloucestershire. Parry-Jones has bred more raptors in captivity than most of us could name: African pygmy falcons, Indian tawny eagles, secretary birds, American black vultures, Aplomado falcons. 'The nice thing about vultures is that most of them are colony nesters,' Parry-Jones said. 'So rather than building one aviary for every pair of birds, you can build one for every fifteen pairs.' From the outside, the aviaries look like warehouses: a hundred feet long, forty feet wide and twenty feet high. The cement walls are broken up by large 'windows', sections of longitudinal bamboo staves that let the air in. The vultures sit on ledges and perches embedded into the walls, below a roof made of strong metal mesh – 'You know,' Parry-Jones said, 'in case leopards or monkeys get on top.' Every aviary has four baths that are replenished twice a week. Whole, skinned goat carcasses are slid in through a door. 'The aviaries are long enough that the birds can fly from one end to the other for exercise, to keep their physical fitness up.' At one point, the breeders experimented with putting individual pairs of vultures in smaller aviaries. The birds lost muscle tone, and their hearts weakened. 'We had to work all these protocols out,' Parry-Jones said.

The first tenants of these aviaries were young vultures taken from nests, before they fledged. Vulture-gatherers shinned down cliff faces, or up trees, to collect them. 'The local villagers never wanted us to take the chicks away,' Parry-Jones remembered. 'We had to explain that these birds probably wouldn't survive anyway, because of the diclofenac out there.' In Pinjore, Parry-Jones and Prakash worked up a system: taking the first clutch of eggs away from parents, incubating them, and returning the chicks when they were six to twelve days old; then hatching the next clutch of eggs and rearing those birds to an adult size over four months, before moving them to the aviaries. Elsewhere, methods had to vary; at Rajabhat Khawa, for instance, the frailty of the electricity supply means that artificial incubation is difficult. 'So there, the mum and dad vultures do all the work,' Parry-Jones said. Of the 700-odd birds in the four centres today, more than half have been born and reared in captivity.

They live in such close proximity, these humans and the birds they raise, and yet they rarely see each other in the flesh. At Pinjore, Prakash watches the vultures through closed-circuit cameras installed in every aviary. Vultures are jittery creatures. They tolerate the staff who slip discreetly and efficiently into the aviaries every two or three weeks to clean up. But if an unfamiliar person – or, for that matter, any other potential threat – approaches suddenly, a vulture will throw up the stinking contents of its gut. It's an ancient reflex; the foul smell puts the predator off, and meanwhile the bird has become lighter, so that it can get away at speed. If Prakash spent plenty of time with his vultures, they'd get too accustomed to him. 'They could easily become like pets. They'd feed from your hand,' he said. 'But then they become useless for conservation, because they won't go back out and mingle with their own kind. So we avoid it. We want minimum human contact with them. Because ultimately, we want them to go back into the wild.'

Of the twenty-three species of vultures around the world, sixteen are facing some startling level of endangerment. In Spain, a slide in vulture populations has been traced back to the old enemy, diclofenac; in Portugal, after the passage of a law requiring farmers to burn or bury the carcasses of livestock, vultures became a rare sight in the skies; in Botswana, Kenya and South Africa, the poisons used by poachers to fell elephants or by farmers to deter predators like jackals have fatally sneaked into the bloodstreams of vultures. And since every kind of vulture is a keystone species, critical to the survival of entire ecosystems, it means that every ecosystem is in trouble. In nature's scheme of things, the role occupied by vultures is a vital one – so vital, in fact, that they've evolved into being twice, in two separate and independent ways. The Old World vultures in Europe, Asia and Africa have different ancestors altogether from the New World vultures of the Americas – a phenomenon known as convergent evolution. It's as if natural selection kept finding that the best way to deploy long-range scavengers was to make a particular kind of bird. A bird with a bald head, because feathers were liable to grow encrusted with bits of rotting flesh during mealtimes. A bird with broad, efficient wings, to fly high and far. A bird with stomach juices stronger than battery acid, to safely digest even carcasses riddled with bacteria. A bird with a bill that can rip and tear, and with a grooved tongue to slurp down slippery gobbets of flesh during a feeding frenzy, and with eyes that can spot a dead deer four miles away.

Without a bird built to such exacting specifications, the carrion would pile up, rot away and spread disease. In India, after the vultures disappeared, the owners of livestock found this happening with their cattle carcasses. Lal Singh Bhujel, a tourist guide who lives near the breeding centre in Rajabhat Khawa, also tends to a dozen head of cattle; his father once kept more, nearly 200. Every time a cow in the village died, it used to be deposited in a shallow ditch near the river, for the vultures to consume. 'There were so many that my parents wouldn't even let me out of the house when a cow was in the ditch, because they were afraid the birds would take me away,' he told me, with a laugh. 'And now, of course, no one does that, because there aren't any vultures left.'

Today the farmers of Rajabhat Khawa, like farmers elsewhere in India, must burn or bury the bodies of their livestock. Leaving them outdoors creates problems. For one, feral dogs get at them, and a swelling population of feral dogs poses a higher threat of rabies. 'Let me be clear. It's not that, because of the lack of vultures alone, more people are dying of rabies now than before, because rabies treatments have gotten better during this same period,' Bowden said. Still, 20,000 or so people die of rabies every year in India. 'And maybe that figure is 20 per cent, or some per cent, larger than it would be if the vultures were all still here.'

The best-known consequence of the vanishing of India's vultures has been suffered by the Zoroastrians, or Parsis as they're called in India – a small, prosperous community whose members live mostly in Mumbai and other parts of western India. Whenever this tale is told, it is inflected with a stern tone of warning: beware the ramifications of meddling with the environment, for they are often unforeseen. Nature's systems are so complex, and her balances so delicate, that a painkiller fed to cows can quickly interrupt the religious traditions of a people half a country away. The really unnerving lesson, though, lies not in the velocity of nature's transformations but in the lassitude of our own. Quite soon, the changing climate will begin inscribing its most drastic alterations upon our world. In all likelihood, it will find us with our heels dug in, reluctant to revise the practices that we've decided are most dear to us.

Zoroastrian scholars like to begin with Herodotus. In the fifth century BCE, Herodotus wrote in *The Histories* of matters 'which are secretly and obscurely told – how the dead bodies of Persians are not buried before they have been mangled by birds or dogs.' A few hundred years later, Zoroastrians built a *dakhma* in present-day Uzbekistan that still survives today: a squat, forty-nine-foot-tall tower of stone near the Amu Darya River, upon which corpses were left for vultures. In photographs, the *dakhma* looks solemn and impassive, almost other-worldly, as if a vessel from another world had touched down upon the flat scrubland. Modern *dakhmas* are strikingly similar: a ring of stone surrounding a central pit. I found a photograph online of Mumbai's main *dakhma*, located in a forested area named Doongerwadi. Four men in white clothes and white caps are carrying a stretcher, on which lies a body draped in white. They walk the band of the stone ring, around the pit. A dozen vultures sit just a few steps away. Despite the sadness of the death that has just occurred, the proceedings have an air of serenity, a sense that the death was a part of the arrangement of nature. In English, the *dakhmas* are called 'Towers of Silence' – a name that made more sense to me the longer I gazed at the photo.

In Zoroastrian theology, though, death isn't a part of the divine order. Instead, it is the temporary triumph of evil over the work of God. As a result, a new corpse has something impure about it – an essence of the evil force that has rudely sundered the spirit from its physical body. 'You don't burn the body, because that is a desecration of fire with the evil force,' Khojeste Mistree, a scholar and historian of the Zoroastrian religion, told me. 'You don't bury it, because that pollutes the earth. You don't drown it, because that sullies the water.' In a *dakhma*, he said, the impurities are contained, even as the sun decomposes the corpse and the vultures consume it. 'It's said that the impure force – the *nasu* – is frightened of vultures.' Eventually, when the flesh has disappeared and the *nasu*'s strength has dwindled, the skeletal remains are tipped into the pit, into layers of lime and rock salt, where they crumble into powder. The time for that to happen varies, Mistree said. 'It could happen in a couple of weeks, but a fat corpse might need anything up to ninety days.'

Mistree is an avuncular man, with a tidy salt-and-pepper beard and eyes that crease up when he smiles. He co-founded Zoroastrian Studies, an institute to spread his knowledge of the religion, in 1977, soon after he returned to Mumbai from England. For a while, he'd been an accountant in London, before he gave it up to study the history and theology of Zoroastrianism at Oxford. Even back when he was in England, he'd heard about a slight fall in the number of vultures in Mumbai, although that was because of how densely urbanised the city was becoming. Blocks of apartments were shooting up around Doongerwadi, in a locality that Mistree calls 'the Mayfair of Mumbai'. But after diclofenac leached into the environment in the 1990s, the decline became steep and terminal. Which prompted the question: if the vultures weren't around, what was happening to the bodies in the Doongerwadi *dakhma*?

In 2005, the issue exploded in the media. Dhan Baria, a Zoroastrian woman who was sixty-four at the time, went to the Doongerwadi to pray soon after her mother was consigned to the *dakhma* and she asked the staff if the corpse had already been reduced to its bones. The staff laughed, Baria said to the journalist Meera Subramanian, who wrote about the many crises in Indian environmentalism in her book *A River Runs Again*. In the absence of vultures, her mother's body would be there for a long time, Baria was told. The following year, she smuggled a photographer into the *dakhma*, who took pictures of its contents: bodies that lay on top of each other, bodies that had bloated and decomposed perhaps a little but were otherwise largely intact, with just small pieces of flesh nipped off by kites and crows. The gentle rate of putrefaction gave rise to a lasting smell. Baria sent the photos to newspapers and circulated them on printed flyers, touching off a furore.

The Zoroastrians form a tight community, folded in upon itself – so closed, in fact, that to its strictest followers anyone marrying outside the faith isn't considered to be a Zoroastrian thereafter. Nearly overwhelmingly, Parsi priests refuse to chant the last rites for the dead if the body is bound for a crematorium instead of a *dakhma*. Many Zoroastrians are traditionalists, Jehangir Patel, the editor of the journal *Parsiana*, told me. 'They're God-fearing people. They worry about their souls and their afterlife, and they want the priests to say prayers. So they were scared about the consequences of the bodies just lying there in the *dakhma* and not decomposing.' These concerns precipitated a schism. The most conservative Zoroastrians – and Mistree counts himself among them – maintained that the sun's ferocity was sufficient to reduce the corpses to bone. (Mistree also disputed many of the details around Baria's photographs.) The *dakhma*'s authorities set up solar mirrors to focus and reflect sunlight more accurately, although the mirrors grew less effective during the city's long, cloudy monsoon. They consulted vulture experts like Vibhu Prakash and drew up plans for a vulture aviary adjacent to Doongerwadi, but these went nowhere. (Patel opened one of his columns, from 2012, with the words: 'Oh no! Not another article on the blessed aviary project!') Another faction, though – Baria included – has been pushing to lift the taboo on cremation, so that priests will agree to consecrate the cremated dead. Isn't it better to burn them, after all, rather than have them suffer the indignity of slowly shrivelling up, like grapes under the sun?

Mistree doesn't agree. A concession on this front, he thinks, would be a betrayal of the faith's fundamental principles. 'It's all right if you see death as something that is the work of God, because then you think: "Why can't I burn the body? After all, it's quicker and easier,"' he said. 'But that is just not what Zoroastrianism believes.' He appeared perplexed by people who aimed to defy this precept of the religion but still wanted Zoroastrian priests to preside over their departures from this world. 'Of course there are alternatives. I get enquiries like: "In Sweden, they use liquid nitrogen to dispose of the dead. Why can't we use that?" The mind can churn up a hundred and one alternatives. But you have to have a link to the theology.'

Mistree's devotion to his theology can sound pickled and hidebound, but despite myself, I felt that I understood his position, and even had a stab of sympathy for him. He has poured himself into Zoroastrianism, but now he's watching the religion dim and fade. There were roughly 57,000 members left in India as of the 2011 census – an ageing populace, in which there are three deaths for every birth. The numbers will only shrink further, because more and more people are leaving the faith by marrying outside it. Facing the prospect that Zoroastrianism will evaporate entirely, Mistree is choosing to hold fast to its tenets while he still can, while they still exist. Somehow, for the orthodox, that is finer and more honourable than contemplating the kinds of changes that might conserve the faith in a different, looser form.

The purpose of the vulture breeding centres was always to return birds to the wild, to pop them back into their slots within the ecosystem. In 2016, the Pinjore centre conducted a test release of a pair of Himalayan griffons, a vulture species not quite as threatened as the long-billed, the slender-billed or the white-rumped. The griffons had been in the centre for a decade, so they were first housed in an intermediate aviary, from where they could see the outside world and get accustomed to its rhythms. 'A lot of people were very sceptical about whether vultures that had been in captivity for so long could even fly properly and survive in the wild,' Prakash said. Then, on the momentous day, a government minister came to Pinjore, tugged on a ceremonial pulley and hoisted up one side of the aviary.

Nothing happened. The birds didn't budge. The minister went back to Delhi.

The vultures stayed inside for the next twenty-four hours. Then one flew out, followed by the second. Twenty teams of spotters kept track of them for the next few weeks, scanning the sky and the treetops, and following them during the day. 'At the time, we didn't have the government's approval to put satellite tags on the birds,' Prakash said. After forty-seven days, the griffons peeled off into the clouds and disappeared.

Encouraged, Prakash prepared to release some of the critically endangered vultures that had been bred in the centre. Last year, eight birds were placed in an intermediate aviary; two of them were adults snared in the wild, intended to guide the others back into the world. They were to have been set free in March, but then the coronavirus struck, and the vultures remained where they were. Perhaps they'd be liberated in September or October, Prakash told me. 'We'll do it when there are some free-ranging Himalayan griffons around also. They usually come around then, in good numbers. And our vultures can join a big flock of them.' He sounded excited and anxious, like a parent who was desperately keen to see his toddlers make friends at preschool.

There's still diclofenac lurking in the environment, a low note of menace. Humans can take diclofenac for their aches and pains, and some of those tablets are waylaid by untrained or unethical veterinarians, who give them out for cows and other livestock. 'We're constantly monitoring the diclofenac out there,' Prakash said. 'We collect carcass samples. We check drugstores. We try to persuade farmers to bury cows that are treated with these sorts of drugs, instead of leaving them out for vultures.' At the same time, he admitted that they couldn't ask for diclofenac to be banned altogether. It's so fast, so effective – 'within fifteen minutes, you get relief' – that patients in pain deserve to be able to take it, he said. Prakash is nothing if not pragmatic. 'It's not an easy battle. But we do see some vultures in the wild that are surviving. So we'll just have to release them and then see what happens.'

In the *Ramayana*, after Sampati tells Rama's search party about spotting Sita, he narrates his own story. When he and Jatayu were young and full of sap, they held a contest to see who could fly higher. They climbed and climbed until Jatayu, the rasher brother, drew so close to the sun that he began to burn. Sampati saved Jatayu by shielding him with his own body. That was how he lost his wings, Sampati says.

But this is the *Ramayana*; there is a prophecy for everything. A wise sage had once forewarned Sampati about all that was to come – about Ravana, about his abduction of Sita, and about the arrival of the searchers. Tell them everything you've seen, Sampati was advised, and you will be healed. And sure enough, as soon as he finished his story, the old vulture grew a handsome pair of new wings. After waiting for decades, Sampati took to the skies once more. ∎

© OLIVE AYHENS
Yellowstone, 1994

OH LATITUDO

Amy Leach

'I loved being young,' says the chorus in *Heracles,* written around 420 BCE, and to this day people are still chorusing about how they loved being young, insisting that someday young people too will have loved being young. Nobody goes up to old people and says, 'I loved being old,' or if they do you can't hear them or see them. I know of a bear who didn't love everything about being young, the bear who his first winter built a den for himself, but it wasn't big enough, so all winter he hibernated with his bottom sticking out.

Platypuses could say to us, 'I loved being young,' since compared to platypuses humans are whippersnappers. Platypuses may condescend to us but we must not condescend to them. If we want to condescend to somebody we can condescend to petunias. Petunias are ridiculously young, having been cultivated in the nineteenth century. (Their parents are old and wild.) But even though they are young and inexperienced, I have seen petunias rallying after a hailstorm, putting themselves back together. I imagine if the supervolcano a little south of here erupted, there would be the insouciant petunias afterwards, shaking the ash off their purple.

Flying around over a supervolcano, the dragonflies of Yellowstone are so insouciant you might think they were superyoung. However they are 300 million years old and over that time have seen plenty of supervolcanos erupt. Maybe that is why their heads are all eyeballs. Anyway, rather than organizing a superbucket brigade in preparation for another eruption, the flame skimmers, cherry-faced meadowhawks and mountain emeralds are zooming backwards, zooming forth, zooming up and down, zooming in place. They possess the insouciance of the old.

The supervolcano has a supersecret underneath the surface, magma and hot mushy crystals. On the surface that secret is expressed in the bluest pools, the most experimental rocks, the burpiest mud and the rainbowiest steam. Looking towards the Grand Prismatic Spring from far off, you can see its prismatic steams rising into the air, red steam, green steam, tangerine steam. The steams are the supervolcano letting off steam, and the colors are the colors of the swimmers in the spring.

Of course in the swimming-pool biz the tradition is to keep the water 'safe', with a pH of 7.4 and a temperature between 83 and 86°F to make it 'comfortable for your swimmers'. However it depends on what type of swimmers you're wanting – if you want fragile big loud pink and brown swimmers then those are good parameters. If on the other hand you keep your pool at 450°F with a pH of 2, like lemon juice, you will get flinty little green and orange swimmers who never shout.

So extreme pools attract extreme patrons; so much for toning things down. Still, the supervolcano is probably at its most brilliant when not erupting. A kept secret is an engine of invention, and Yellowstone's supervolcano is flamboyantly secretive. Because it does not eject its secret, its secret is ever-imminent, effecting pools so turquoise, so russet, so lime, so lemon, waters so swashbuckling and rocks so imaginative, those beehives and mammoths and urchins and elephants and hoodoos. Landscapes with no secret can be a snore.

Hoodoos are imaginative rocks; they are people-looking columns with a hard little limestone cap that keeps their softer sandier torsos and legs from eroding. Actually the hoodoos of Yellowstone are not hoodoos but boulders that tumbled down a hill. However they resemble hoodoos and hoodoos resemble hooligans. Hoodoos resemble hooligans both externally and in a deeper way: as a hooligan is not just a hooligan, so a hoodoo is not just a hoodoo. That is why hoodoos and hooligans are never disappointing.

Sandhill cranes fly up from Arizona to Yellowstone to have their babies on the supervolcano. Their babies are destination babies. The cranes must know what they are doing because like the dragonflies they are very old, dating from the Pleistocene, when some extinct humans appeared. As it turns out, those humans were fifth wheels – who misses them now? – who cares if a fifth wheel falls off? Anyway, maybe they went extinct because they were impatient. The patience of the sandhill crane is exemplified by that mother sitting on her egg in the spring blizzard. While the snow piles up to her eyes, her baby bird never even knows it's snowing. She is patient like Monteverdi, who had terrible headaches but you'd never know it from his music. (With some music, you can tell the composer had headaches.) Here's to all you mothers out there sitting on your babies in the snow.

Our mother the world is very old, and like a lot of old and wild parents – Abraham Lincoln and God and the parents of petunias – she is quite permissive. She gives us plenty of latitude and longitude and endless examples of what is permissible. The bubbly fresh springs give us permission to think bubbly fresh thoughts; the boiling mud give us permission to think boiling muddy thoughts. Winter gives us permission to think dark icy thoughts, especially if our dens aren't big enough. The aspen, immovable of trunk and movable of leaf, gives us permission to be both movable and immovable and dragonflies give us permission to zoom in place in the presence of great explosivity.

These authorities like dragonflies and coyotes outnumber the bigwigs, and are worthier of respect. The coyote authorizes us to possess some bite and the bump on the log authorizes us to be a bump on a log. The petunia authorizes us to be ridiculously young and the platypus to be ridiculously old as well as ridiculously ridiculous. The volcano erupting authorizes you to erupt, even if you are no longer three, even if you are a million years old. The volcano that abstains from erupting authorizes you to contain your volcanic feelings and thus to bubble up the 'Ode to Joy' in arpeggios or watercolors or spumone or whatever your medium might be. I know some people whose medium is mud. Composing the 'Ode to Joy' is better than burning down Wyoming. Wyoming has all those beloved forest-floor animals.

In my house lives a toy rabbit holding a basketball who, I am told, likes everything except for death. He is friends with a macaroni penguin who likes everything including death. She is the kind of penguin who would not only say 'I loved being young' but also 'I loved being old' and 'I loved being dead'. Somehow the rabbit and the penguin have resisted the pressure to rue everything. We live in a world so full of quality bears and quality beers, quality skunks and clowns and thimbleberries, quality Waynes and walnuts and whatnots, and we have such a quality satellite, such a quality star. The basketball rabbit and the macaroni penguin are good examples, good Emersonians, to like everything including headaches and sleeplessness and snowstorms and then even after death – to maybe go on liking. ∎

ORNITHOGRAPHIES

Xavi Bou

Introduction by Tim Dee

In the 1940s, during the early years of radar, systems operators regularly reported inexplicable blooms and blurs of light moving across their screens. They called them *angels*. During the Second World War these illuminated echoes even prompted an invasion scare in Britain; only later, in peacetime, were they identified as ordinary things and everyday occurrences – birds flocking in flight.

Starlings, gulls, swallows, kites, fulmars . . . many grey-black angels are to be seen for real in Xavi Bou's photographs. Each of his *Ornithographies* shows actual birds undertaking actual journeys, and all the images here reveal *wing work* – the specifics of flying and how every species flies in its own way. No scientific photography or technical illustration known to me has rendered bird locomotion as legible. No artistic treatment of the same has been so literally built from the real world.

Most of these images record roughly twenty seconds of flying time. Each flight is rendered as a line, thin or thick and curved or straight depending on how the bird flies. The line is a capture of a flight path and is made from a thread of snapshots of the moving bird harvested from hundreds or more frames and collaged into one. Wingbeats are first stopped, as it were, and then reanimated. Every final print contains within it a sequence. The *now* (Cartier-Bresson's 'decisive moment') of each is stretched by Bou, so that each has a past – earlier moments of the bird's flight – within its present. The effect is similar to looking at a zoetrope or a flicker-book except everything happens in a single image. A whole movie is condensed into one photograph.

No bird could ever be seen by our naked eye as Bou shows it, but every flying bird actually moves in that way. Paradoxically, his artfulness increases each picture's truthfulness.

Three yellow-legged gulls and four white storks circle together up a column of rising air. Their flight paths make up the seven inky lines that alone mark this print. Even as calligraphy the birds' *jizz* is apparent – jizz is the term for the combination of features and behaviour that constitutes the quintessence of every species and enables its identification. The bulky and broad-winged stork is a soaring bird that, if thermals permit, is not keen on wing flapping. These four are in luck: smooth brush-like strokes record their easy ride. Gulls soar too but are mostly flappers; that flight action is also recorded with their wings making more effortful undulating marks. We might even calculate energy spend: it takes on my count twenty-six flaps for a yellow-legged gull to rise as far as one soaring movement will lift a white stork.

Icarus would have pored over these photos and have learned from them; so might Amelia Earhart, or Leonardo, or the Birdman of Alcatraz, or David Lack, the radar operator turned ornithologist. ■

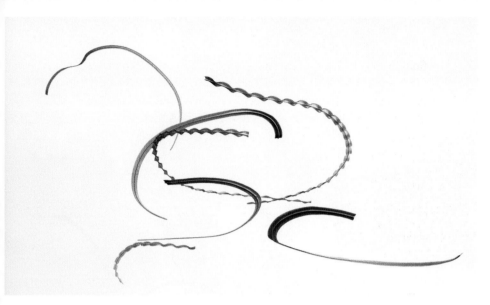

Yellow-legged gulls and white storks, Parc Natural dels Aiguamolls de l'Empordà, Catalonia

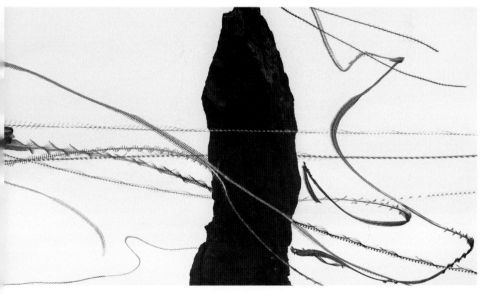

Northern fulmars and puffins, Vík, Iceland

Barn swallows, Yellowstone National Park, USA

Common starlings, Parc Natural dels Aiguamolls de l'Empordà, Catalonia

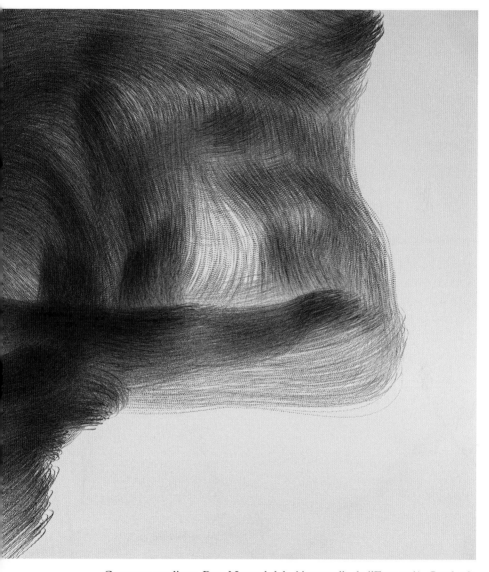

Common starlings, Parc Natural dels Aiguamolls de l'Empordà, Catalonia

European goldfinches, Girona, Catalonia

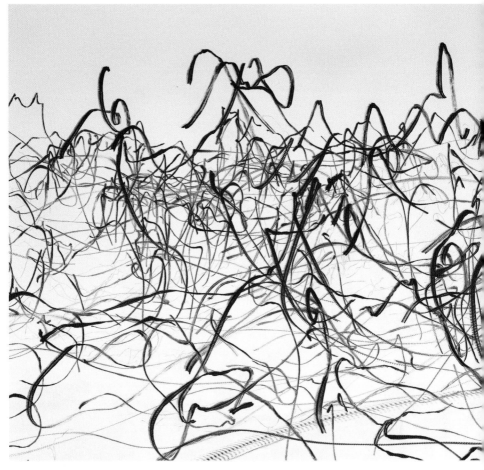

Black kites, Tarifa, Spain

Northern fulmar, Hvalnes, Iceland

Northern fulmars, Vík, Iceland

Griffon vultures, Tremp, Catalonia

Red kites, Lleida, Catalonia

Give the gift of Membership

Set someone special on a journey through human history with 12 months of extraordinary exhibitions and events at the British Museum.

Buy now

Ways to buy
britishmuseum.org/membership
+44 (0)20 7323 8195

The British Museum Friends is a registered charity and company limited by guarantee which exists to support the British Museum.

Registered charity number 1086080
Company registration number 04133346

Large vase, tin-glazed earthenware (maiolica), from the workshop of Orazio Fontana, made in Urbino, Italy, about 1565–1571, with gilt-metal mounts made in Paris, France, about 1765. Part of the Waddesdon Bequest.

Wolves, 1926
Gallery Sylvia Kovacek

THE WOLF AT THE DOOR

Cal Flyn

There's a monument near Brora, sixty miles short of John o'Groats, that claims to mark the spot where the last wolf in Sutherland was killed. I pass it often in the car. The wolf, it says, was KILLED BY THE HUNTER POLSON IN OR ABOUT THE YEAR 1700.

I know this story. Polson, so it goes, was standing watch outside the wolf's lair while his sons laid waste to the pups inside. When the she-wolf returned from the hunt, racing to the aid of her young, she bounded past the hunter and as she did he grabbed her by the tail. From inside the den – now plunged into darkness as Polson and the wolf struggled at its entrance – came, in Gaelic, a shout of alarm: 'Father! What's blocking the light?' To which Polson replied: 'If the tail comes away at the root, you'll soon find out!'

It's an unlikely story, even as such stories go. The memorial itself hedges its bets, doubt sown into the wording: unusually for a work of statuary, those repositories of heroics and hyperbole, its erector felt the need to cite its sources, pass the buck (ACCORDING TO SCROPE'S 'ART OF ÐEERSTALKING'), a detail that has always tickled me. The history of wolves is saturated with this kind of machismo and myth-making. Here are all its stock ingredients: the lupine villain, the plucky hunter, the lucky break. Did it really happen? Probably not. Still, whether Polson is to blame or not, there are no wild wolves left in Scotland.

By 1700, they had also long been extirpated from England and from Wales – though their old territory is commemorated in the form of names: Ulthwaite, Wolfenden, Wolfheles, Wolvenfield. Their deaths too: Woolpit, Wolfpit, Woolfall. All across Europe there were centuries of open warfare against the wolf – that universal anti-hero, folkloric villain, sharp-toothed grandmother with a glint in her eye – which saw it hunted relentlessly wherever people lived, persecuted across continents and cultures.

In Europe, those that survived retreated to rare enclaves, finding sanctuary on the high ground of the Apennines, or fleeing east into the debatable lands where Europe bleeds into Asia: Carpathia, the Balkans. There, the wolves in exile clung on, waiting for an opportunity, preparing for their victorious return.

If the trajectory of the European wolf is dispiriting, it is also familiar. We have become well acquainted with graphs that plot the advance of humans against the decline of all else. Everywhere we go, it seems, we wreak death and destruction, chipping away at the natural world.

But over the last century, a different narrative has been writing itself into existence. In Europe, patterns of farming and land use have been changing on a grand scale, as marginal land – too steep or too depleted to be worth the effort of farming – falls into disuse. As the value of livestock has dropped, young people too have increasingly abandoned rural areas for cities. When they do, ever more land often goes unclaimed, unploughed, unrestrained. Some estimate that over the three decades leading to 2030, an area the size of Italy will have been abandoned within the European Union alone.

While our attention has been elsewhere, nature has expanded into the gaps left behind. As annual crops fade away without human input, shrubs and fast-spreading thorns take their place. Then tiny trees take root and the ground starts to bristle with new life as soft, and hard, woods, hoisted from the earth, spread a densely embroidered tapestry of life across the landscape. The still summer's air is soon vibrating with the tiny wings of insects. Songbirds raise their voices, trail up and down the scales, an orchestra coming into tune. Rabbits, badgers and foxes dig their homes between the roots. Deer graze in shabby pastures, leap tumbledown gates. Along the rivers' edges, otters dive and beavers build their dams – some reintroduced, many recolonising territory of their own accord. Mice nest in old barns. Wild boar rootle in new woods.

All this Arcadian plenty has tempted in the carnivores, who crept in quietly at first, testing the waters. Lynx: low to the ground, ear-tufted, slinking through the shadows, rarely seen. Some 9,000 of them or more are now thought to live on the Continent, having been hunted to local extinction in western and central Europe by the middle of the twentieth century. Brown bears: 17,000 of them, spread through Scandinavia, the Dinaric Alps, the Carpathian Mountains, Bulgaria, Greece, Cantabria, the Alps . . .

And, of course, wolves. There are an estimated 12,000 of them in Europe now, far more than in the contiguous United States – where the grey wolf was similarly persecuted, until legal protections came into force in the 1970s – and they have now been documented in every single country on the European mainland. In 2017, the first wolf was spotted in Luxembourg for more than a century and the first wolf in Denmark for 200 years. Last year, wolves were confirmed to have set up home in a Dutch national park. These are all crowded countries, intensively farmed and densely populated, and the wolves' presence there indicates how closely our ranges have come to overlap. Recently, while the residents of Scanno, Italy, were confined inside to halt the spread of Covid-19, four wolves were seen to hunt a herd of deer through the town; they took down a hind and devoured it right there in the street.

Mainly, however, the wolves live where we have ceded ground. Iberian wolves now wander the ghost villages of Galicia, and Eurasian wolves haunt abandoned Cold War-era military sites along the former Iron Curtain. In the early 2000s, they crossed the border into Germany from the dense forests of Poland, finding sanctuary in former army testing ranges and post-industrial ruins. There are now more than a hundred German wolf packs, each numbering five to ten animals, occasionally more. Where we have withdrawn, they have grown. Our loss has been their gain.

Although maybe that's the wrong way to think about it. Perhaps their gain could be our gain too; perhaps their return heralds change for the better, for the whole ecosystem. In recent years, scientists have come to appreciate the full impact that an apex predator, such as the wolf, can have upon its wider environment. The seminal case study that guides thinking on this issue is that of Yellowstone National Park, 3,500 square miles of protected land in north-west Wyoming. There, the 1995 reintroduction of grey wolves into the environment after a seventy-year absence has offered insight into the influence of large predators upon the behaviour of grazing animals, their prey.

As far as the elk and mule deer of Yellowstone were concerned, the return of the wolves changed everything. Though they had faced some predation throughout – not least from humans with guns – they had grown used to milling freely through the open landscape, grazing hither and thither. Heretofore relatively peaceful sunlit glades and fragrant sagebrush meadows became gauntlets to run, through which they moved as targets. They grew nervy, hesitant. They kept on the move through the clearings, bunching tightly together in agile, watchful groups. They snatched mouthfuls on the move, and ate less overall.

Around the same time as the wolves were released, the mountain lion population, once hunted to local extinction, was becoming re-established as well – having crept back in from wilderness areas in central Idaho. Under these twin pressures, over a period of about fifteen years, elk numbers halved.

Those that did survive behaved differently too: when the wolves were on the prowl, they retreated to the dimly lit comfort of the woods, where they might wander in clandestine bands. They avoided the cougars, most active at night, by steering clear of landmarks where they might be trapped or surprised from above in the dark – ravines, outcrops, embankments. No longer did they live in an environment defined by its waterholes and pastures, or even by its ridgelines and ravines, but by areas now suffused with danger and relief. A psychological topology, this – one marked with hillocks of anxiety and peaks of alarm. Ecologists know this as 'the landscape of fear'.

And as the deer's landscape of fear metamorphosed in the presence of the wolves, so too did the physical landscape that underlay it. As deer numbers fell and grazing habits changed, the willow, cottonwood and aspen seedlings they had been stripping from the clearings were granted a reprieve. Undergrowth thickened. Leafy stands grew up along the river edges. In this way, fear is a force that shapes the world.

Across the Atlantic, European environmentalists were paying close attention. Some were interested in what change these self-willed wolves might wreak upon their old haunts. Others were more interested in, essentially, their *application* – how wolves might be used as a tool of rewilding and reforestation. Wolves might, they hypothesised, be a way by which ecosystems thrown wildly out of kilter could be brought back into some form of balance. The big bad wolf has returned to favour, in certain ecological circles, at least.

Here in Scotland, red deer have been running rampant for decades. Thanks to the lack of natural predators, and the sporting estates' habit of feeding them through winter, numbers have more than doubled since 1959, rising from 155,000 to an estimated 400,000. Highland landowners have been pressed into service as ersatz wolves and are now required by law to spend months stalking smooth-skinned hills – bitten down to the quick by hungry mouths – with loaded rifles; and they do so, some more enthusiastically than others. In this way, last year, 80,000 red deer were culled.

Many believe this is nowhere near enough, but it's a time-consuming, expensive process that swallows up thousands of man-hours each year. For this reason, our old enemy has been looking a lot more attractive of late.

But wolves will not return on their own. We are separated from the wolf packs of continental Europe by the sea; if we want wolves in Scotland, haunting the hills, we will have to *invite them in*.

LITTLE PIG,
LITTLE PIG,
LET ME COME IN.

The hunting lodge at Alladale sits on a low rise, overlooking the glens that form the body of Paul Lister's Highland estate, thirty miles inland from the monument at Brora. It's a grand, stone-built Victorian country house with bay windows and high ceilings. When I arrive there on a hot summer's day I find a half-dozen stags dozing peacefully on the lawn, looking sleek and lithe, docile as cows, their antlers trimmed with a velvet of russet and gold.

I step towards them, right up to them, almost – I'm maybe three metres away when they finally heave to their feet and swing to face me, almost defiantly, before trotting into the trees that mark the edge of the garden.

'No fear,' comments Paul. That's the problem.

The land at Alladale is steeply pitched, dramatic, desperately beautiful. It's a place that will grab you by the hand, by the hair, make you gasp. But as a landscape of fear, this time of year, it is smooth and almost featureless. The deer will head up to the high ground over winter, he says, during the stalking season, when all bets are off. But for now they are safe. 'They know, well enough, when it's time to go.'

Paul is a vigorous man, slim and tanned, in his sixties. The heir to a vast fortune made in furniture, he has been sinking a sizeable part of it into the rewilding of this Highland estate since he bought it in 2003. Back then, there were twenty-five deer per square kilometre; today, through a combination of 'population management' – that is, shooting them – and extensive deer fencing, his staff have brought that figure down to four or five. These days, he doesn't call it an estate, but a 'wilderness reserve'.

Whatever you want to call it, the results of the work are tangible, easily visible to the naked eye. We bump down a track in a Land Rover to view how this is a place shivering with summer foliage, so unlike the naked hollows of the glens I know so well – those cavernous spaces, those glacial curves. Birch and aspen tremble along the river's edge, swollen with the very last of the snowmelt. Scots pine shin up the very steepest slopes, bilberries blooming in their shadow.

None of this came about by accident. These trees were planted in batches, tens of thousands of them at a time. The oldest are now approaching two decades in the ground, and are maturing in safety, behind fences six feet high that march along the road's edge and then up and over the ridgeline. Between their branches, unseen, scamper red squirrels: native to the area but boosted with releases from elsewhere. Back at the lodge, wildcat kittens romp in a pen, part of a reintroduction project that could see them set loose within a couple of years. All of it part of the same grand plan.

But what Paul really wants is this: a 50,000-acre enclosure within which wolves run free alongside the deer and the rabbits and the squirrels and the wildcats and all else. The hope is that the wolves would take it upon themselves to 'manage' the deer population, starting with the weakest – the old, the sick, the starving – and working up, keeping them on their toes, on the move, relieving the grazing pressure on the hills and thus liberating the land to attain a level of fertility not seen for centuries.

Paul views this as a way to restore a crucial self-righting mechanism to an ecosystem thrown haywire, an ecosystem where 'nothing makes sense' any more. Morally speaking, he says, 'it's the right thing to do'. Before, we killed the wolves and the bears and the lynx – trapped them, bludgeoned them, flayed them alive – 'because they were inconvenient to us. What gave us the right to eliminate other species? It's disgusting. So when we have the opportunity to put something back, albeit in a controlled way, it should fill us with joy.'

Still, his plan – heavily modelled on the game reserves of South Africa – retains a great deal of hands-on interference with the 'natural way of things'. The wolves themselves would require population management: 'If you put a pack of wolves in here, they're soon going to make two packs, then you have to step in and neuter the females. It's the only way to do it.' The game reserves do it all the time – 'play God' – but perhaps it's the best we could hope for in a broken world: 'either that or nothing,' Paul tells me.

'Look', he says suddenly, leaning over the passenger seat and pointing high up to the ridge to the east. 'Imagine a wolf pack coming over that pass. Can you see it?'

I look up: to bare rock, heather, dry grasses whipped by the wind – and find that I can.

L ater, I am driving home in the deepening dusk when suddenly I find myself surrounded on all sides by a dozen sets of flashing eyes. I touch the brake, heart pounding, and silhouetted forms rise up from the gloaming: antlered figures on stony outcrops, cervine faces emerging from the thicket. They are unspeaking presences with an unpredictable, almost chaotic, energy – what seems like rock will reanimate and rush out in front of me, bounding, leaping, with athletic grace.

I hunch over the wheel, foot poised on the brake, eyes narrowed as pale shapes pass soundlessly through the gloom. Perhaps it's the late hour, the moonlit hills, the solitude of the open road, but their boldness – *insolence* – makes me uneasy. I slow to a crawl, then stop, as a red hind picks her way purposely across my path, turning her head into the glare of my headlamps with a slow, almost alien, calm.

On islands, over time, wildlife isolated from any natural predators tend to lose their defence mechanisms: their flight response, their sense of fear. 'Island tameness', as this is known, is an enchanting evolutionary act of self-harm, producing naive, docile creatures who do not recoil from danger. Take the Falkland Islands wolf, or warrah (*Dusicyon australis*, literally the 'foolish dog of the south'), whose dopey, curious demeanour disconcerted, then amused nineteenth-century sailors. It could be killed quite simply by holding a piece of meat in one hand and a knife in the other. It has been extinct since 1876.

Island tameness, as a phenomenon, applies to islands far smaller than our own, but it's what comes to mind as I face off with the hind. An allegory of our age – not just for the deer and their oblivious manner, but for our own.

Paul's wolf plan – limited though it is in scope – has met with stiff resistance from almost every corner. Trembling voices speak up at public meetings, frightened for their safety. Bureaucratic hurdles emerge that may prove insurmountable: animal welfare controls prevent the keeping of predators and prey enclosed together; hikers point to their right to roam Scottish lands, enshrined in law. People here, says Paul, have forgotten what it means to live alongside predators. They are obsessed with livestock, their helpless pets. They kick and squeal, refuse to adapt their ways for a wilder future.

What could it cost us, this risk aversion? While we've been wringing our hands over a few dozen beavers, refusing even to countenance the reintroduction of lynx, Europe has been rewilding of its own accord. Wolves brook no bureaucracy. They do not believe in borders.

It has been years since we have come face to face with apex predators in our own country. If our fear was a landscape, it would be a prairie, a great plain. The threats we face now are constructions of our devising.

L isten. I'm a woman. I know of men. I have walked city streets with keys pressed between my fingers. I've wrenched my wrist from a strong grip, stepped from a moving vehicle as it swung off the road, confronted strangers under street lights rather than leading them to my door. But what has stayed with me is those other times, in other places: that night I woke to hear the breathing of an animal, large and close at hand, through the canvas of my tent; that time, in bear country, I smelled a bestial stench so strong the hairs on the back of my neck stood up, and my horse spun and danced beneath me, flaring its nostrils and rolling its eyes. This is a different plane of fear: a fire of the body, a fear without reason.

I say without reason. This is true in both senses of the term, for our fear of wolves is out of all proportion to the danger they pose us. Wolves very rarely attack humans, even actively avoid us. One might live a lifetime in the woods with a pack of wolves for neighbours and never see a single one. When thinking of reintroductions, we must be circumspect, realistic: the risk of wolf attack is small. Tiny, even. Still, it is not *zero*.

In the past, every so often – maybe every hundred years – a country supporting a large population of wolves might find itself scene to a lupine horror story. In the eighteenth century, for example, the so-called Beast of Gévaudan terrorised the south of France, allegedly killing and eating more than a hundred people. Royal huntsmen were called in to slay the local pack, and in 1765 they did, bringing down a massive, scar-faced wolf. Yet after a brief pause, attacks resumed until 1767, when a second monstrous wolf was killed, said to have human remains in its stomach. Fifty years later, in the Forêt de Longchamp, nine children would be killed and a further seven injured by mysterious forces. Again, the killings only stopped once a wolf of exceptional size and stature was brought low.

These cases are infamous: exceptions to the rule that fuel the fantasy, the kernels of truth at the core of European folklore – those tales of wolves in the bed, wolves at the door, werewolves stalking the halls at night, driven wild for the taste of human flesh. They sure stick in the mind.

Mark Mennle knows well the risks that wolves can bring. Mark is in his mid-forties, a shepherd from Prignitz, in Brandenburg, in the east of Germany. An itinerant shepherd, he grazes his flock of 600 sheep on state-owned grassland and between the panels of solar farms in a region where wolves have firmly re-established themselves in the space of a decade.

He, like all farmers in the area, has had to adapt his practices to the wolves' return. In some parts of Europe – mountainous regions, where the sheep roam free – shepherds have reverted to rearing more 'primitive' breeds, better able to fend for themselves against a predator's threat. In Brandenburg, a flat, rather sandy, plain criss-crossed with rivers and ribbed by dykes, Mark uses specialist electric fencing, pinning it to the ground to stop wolves getting in underneath.

He uses more traditional methods too: he had to trade in his quick, compliant sheepdogs for a powerful, bear-like breed that lives in among the sheep as their protectors – the Illyrian shepherd dog. But the dogs themselves can be difficult to handle. It's a hard balance to strike: they must be safe to coexist with ramblers and cyclists, but aggressive enough to start a fight with a wolf. Like hiring Hells Angels as security: things can go sour fast. Last year, a man came by, walking a pet dog – a scrappy little thing that strained at the lead and barked.

One of Mark's guard dogs grabbed it, pulling the lead from its owner's grip, and killed it. The furious man came at Mark with a stick. He has seventeen of these guard dogs now. These are expensive animals, each one worth far more than a sheep. 'Last year, I had to explain to my seven-year-old daughter I couldn't get her a Christmas present because I had to buy a new dog. That was heartbreaking.' Mark doesn't own his land. At this rate – the extra costs of security, the growing losses – he never will. For even with the dogs, his flock is not safe.

On 1 March, his phone rang at 7.30 a.m. It was the police, calling to tell him there had been an attack. When Mark reached the paddock where the assault had taken place, he could see the ravens circling. He knew at once, he says now, that something terrible had happened. What he found there was carnage, a desperate scene: twelve sheep dead – shredded – a dismembered mess. Eight more ewes lay broken and bleeding in the grass, some still breathing, heavily pregnant, in the process of dying. One's uterus had been torn from her body, the lamb still moving in her open womb. Others had gone into labour out of shock, only for the wolves to kill the infant lambs as they emerged. Another thirty, Mark later realised, had been taken, never to be seen again.

Massacres like this – killing beyond all possible hunger, as if for sport – are not unknown among wolves. When hunting deer, they will separate their victim from the herd and seize it; when it falls, its fellow deer will run, abandoning it to its doom. But sheep are different. They stay together. Even as the wolves are stripping their sisters for parts, they herd ever more tightly together, bleating, ready for slaughter. Blood-crazed wolves, adrenaline pumping, will kill, and kill, and kill.

As Mark rushed to the scene, he had been struggling to align what the police had told him with what he knew of his animals. He had left the flock miles from here, grazing contentedly, only the night before. 'The wolves hunted them for five kilometres,' he says. 'Can you imagine that? Maybe you can,' he adds, after a moment. 'As a woman.'

He gets financial recompense from the state, but – he says – not enough to cover the costs. That's not the worst part. 'It's the images I can't get out of my head. You feel for your sheep. You don't want them to suffer. The bloodbath in the field is not comparable to what the butcher is doing.' This was Mark's sixth attack since 2016. They're getting worse. Altogether, he's lost around 300 sheep to the wolves. Still, he hasn't thought about giving up. The prospect confounds him. What else would he do?

As wolf numbers rise across the Continent – as packs grow, split and re-form – here we sit on our island, watching through our fingers, patrolling our perimeters.

There is no serious consideration of releasing wolves into the UK countryside – at least, not in the foreseeable future. Efforts to reintroduce the comparatively small and harmless lynx, for example – seen by some as a stepping stone to the ultimate goal of bringing back wolves – remain extremely controversial, while beavers 'unofficially' released into Scotland's Tayside fifteen years ago – where they continue to thrive – are a major source of contention. Farmers, perhaps fairly, feel they have enough to contend with already. The wider public is wary too. Still, proponents of rewilding hope that, one day, wolves might run free through our wild and rewilded lands. But many barriers stand between now and then. Even under Paul's hampered plans, returnee wolves would not be reintroduced, but contained behind high fences. The only thing marking them apart from other captive wolves – of which we have a small number in this country – would be the size of the enclosure.

At the Highland Wildlife Park near Kingussie – a 260-acre facility run by the Royal Zoological Society of Scotland – I stop in to observe the resident wolf pack at feeding time. Here, a family group of six animals lives in a high-sided compound: a square of pine trees, cordoned off and scattered with wood piles and platforms. I watch them through Plexiglas, racing for scraps thrown in over the side. Large animals – perhaps the size of a Great Dane – but limber, agile, flowing over obstacles like water, their legs pistoning. They are shaggily dressed in furs of tawny and buff, with bulky leonine ruffs around their necks. Main course is rolled in in a wheelbarrow: the barrel of a large animal's ribcage, the fur scorched off. After a feast like this, the wolves will come together to sing. This is bonding.

They are strange, and yet familiar. I keep a dog at home – a retired sled dog I brought back from Finland, where she ran in teams of six or eight or ten. Groups of dogs like these retain something of that pack mentality. They strain at their harnesses, snap, turn on one another. While they wait, they lift their heads and howl, voices coming together and apart. My dog is soft now, submissive. A pet. But sometimes I see the predator in her flicker awake. It's in her eyes, the way she moves, the way she pricks her ears.

But these are not dogs. Look at their pelts, their strength, the size of their heads, their claws! Wild creatures. Or nearly. This pack, the keepers remind me, is an artificial construction. The male and female at its head have an uneasy relationship. They bicker, undermine the other's authority. They would not have settled for one another, given the chance. Still, they breed. Wolves are good like that. Pragmatic.

The question is: now what? The female keeps her adolescent daughters in check. Soon, in the wild, these young females would leave the pack in search of mates; roam as lone wolves through strange lands. But there is nowhere here for them to go. They cannot be released – they likely never will be free. So these captive wolves have taken on an uneasy status: not wild, nor yet domesticated. Are they truly wolves at all?

Once, in Finland, I woke one still white morning to find wolf tracks threading through the snow right by my cabin. Something fired within me then – something primal, an instinct half-buried. I've never forgotten it. I feel it rise again in me now as I watch the wolves in their enclosure: the way my eyes snag on their powerful gait, their carnivore swagger. This is morbid fascination, and a reckless compulsion. What it demands of me is this: open the gate. Let all hell break loose – or not.

Look up: can you see it? The wolf pack on the high ground, passing between peaks. Roaming the darkened glens, raising their voices in dissonant chorus. And us, in our houses, locking the doors. If I squint my eyes, I find that I can. ∎

© JILL PELTO
Landscape of Change, 2016

PREPARE TO BE KIND

Rebecca Priestley

I'd survived blizzards, white-outs and minus 20°C in Antarctica so there was no way Wellington's autumn rain was going to stop me venturing outside. The daily walk had become an essential lockdown activity – a change of scene, a bit of relief from the computer screen. On top of my leggings, T-shirt and Scott Base hoodie, I pulled on Antarctic-issue woollen socks and gloves, an oilskin parka and a woolly hat. When we set off on our government-sanctioned 'local' walk, a three-kilometre hike up muddy paths on forested slopes, it was 11°C, but with the wind chill – a southerly gale gusting to eighty-seven kilometres per hour – it felt like 8°C. We walked up the hill, travelling fast across grassy clearings and taking our time on sheltered paths, watching the water make little streams through the pine needles. Without the pre-lockdown roar of traffic and whine of jets, we could hear the birds: the peep of a pīwakawaka, the mad warble of a tūī, the primordial screech of a kākā. By the time we reached the iridescent ceramic pyramid of the Byrd Memorial, near the top of Mount Victoria, my legs were sodden, soaked, drenched. My ill-considered medley of inside and Antarctic clothing was great for the cold but not much good in the rain.

The memorial to the American admiral Richard E. Byrd, who used New Zealand as a base for his many Antarctic expeditions, featured a bust surrounded by a patchwork of rocks from Antarctica – granites, diorites, basalts. The ceramic-tiled triangle above him, designed to look like a polar tent, stretched back to a point and was glazed in blues, yellows, pinks and greens to represent the aurora.

We stood beside Admiral Byrd, facing the wind, eyes squinting against the southerly onslaught. To the east was the flat isthmus between Lyall Bay and Evans Bay, a low-lying grid of streets lined with wooden houses, two schools, two shopping centres and the now-quiet airport runway sitting just 4.5 metres above the rising seas.

I followed Admiral Byrd's gaze. To the south, past the houses, was Lyall Bay beach, the Southern Ocean and – beyond that – some 3,300 kilometres away, Antarctica. But the rain was heavy and the skies were low and all I could see was white.

On my first trip to Antarctica, in 2011, I'd found another bust of Admiral Byrd at McMurdo Station. The US base, along with New Zealand's Scott Base, sits on the volcanic rock of Ross Island, in view of Mount Erebus. McMurdo's ragtag assemblage of buildings and reddish-brown dirt roads provides a splash of murky colour in an otherwise white landscape.

Most of the year, Ross Island is covered in snow and surrounded by ice. On the northern coast of the island, the annual sea ice – a two-metre-thick layer – sits on top of the ocean, creating habitat for penguins above and algae and fish below. South of the island, the Ross Ice Shelf stretches, flat and white, towards the horizon. This floating slab of ice, up to 750 metres thick and extending over an area the size of France, covers most of the Ross Sea, the southern extent of the Pacific Ocean. To the west, the Transantarctic Mountains form a barrier between the ocean and the massive East Antarctic Ice Sheet, which covers the continent with a layer of ice up to four kilometres thick. In the gaps between the mountain peaks, massive glaciers pour through steep-sided valleys to drain the ice sheet. North of Ross Island, the glaciers flow towards the ocean; south of Ross Island, these ice rivers – along with massive ice streams from the smaller West Antarctic Ice Sheet – feed the Ross Ice Shelf.

As a science writer on an invited media programme, I got the VIP treatment: helicopter trips to Scott's and Shackleton's historic huts and to an American field camp in the Taylor Valley, with spectacular aerial views of the mountains and glaciers. I spent eleven nights at Scott Base and one in a tent on the Ross Ice Shelf.

Now, nearly a decade later, as I stood on a Wellington hill, looking south towards Antarctica, the World Health Organization was reporting nearly half a million cases of Covid-19 and more than 20,000 deaths. While New Zealand, with 102 cases of Covid-19 and no deaths, was hardly the centre of the crisis, our prime minister, Jacinda Ardern, had on 23 March closed the borders and provided forty-eight hours' notice to prepare for a strict lockdown – Alert Level 4 of four possible levels. 'Be strong and be kind,' she urged our island nation of 5 million people at the end of her televised message.

Antarctica had always felt like another planet, and now it really was a world away. Shut off from the rest of humanity, with its bases now staffed by winter-over crews, it was the only continent in the world that was Covid-free.

We were quiet as we walked downhill, soaked to the skin. Close to home, my daughter ran ahead, while I plodded along in my water-laden boots. At the top of a muddy slope, where the mountain bike track joined a paved path and a field, were three yellow signs on a wooden pole. Two yellow diamonds showed black figures – two children holding hands, a purposeful-looking walker. Below them, an orange rectangle carried a warning. But someone had used silver spray paint to write over PREPARE TO STOP, and those of us leaving lockdown and braving the outside air were now being cautioned to PREPARE TO DIE.

I had adapted easily enough to lockdown. As an academic, I was on salary and able to work from home. I spent my days in Zoom meetings: virtual morning teas with my team, emergency faculty meetings, Māori language lessons, student supervisions. When I had time, I progressed some research I was preparing to submit to a scientific journal. I led a public engagement workstream for the NZ SeaRise programme, a five-year effort to improve sea level rise projections for New Zealand. But before we told people what to expect in the future, I wanted to gauge what they already knew. People were worried about sea level rise, our survey of 1,000 New Zealanders revealed, but they didn't really understand it. First, they tended to think the main cause of sea level rise was melting sea ice, but we knew that when sea ice melts it has no direct impact on the volume of water in the ocean. They also seemed to think things could get a whole lot worse than any of us did. If things really all went to shit, under what we called a 'scientifically credible worst-case scenario', one third of respondents rightly assessed that sea levels could rise up to two metres by the end of the century. But another one third of respondents thought things could get much, much worse, checking the boxes for five metres of sea level rise, eight metres, twelve metres, or even 'fifteen metres or more'. Fifteen metres of sea level rise by 2100? Was that even physically possible? My house would be completely under water if the oceans rose that much.

It was more than two years since I'd returned from my third trip to Antarctica and I doubted I'd ever go back. I'd written magazine articles, compiled an anthology of Antarctic science writing, filmed lectures for an online course taken by students around the world and written an Antarctic memoir. Given the carbon emissions involved in a flight to Antarctica, I'd need a new and compelling reason to try and go back.

On my first two trips, in late November and early December, I'd enjoyed daily walks on the pressure ridges. Here, the moving sea ice in front of Scott Base is deformed into rolling hills and jagged peaks, bent and broken slabs of ice separated by vivid turquoise melt pools, a miniature landscape in blue and white. My most recent trip was in late January – high summer – when this icescape gave way to open water around Ross Island, meltwater streams flowed over volcanic rocks, and green mosses and orange lichens emerged to add colour to the monochromatic landscape. While the weather I had experienced – sunshine and temperatures around minus 5°C – was typical for summer on Ross Island, it all felt ominous, a sign of things to come. In other parts of Antarctica the environment is changing rapidly. The Antarctic Peninsula is one of the fastest warming places on the planet and just a few weeks before my lockdown walk, Esperanza Base, at the northern tip of the peninsula, had a temperature of 18.3°C, the highest ever recorded on the continent. The rising temperatures, on land and in the surrounding ocean, are causing ecosystem changes and Adélie penguins are suffering, while other species, like exotic grasses and predatory king crabs, are thriving. Most dramatic, though, are a series of ice shelf collapses, forming giant bergs that are photographed by satellites and shared around the world.

When floating ice shelves collapse, the land-based glaciers that feed them are free to melt into the warming ocean. This kind of ice loss *does* cause sea level rise. Antarctica, the biggest repository of ice on the planet, is home to 90 per cent of the world's ice and 70 per cent of the world's fresh water. If all of it melted, it could raise global sea levels by sixty metres or more. The Ross Ice Shelf remains intact, but in West Antarctica, the warming ocean is melting the floating ice shelves, and the ice sheet is thinning and retreating. The net result of the melting is that ice is currently being lost from Antarctica at a rate of 252 gigatonnes – that's 252 *billion* tonnes – per year. It's hard to comprehend. One gigatonne of ice would cover New York's Central Park to a height of 1,119 feet, say NASA, who estimate that 49,000 gigatonnes of the planet's ice has melted since 1901.

On my second trip south, I travelled with a colleague, Cliff Atkins, and a camera, making video lectures for an online university course about Antarctic science and culture. While I visited huts from the Heroic Age of Antarctic exploration to give field lectures on Antarctic history, Cliff filmed me. When he visited rock outcrops and field camps to give lectures on Antarctic geology, it was my turn behind the camera. On the second week of our trip, we were helicoptered into the Friis Hills, a 1,300-metre-high ice-free plateau in the Transantarctic Mountains. Here we joined a team of geologists and palaeoclimatologists – some of whom were now working on the NZ SeaRise programme – investigating what this part of Antarctica was like during a period they called the Miocene climatic optimum, when atmospheric CO_2 levels reached 700 parts per million, temperatures were 4–5°C warmer than today and sea level was up to thirty-five metres higher. Tim Naish, one of the expedition leaders, had told me that when it came to the CO_2 we were pumping into our atmosphere today, 'We know the endgame. We know that if we keep 400 parts per million or more in the atmosphere for long enough, we're heading towards a world like the mid Miocene.'

One lockdown morning, I received an email from Tim, with a journal article attached. 'Assume you have all seen this?' he wrote to the NZ SeaRise team. The article, published in the journal *Science*, reinforced the scientific view that when it came to sea level rise, there was a tipping point at around 2°C of warming, after which Antarctic ice melt would be unstoppable and sea level would keep rising for centuries. Tim described it as 'a commitment to multi-metre sea level rise if we miss the Paris target'.

In 2015, at a United Nations Framework Convention on Climate Change conference in Paris, the nations of the world agreed to try to limit global temperature increase by 2100 to 1.5–2°C above pre-industrial levels. The ambitious 1.5°C target was led by a coalition of small island and low-lying nations whose homes would be inundated if higher temperatures caused sea level to continue to rise. '1.5 to stay alive' was their call.

A few days after Tim's email, I was in a Zoom call with Tim and NZ SeaRise leader Richard Levy. Tim had the standard home office set up behind him – bookshelves, some framed awards, a bit of art – but Richard had used Zoom's virtual background feature to place himself in the Friis Hills. It looked like a helicopter shot, perhaps taken on approach to our campsite. Snow was speckled across the dark brown, rocky landscape of 500-million-year-old granites, 180-million-year-old dolerites and 14-million-year-old glacial deposits. In the distance I could see the vast expanse of ice that feeds the Taylor and Ferrar Glaciers, the steep-sided Kukri Hills that separate the Taylor from the Ferrar, and the distant peaks of the Royal Society Range. The sky was a brilliant blue and the sun glinted off the ice.

They started the meeting by catching up with each other, talking about conferences cancelled, Antarctic Treaty meetings postponed, but I eventually got their attention. Over the last week I'd been reading news reports of dropping global carbon emissions. People were talking about 'silver linings' and 'golden opportunities' to turn things around, to use the post-Covid recovery to reinvest in a green economy. I felt cautiously hopeful about the future, but I knew that even if we 'solved' climate change, even if we cut global carbon emissions to zero tomorrow, that sea level would keep on rising.

Even under the best-case scenario, Tim said, where we achieved our Paris Agreement targets to keep global warming close to 1.5°C, we were still in for a significant amount of sea level rise. 'Most models for that pathway suggest we're going to get at least forty centimetres of sea level rise by 2100. We can't avoid that.'

Scientists are in fair agreement about what will happen under a 1.5°C warmer world as the sea level rise under that scenario is mostly associated with thermal expansion – water takes up more space when it is warmer – and melting of mountain glaciers. The physics is relatively simple and it's all pretty quantifiable. But under warmer scenarios, projecting sea level rise is complicated. What gets the scientists perplexed, and has the modellers disagreeing with each other, is the response of the Antarctic ice sheets to a warming world and how much they will contribute to sea level rise.

As we warm the oceans, the sea ice will go first – we're already seeing that happening in the Arctic. Without the buffer of the sea ice, the ice shelves will be further exposed to the warming ocean and will start to melt. If the ice shelves are lost, there will be nothing holding back the glaciers that flow from the massive ice sheets towards the ocean. That's when something called marine ice sheet instability, or MISI, kicks in.

'That's where the real tipping point is,' said Richard. 'If we blow through that two degrees, then we're really committed to long term, major sea level rise.' With MISI, he explained, there's a runaway non-linear retreat of the ice sheets. While the more stable East Antarctic Ice Sheet covers the Antarctic landmass, the smaller West Antarctic Ice Sheet sits over a massive marine basin, a giant ice-filled bowl, The grounding line of the ice sheet – the line where the grounded ice *sheet* meets the floating ice *shelf* – is around the rim of this basin. For millennia, the ice sheet has been stable: the flow of ice from the centre of the ice sheet is balanced by the loss of ice where the ice shelf meets the ocean. But the warming planet is upsetting this equilibrium. If warmer water melts the base of the ice shelf, it thins and – with less mass to hold the ice sheet in place – the grounding line could retreat back from the lip of the marine basin and turn the grounded ice sheet into a floating ice shelf. As the ice sheet thins and the grounding line retreats deeper into the basin, a thicker and thicker layer of ice is free to go afloat, where it is vulnerable to melting and calving, leading to more retreat. It's a self-sustaining cycle.

'It's non-linear, like Covid,' added Tim. 'We'd end up with exponential loss of the ice sheet.'

We've all become familiar with non-linear growth curves from looking at plots of each country's total Covid-19 cases over time. But I've been looking at exponential growth curves for years. Exponential growth of CO_2 levels in the atmosphere is happening now. If we don't reduce CO_2 levels, exponential growth of sea level rise will follow. The difference with Covid-19 is that the exponential growth can only last so long. New Zealand's elimination strategy lockdown, and other countries' attempts to 'flatten the curve' through border control, social distancing and mask wearing, have seen new cases level off, then start to decline. We're not doing so well on the climate change metrics. Those curves keep on steepening.

If we fail in our efforts to reduce CO_2 levels, the impacts will be felt over generations. If we hit two metres of sea level rise by the end of the century, it won't stop then. 'After that you're talking multi-metre sea level rise, up to ten metres over the next five hundred years,' said Richard. 'And that can't really be avoided by reducing CO_2 because you've got other non-climatic processes pushing the ice sheets along.'

Sea level has already risen by twenty centimetres over the last century. Looking forward to 2100, it's a choice between another thirty centimetres of sea level rise if we do everything we can to cut our carbon emissions, and up to two metres of sea level rise if we don't. Even forty centimetres of sea level rise could displace millions of people in low-lying countries like Bangladesh, and Pacific Island nations such as Kiribati and Tokelau. Most of the world's major cities are coastal, and two metres of sea level rise could inundate 1.79 million square kilometres of land and displace up to 187 million people, leading to millions of climate migrants and 'social breakdown on scales that are pretty unimaginable,' said physicist Jonathan Bamber, who led a 2019 study into sea level rise.

But it's not just about seawater flooding the coastal regions that are dry today – rising sea levels will cause storm flooding to reach much further inland, saltwater contamination of drinking water and crops, and failure of storm water, sewerage systems and transport networks.

In our research project, we were hoping that if people understood sea level rise better they would be more willing to take action to *adapt* – to prepare for the sea level rise that was inevitable – and to *mitigate* – to reduce carbon emissions to stop things getting even worse. Around the world, we were now seeing radical societal change in response to the threat from Covid-19, and while many people and businesses were finding it painful, and difficult, it was saving lives. It was encouraging to see that change was possible, that when people and governments really understood the nature of a threat, they were – well, most of them were – willing to make sacrifices now to avoid something worse in the future.

As the days went on, I fell into an adrenaline-fuelled routine. In the early mornings, I baked bread and walked in the hills. During the day, I sat at my computer and worked, with frequent interruptions from children wanting food, or help with their schoolwork. In the weekends, I gardened, made crumbles from the quinces and figs that were ripening on my trees, and used the sewing machine to tackle a pile of mending that had been building up for years. As a teenager in the 1980s I had thought we were heading for nuclear war, and as an adult that anxiety had transferred to climate change. Global pandemic? That'll do. It seemed to trip the 'existential threat to humanity' switch that was hardwired into my psyche. On some level, I felt like I'd been preparing for this for years.

In the evenings, I poured a gin and tonic and watched the Al Jazeera world news. Half the world was now in lockdown. There were drones in the streets of Spain telling people to go home. In South Africa, police were firing rubber bullets at shoppers breaking lockdown rules. In the UK, an old man with a Zimmer frame was walking laps of his backyard to raise money for the NHS. In the US, President Trump was telling lies and firing dissenters.

But the focal point of each day was the Covid-19 briefing. At 1 p.m. each day I tuned in for the daily briefing from Prime Minister Jacinda Ardern and Director-General of Health Ashley Bloomfield. New Zealand's first Covid-19 death was reported on 29 March. Daily cases peaked ten days into lockdown, by which time global cases had passed 1 million. Jacinda, while standing firm on the lockdown measures taken to halt the spread of the virus, also continued urging calm and kindness.

While looking at Twitter one morning I noticed the MetService was forecasting six-metre southerly swells. I scrolled further down. Someone had posted a video of a ferry battling the waves as it turned out of Wellington Harbour and into Cook Strait. As the swell hit the front of the ship it rose high on the water, exposing a bulbous bow that should have been way below the waterline. The bow crashed down as the swell passed and lifted the back of the turning ship. I continued to scroll down. Another video showed waves crashing onto Lyall Bay beach and surging across the road only two kilometres from my house. A tweet from the city council announced that the south coast road was closed.

The government had made the rules clear – if you're not an essential worker you should only go out, locally, for exercise, food shopping or medical appointments. I had to go to the supermarket, and if I dropped some supplies to my mother, I could justify driving to Lyall Bay, where a wide sandy beach stretches from the airport at one end to the hills at the other. The airport end of the beach is usually populated by surfers and dog walkers. At the suburban end of the beach is a cafe and – in warmer months – swimmers and paddlers.

When I arrived, just past midday, the Esplanade was busy – or what passed for 'busy' under this new normal – with dog walkers, cyclists and parents with prams. I parked and scurried across the road, avoiding a pile of slimy brown kelp and sand, and leaned over the sea wall. The beach was gone. On the other side of the low concrete wall the water swirled over tussock-covered dunes, submerging the dunes with each incoming wave, and exposing the golden grasses as the water retreated.

It was unrecognisable. At the western end of the bay, where the coastline curved towards the hills, the water flowed in multiple directions as the waves swept in from the south, bounced off the sea wall and travelled east, to intersect with the next set of southerly waves.

I started to walk around the curve of the bay, stepping carefully on the sandy footpath, popping kelp bubbles and trying not to slip while I immersed myself in the roar of the waves, the smell of sea and kelp, the squawk of an oystercatcher.

As I walked, I looked through the gaps between a row of beachfront houses. One had a launch on a trailer in the driveway. Another a kayak on the lawn. Useful. I found myself standing with an older couple and a woman with a camera, looking past a wooden house where waves were surging across a stone wall and into its yard.

'Are you a reporter?' asked the man, with a nod at my notebook and pen.

'I'm a writer,' I replied. 'I'm writing about sea level rise.'

'Ah!' He nodded. 'Good thing the land keeps rising.'

'1855,' he added with a raise of his eyebrows.

He was right but he was also wrong. In 1855, a magnitude 8.2 earthquake hit the Wellington and Wairarapa regions. It lifted this shoreline by up to one metre, creating the raised wave-cut platform that our coastal roads now followed, and drained the swampy isthmus between Lyall Bay and Evans Bay that was now home to more than 5,000 people. Further east, the uplift reached six metres. Earthquakes like this, though, work against a long-term slow subsidence of about two millimetres per year. Other parts of New Zealand are subsiding by up to four millimetres a year. This is another reason why projecting sea level rise is complicated – projections of forty centimetres, one metre, two metres or more are global averages, but sea level rise will differ from place to place. One factor that impacts local sea level rise is where the melted ice comes from. Because large ice sheets have a gravitational pull on the ocean surrounding them – they pull the sea up towards the ice sheet – when an ice sheet melts, local sea level will actually *fall*, meaning that sea level on the other side of the planet will be higher than the global average. So if most of the melting ice comes from Greenland and other northern hemisphere sources, sea level rise in the southern hemisphere will generally exceed the global average. When Antarctica starts being the major contributor to sea level rise, sea level will increase more in the north. Add to this any local effects such as uplift caused by isostatic rebound – some parts of Europe and Canada are still bouncing back from the pressure of being covered with continental ice sheets some 10,000 years ago – and subsidence related to plate movement or groundwater extraction, and projecting sea level rise for any specific location gets even more complex. New Zealand is prone to earthquakes, which can uplift significant stretches of coast, but earthquakes are unpredictable; they aren't something we can rely on to solve sea level rise.

High tide had passed and the beach was re-emerging. I walked to my car, head down, reading a news article on my phone. A person swept out to sea that morning had been 'recovered with moderate injuries' and a police spokeswoman was telling locals, 'Do not come down to take pictures or just to have a look.'

A police car drove slowly past, flashing its hazard lights. Sprung.

Climate change is already increasing the frequency and intensity of storms. When an extreme coastal event happens – a storm surge, a king tide, or both at the same time – if it happens on top of a higher sea level the impact will be greater. On average, the sort of coastal floods that we now know as '1-in-100-year events' are projected to happen once a year by 2050. After one metre of sea level rise these sorts of water levels will happen at every high tide. We need to start protecting our coasts, with sea walls, sophisticated drainage systems and wetland and dune restorations. In some places, we need to think about coastal retreat – we need to start moving away from the coast before the decision is made for us.

Other parts of Wellington have already made the hard decisions. At Mākara Beach, residents have decided to stay and adapt, but money will need to be spent on a sea wall and drainage. Kāpiti Coast residents have decided on a managed retreat, with a surf club, parking and picnic areas, and tracks to be relocated or abandoned after a series of damaging storms. Either option – adaptation or relocation – costs money. At Lyall Bay though, the existing sea wall – built in 1932 to reduce sand drift – is going to be restored as a heritage structure. I wonder how many more storm events it will take before a new plan is needed.

Winter was approaching, and I continued my daily walks as the weather got wilder, but things calmed down – locally at least – on the Covid-19 front. Daily cases were dropping and a public health professor was calling New Zealand's success in responding to the pandemic a 'triumph of science and decisive leadership'.

Is that what we needed for climate change? Science and decisive leadership?

'The challenge we have with climate change,' Richard told me, 'is it's very slow; it hides in the weeds and you don't see it until it jumps up and bites you in the arse. So it's hard to get the same social response, it's just not so in your face.' The climate change graphs I'm familiar with show atmospheric CO_2 levels over years, decades, centuries, millennia – the Covid-19 graphs show daily figures. But lately, said Richard, people were starting to notice the increased frequency of extreme weather and flooding events. 'People are saying, "Holy shit, this is actually starting to have an impact on *me*".' On my Lyall Bay excursion, the waves were exciting, entertainment for the locked-down masses. But when your beachfront house falls into the sea because of coastal erosion, when you can no longer get insurance for your family home, when the rising seas start eating your country. That's when people take notice.

I knew that while science and leadership had contributed to New Zealand's successful Covid-19 response, no amount of science and leadership would stop the sea from rising – the carbon we had already pumped into the atmosphere had committed us to a certain amount of sea level rise. And our country couldn't go this one alone, pull up the drawbridge. 'As an island nation, we have a distinct advantage in our ability to eliminate the virus,' said Jacinda Ardern at one of her daily briefings. But that's no advantage to us when it comes to climate change, to sea level rise – we're all on the planet together on this one. When the ocean really does eat people's countries, the people displaced by rising sea level will need somewhere to go. Our response to Covid-19 is to close the borders, lock everything down. But as sea levels rise, we'll have to start opening our borders. New Zealand will likely become home to thousands of our Pacific Island neighbours escaping coastal erosion and freshwater contamination. People in large or mountainous countries, like the United States and many European countries, can retreat inland. But what about Bangladesh, with a population of 160 million and two thirds of the country less than five metres above sea level? Where are all those displaced people going to go?

As people started speculating about when lockdown might be lifted, when we might move to a lower alert level, I began to feel anxious. I had settled into this newly simple life. The roads were quiet enough for me to ride my bicycle. We were spending wisely and not wasting any food. We'd stopped flying and were barely using the car. I was enjoying more time with my family, in the garden and on personal projects I'd been neglecting for years. And I felt a new sense of community. We would smile and say hello to neighbours on walks. People were looking out for each other and students were delivering groceries to elderly people, the over-seventies who had been told to stay home. It all felt more like the life I wanted to be living.

But I wasn't exactly *happy*. I felt the same sense of dread as everyone else. But I felt this dread all the time – I'd been lying awake at night worrying about climate change for years. It felt like the rest of the world was suddenly acknowledging that yes, things were fucked. What upset me, what made me feel like things were out of control, was when we kept living, kept on consuming, as if everything was OK *when it's not*. At last, there was a response that seemed commensurate with the shit that we were facing as a planet and a civilisation.

In New Zealand, our strict lockdown was lifted on 28 April, after thirty-three days. We spent sixteen days in Alert Level 3, then settled in Alert Level 2 on 14 May. Inside New Zealand, most restrictions were dropped, but the borders remained closed. We ate takeaways for the first time in five weeks. My three children returned to university and school. We started to share meals with my mother and her husband. While I was pleased to have a quieter home workspace, the world around me started to feel noisy and busy. I felt tense. I was spending less time in the garden. My impressive daily step count had dropped, so I planned a long walk that took in the waterfront and the hills.

I walked down our street, over a flat park built on reclaimed land and across a busy road to the Evans Bay Marina, home to 140 yachts and launches, a row of boat sheds, a small coastguard station. It was high tide and the boats were high in the water, which was lapping just fifteen centimetres below the parking lot and the marina walkways. Lyall Bay's sea wall should hold back the water for a while, but the sea will overflow this marina in my lifetime. In his 2017 book *The Water Will Come*, American journalist Jeff Goodell reports from the front line of sea level rise about how the rising ocean is already impacting nations around the world: in Venice, engineers are building a set of inflatable booms to hold back storm tides; in the Marshall Islands, saltwater is contaminating the atolls' scarce freshwater supplies; in New York, the city is planning a sea wall around Manhattan Island. I saw Goodell speak at a writers' festival, where he said that scientists were projecting that sea level rise by 2100 would be 'three to nine feet – and the numbers keep getting higher.'

That's more than the scientists I work with are expecting, but not by much. The trouble with overestimating sea level rise, though, is it can make people feel helpless. It's much better to tell it like it is. We will have thirty or more centimetres of sea level rise by 2050. We could have a metre of sea level rise by 2100, perhaps even two metres – and we need to prepare for that. One of the interesting things I've learned in my research is that if people acknowledge the sea level rise that is coming, and realise they need to adapt to it, they will also be much more likely to mitigate, to try and reduce carbon emissions, reduce global warming, to avoid the more extreme sea level rise scenarios.

From the waterfront I walked up a suburban road, through a small shopping centre, across a footbridge and into the bush-covered hills. I might have been far from Antarctica, but I knew that the rocks beneath the tracks and the trees were greywacke – deformed layers of sandstone and mudstone that were once, some 200 million years ago, layers of sand and mud on the sea floor off the coast of the ancient supercontinent Gondwana, before it broke into Antarctica, Australia and several other continents.

As I walked I listened to a podcast, the first in a series called *After the Virus*. In New Zealand, following our prime minister's decision to 'go hard' and 'go early' with one of the strictest lockdowns on the planet, there had been 1,504 cases of Covid-19 and twenty-two deaths, but now, in early June, only one person in the country remained sick. I listened to journalist Guyon Espiner interview Christiana Figueres, who chaired the United Nations meeting that led to the 2015 Paris Agreement. The global lockdown, she said, had led to a drop in carbon emissions that is projected to reach 8 per cent by the end of 2020, more than the 7.6 per cent per annum needed to reach our Paris Agreement goal to halve carbon emissions by 2030. But it's not good news, she said. 'The drop in emissions has come at a very, very high human cost. We have lost thousands of lives. We have lost millions of livelihoods. That is not the way we are planning on decarbonising the economy.' What we need, she continued, is 'a drop in emissions and an *increase* in the quality of life of the human population. So this is almost getting to the right destination with absolutely the wrong path.'

Can we now treat climate change with the same urgency that we felt in trying to manage Covid-19? asked Espiner. Given the trillions of dollars that are now being committed to economic recovery, we have to, said Figueres.

'We thought this was the decisive decade for climate change,' she said. 'No. Forget it. This is it. Those ten years that we thought we had have now been shrunk, I would say, to anywhere between three to eighteen months. *C'est tout*. Because by the end of those eighteen months all the decisions, and most of the allocations of the recovery packages, will have been made.' But it's not just climate change we have to respond to, she said; four global crises have collided: an acute health crisis has come on top of the climate crisis, an inequality crisis and an acute oil price crisis. We have to converge the solutions to these crises, she said, with policies and injections of capital that address them all at the same time, 'because sequentially addressing them will only get us out of one frying pan and into a raging fire.' Economic recovery packages must be focused on initiatives that are clean, green, lead to more social inclusion and build the health resilience of both humans and the planet, she said.

There were two other guests on the podcast – New Zealand's Parliamentary Commissioner for the Environment Simon Upton and the head of the United Nations Development Programme Achim Steiner – and each spoke from a different perspective, but they seemed in agreement when they talked about the need for multilateral cooperation, collaboration, fairness, transparency, solidarity . . . Perhaps what they were talking about was kindness. Kindness on a global scale – not just for each other, but for the planet, and everything on it.

The track wound down the hill through the pines.

We had managed to crush Covid-19 in New Zealand but around the world the virus was raging and people were getting angry. Globally, there were now 6.6 million cases of Covid-19 and 389,000 deaths and there was talk of a second wave of Covid-19 in the northern hemisphere. I had become acutely conscious of how privileged I was to live in an island nation with a sensible leader and a populace who – mostly – trust scientists and care for each other. Things felt positive here, but what about the rest of the world? Could we do it? Could we use this period of upheaval and unrest to segue into a better world? A better world for *everyone*? We have to, I thought. And I felt hopeful about the future because it's the only way I know how to survive.

I was nearly home.

On the track above the field there was a new embellishment to the orange sign.

Someone had used marker pen on paper, and a mass of sticky tape, to cover the words STOP and DIE so the sign now read PREPARE TO BE KIND. ■

THE DRAGON'S DEN

Tim Flannery

I was carrying my five-year-old son on my shoulders, watching Komodo dragons doze in the heat of a tropical afternoon. Covered in knobbly scales and dust and with saliva dripping from their jaws, they are formidable, crocodile-like reptiles, up to 3.5 metres long and weighing as much as ninety kilograms. I walked among them as they lay clustered in groups of three or four, seemingly imperturbable in the scattered shade offered by the scanty trees on Indonesia's Rinca island. With poor hearing and even worse sight, they seemed like the most hapless of predators. Then I tripped on a cobble, and my son began to cry. Instantly, every dragon sprang to life, their great forked tongues flickering, questing. They turned as one and strode rapidly towards us. But when I quieted my son, the giant lizards fell back into a torpor – as though I had turned off a switch.

Before humans arrived some 45,000 years ago, Australia was home to a diverse megafauna, creatures that weighed more than forty-five kilograms, including the megalania, a gigantic relative of the Komodo dragon that grew up to five metres long and weighed half a tonne, as well as the Komodo dragon itself. The megalania was Australia's top land predator and almost certainly fed upon the largest marsupials, while the Komodo took smaller megafaunal species.

Long extinct on the Australian mainland, and today surviving only on the island of Flores and its satellites in Nusa Tenggara, Indonesia, Komodo dragons are the last surviving Australian land-based predatory megafauna. Forty-five thousand years ago they roamed northern Australia and islands to the north, all the way to Flores. Today's Komodos kill goats, deer and water buffalo, all of which have been recently introduced to Flores and other nearby islands. As an Australian palaeontologist obsessed with understanding what my continent was like before extinction robbed it of its megafauna, Komodo dragons have an enduring fascination.

A continent that has lost its megafauna is a profoundly impoverished place. Much of the challenge and excitement of life is gone, as well as the environmental dynamism stimulated by browsing, grazing and predation on a gigantic scale. Just imagine the Australian inland with herds of rhino-sized diprotodon, as well as other gigantic marsupials, being preyed on by marsupial lions and Komodo dragons. Large predators and herbivores are landscape architects, capable of turning forest into woodland or even grassland through their various interactions with other flora and fauna. But in addition to these large-scale changes, they can create intricately varied habitats for smaller species through vegetation disturbance, seed dispersal and the moving of nutrients across landscapes.

The introduction of alien megafauna by the Europeans has been one of many ways in which ecological systems have been degraded, along with colonial farming practices and other extractive industries like logging and mining. And in recent decades, the climate has been changing. As Australians struggle to limit the damage from these changes, it's vital that we understand what Australia was like before its original megafauna was lost. We may even find that restoring its few banished but surviving megafaunal species, like the Komodo dragon, might help limit degradation of its ecosystems.

M y fascination with Australia's prehistoric past is deep. While still a teenager, I accompanied a scientific expedition into what is referred to as the 'dead heart' of Australia – the Lake Eyre basin. We were looking for fossils, and for days we traversed a landscape of muted pastels (so different from its name, the 'Red Centre') – sand dunes, parched bushes and salt lakes. The geological memory of a continent is stored in layers of rock. Most continents have very good geological memories, the evidence of the past packed in abundant layers, but Australia is the exception – a forgetful land whose tectonic lethargy has resulted in a great geological amnesia. Yet occasionally, like an elderly relative whose memories of childhood can be startlingly vivid, Australia's scant geological recall can spring into focus, bringing a long-lost world to life.

In this land without streams, beside a salt lake we found something unusual: rounded pebbles. I set to work with a mattock. After digging down fifty centimetres into the acrid, black mud of the lake's margin, I encountered a layer of grey clay. I pulled a piece from the mattock blade and sniffed it. The sweet smell of humus – the scent of rainforest – filled my nostrils. Plucking a mummified leaf from the clay, I bent it between my fingers and watched as it hardened and crumbled in the desert air. Ten million years ago, this leaf had fallen to the floor of a vanished rainforest. It was an unforgettable moment. Ever since, I've had a thirst for a sensory understanding of Australia as it was during the Ice Age (2.5 million to 45,000 years ago), after it had dried out during the Pliocene, and its interior was home to a host of lumbering marsupials, reptiles and flightless birds.

A few years after my expedition to the Lake Eyre basin, I excavated a deposit of megafaunal bones in western Victoria that was more than 50,000 years old. I remember my trowel slicing into thick black mud and revealing the surface of a massive bone the colour of mahogany. I realised I was the first to see anything of this creature since its demise. Once it was at the lab I discovered it was the thigh bone of a gigantic grey kangaroo that must have weighed 200 kilograms – twice the weight of any grey kangaroo that exists today. Nearby, I found a collarbone from the same species, bearing the tooth marks of a marsupial lion, and felt the sudden, electric thrill of connecting with the drama of life tens of thousands of years ago: my hand was where the mouth of a mysterious predator had been, tearing into its meal.

The marks on the bone took the form of long gouges. Strangely for predators, marsupial lions lacked canines. Instead they had blade-like premolars suitable for slicing flesh from bones. Just how they killed remained a mystery until claw marks found on the walls of caves on the Nullarbor Plain – a vast limestone plateau where the vegetation today grows no higher than the human knee – revealed that they had great, sheathed 'thumb claws' on their forelimbs. The stash of bones I uncovered proved to be the remains of a marsupial lion feast, 11 per cent of which bore the lion's distinctive premolar marks – the highest incidence of remains with these marks yet reported. The discovery showed me that it was possible to put flesh on the bones of Australia's deep past.

Around sixty species of large to gigantic marsupials, reptiles and birds are classified as Australia's megafauna. The largest, at around three tonnes in weight, was the wombat-shaped diprotodon. Australia's equivalent of the much larger African elephant, it roamed the arid inland in herds, consuming the twiggy browse of desert bushes and trees. The diprotodon's huge head was mostly filled with air (the skull being riddled with great sinuses) and its brain was barely the size of a human fist. It must have been dull-witted and, given its infertile environment, slow to reproduce.

Unique among the continents, Australia had very few species of grazing megafauna. Most of its marsupial giants were browsers, feeding off trees or the kinds of desiccated bushes where I had camped in the Lake Eyre basin as a teenager. Among the most abundant were several dozen kinds of short-faced kangaroos, the largest of which weighed a quarter of a tonne. Most of these creatures were the ecological equivalents of deer and antelope on other continents. But some were very odd indeed, with skulls and teeth superficially similar to those of *australopithecines* (extinct relatives of humans). I imagine a furry, three-metre-tall creature with a face like an apeman, mounted on a kangaroo's body, with powerful hopping legs and long arms tipped with two elongated, clawed digits used to pull branches within reach of their lips.

Other megafauna were equally odd-looking, including a short-trunked marsupial sloth that may have fed on bark, a hippo-like relative of the wombat that lurked in rivers and lakes, and a carnivorous kangaroo the size of a cougar. Among the most perplexing of the extinct marsupials are the tree-climbing kangaroos of the interior. Today, seventeen species of tree kangaroo survive in the tropical rainforests of New Guinea and Australia's north-east. They are among the most spectacular of the surviving marsupials, one species resembling a miniature giant panda, while another has blue eyes and bright yellow stripes running down its back. My PhD involved research on kangaroo ankle bones, and I had the privilege of discovering and naming the very first extinct tree kangaroo to become known to science. *Bohra paulae*'s leg bones, which were the size of a female orangutan's, had been found in a cave in New South Wales, but had lain unrecognised in a museum drawer for 150 years. I still recall the disbelief of many of my colleagues at the idea that a gigantic tree-climbing kangaroo once inhabited Australia's dry inland.

More recently, the remains of two smaller species of tree kangaroo have been found in caves on the Nullarbor Plain. Fossilised snails found with these bones suggest that the Nullarbor Plain was as dry as it is today when its tree-climbing kangaroos were alive. Despite its aridity, it seems that the Nullarbor must once have been covered in arid-adapted trees which are now locally, if not entirely, extinct. The find reveals how very little we know about the nature of Australia when its megafauna thrived. Indeed, astonishing new species of extinct Australian megafauna are still coming to light.

Around the time Australia's marsupial giants became extinct 45,000 years ago, the continent also lost a number of smaller species, including the giant megapode (a relative of the chicken that lays its eggs in mounds of rotting vegetation and leaves them to hatch without brooding) and a small, primitive wombat that might have resembled a porcupine. Other species that also became extinct on the Australian mainland left relatives that survived on offshore islands, including a half-metre-tall, probably flightless coucal (*Centropus maximus* – a member of the cuckoo family), whose nearest living relative is the splendid sixty-four-centimetre-long violaceous coucal of the Bismarck Archipelago, north of New Guinea.

New Guinea itself provided refuge for another megafaunal giant: the long-beaked echidnas of the genus *Zaglossus* are the world's largest egg-laying mammals, reaching a metre in length and weighing up to seventeen kilograms. Australia's surviving echidna is less than a quarter the weight. The bones of *Zaglossus*-like creatures have been found in sediments in eastern Australia, but the species vanished there along with the rest of the megafauna 45,000 years ago. Perhaps long-beaked echidnas survived in New Guinea because its dense and extensive rainforests provided a refuge from human hunting.

Meeting a long-beaked echidna face to face is unforgettable. I first encountered them in 1981, high on Mount Albert Edward, on my first expedition to New Guinea when I was still a doctoral student. The chilly alpine grasslands were pitted with holes from where they had inserted their long beaks into the earth to feed on worms, but the creatures remained hidden, being exceedingly difficult to track in the impenetrable scrub that surrounds the grasslands. When I finally saw one I was astonished by its long black fur, which hid the spines. Their beak-like faces are devoid of expression, yet they are highly intelligent, having brains that are the largest and most complex of any Australian land-based vertebrate. After caring for one for weeks, I deposited it in a wildlife sanctuary. When I visited years later it inserted its long snout into my boot and tickled my toes with its tongue. I got the distinct feeling that the creature had fond memories of me.

But the most astonishing survivor is surely the Komodo dragon. Why should this gigantic predator have survived only on small islands at the very north-western limit of its distribution? Flores and its satellites are unusual in that they are also home to a giant rat weighing around two kilograms which, like the Komodo dragon, is something of a living fossil. More famously, Flores was also once home to the hobbit (*Homo floresiensis*). The ancestors of this tiny hominin, which was the size of a three-year-old child, smaller than my son sitting on my shoulders, reached Flores around 800,000 years ago. Back then, they resembled *Homo erectus* and were presumably similar in size to ourselves. But a million years of island solitude does strange things to any beast, and isolated on Flores, the hobbits dwarfed to survive. Yet they remained able hunters who probably exterminated the giant land tortoises that roamed Flores prior to their arrival; and scraps left at campsites reveal that they could kill the newborns of the pygmy elephants that shared their island home. Doubtless they also hunted juvenile Komodo dragons and giant rats; yet they did not drive these species to extinction.

Modern humans reached Flores around the same time they reached Australia. They were more able hunters than the hobbits and probably exterminated both them and the island's pygmy elephants. But the Komodo dragon and giant rat survived, perhaps because coexisting with the hobbit had made them wary enough of upright apes that they were not sitting ducks for *Homo sapiens*.

The cause of the loss of Australia's grandest, fiercest and most intriguing species around 45,000 years ago continues to be debated. Ten times over the past million years the globe has gone from icehouse to greenhouse conditions. At the coldest of times, the areas of Australia that are west of the Great Dividing Range were all but devoid of trees, and much of the centre lacked vegetation altogether. Cyclonic winds – with the eye of the cyclone situated over Uluru, known by colonials as Ayers Rock – drove fields of Sahara-like sand dunes across 80 per cent of the continent. With the sea level 120 metres lower than today, New Guinea and Tasmania united with Australia to form a land surface of 10 million square kilometres known as Meganesia, the margins of which provided humid refuges. Paradoxically, these cold, dry periods also saw the inland rivers and lakes fill with water, probably due to reduced evaporation. Then, during brief warm periods, the sea rose and the forests regrew westwards. And through all these fluctuations, Australia's megafauna survived.

The giants only became extinct when the first humans arrived in Australia, around 45,000 years ago. Humans arrived much later in the Americas, around 13,000 years ago, and that is when American megafauna disappeared: forty-five species in North America, and a staggering fifty-eight species in South America. Much later, just after William the Conqueror crossed the English Channel, the Māori arrived in New Zealand, at which point the moa, a large, flightless bird similar to the emu, began to vanish from New Zealand's forests. So it appears that, in whatever era it happens, the arrival of people is bad news for big animals. Scientists are only just beginning to understand how profoundly the disappearance of these great creatures impacted ecosystems and biodiversity. There is only one continent humans never arrived in – Africa – because that is where we evolved. Consequently, Africa is the only continent to have retained a diverse megafauna and to have incurred relatively few (only eight) megafaunal extinctions. Co-evolving with humans gave African animals the chance to develop strategies of evasion and self-defence.

I have often tried to imagine my way onto the raft that must have carried the first humans to Australia. They would have been expert big mammal hunters, for the campsites of their ancestors are full of the bones of large, fierce mammals. And over the millennia their prey had either found ways to cope with them, or became extinct. If the first humans in Australia were anything like modern hunters they would have had their charms and prayers to the ancestors for a successful hunt. How surprised they must have been when they met their first diprotodon. The diprotodon, whose predators were crocodiles and Komodo dragon-like lizards, would not have seen humans as a threat. As if bid by the ancestors to give its life to the hunter, it would have stood there, unperturbed, until a spear pierced its vitals. That first Australian hunter must have felt like a god himself, or at least one abundantly blessed by them. And surely the experience of successfully hunting one great beast after another, almost effortlessly, must have been intoxicating.

As has been said, Australia's megafauna was not only naive, but small-brained and slow to reproduce. Even the hunting of just a few individuals in such a population can, over time, lead to its extinction. In the 45,000 years since their arrival, Australia's Indigenous peoples have become accomplished conservationists. But when newly arrived, they could not have anticipated the extreme sensitivity of Australia's megafauna to extinction through hunting.

In my view, not one convincing depiction of any of the megafaunal species that vanished 45,000 years ago survives in rock art. The extinctions may have just been too swift to have been recorded, or perhaps the mobile, frontier life of the first Australians precluded artistic endeavours. Whatever the case, we must look elsewhere, sometimes in the oddest places, for clues as to how Australia's megafauna lived.

Australia is renowned for its invasive species – colonial introductions like the red fox, rabbit and blackberry that wreak havoc on the Australian environment – but it is less well appreciated that some Australians have become pests overseas. One of the most pernicious is *Acacia cyclops*, a shrubby wattle native to Australia's south-west that is now overrunning much of South Africa. In Australia nothing feeds on it and it is entirely unexceptional. But in South Africa it is browsed upon by small antelopes, and when they consume its leaves it does something very strange: the outer branches die off and curve upwards and inwards to form a basket of harsh, dry twigs. From the centre of this protective basket emerges a strong, central stem which does not branch until it reaches a height of several metres above the ground. This genetically determined behaviour defends it against herbivores, perhaps some long-extinct short-faced kangaroo.

A similar strategy is deployed by the leopardwood tree, *Flindersia maculosa*. One of Australia's most beautiful trees, with mottled bark and a graceful canopy, it thrives on good inland soil, where it can reach a height of ten metres. Seeing a leopardwood grove, you could be forgiven for thinking that the younger plants, consisting of a great tangle of spiny branches, belong to an entirely different species. Only once they exceed diprotodon head height does a strong, central stem with spineless branches emerge, carrying wispy, pale green leaves safely out of diprotodon grazing reach. It seems strange to me that, for over 40,000 years now, the leopardwood has maintained its defences against the ghosts of browsing megafauna.

The ancient forests of Australia's warm periods were not like today's forests. A vital ingredient was lacking: fire. Fire so dominates Australia's landscapes today that it is hard to imagine the continent without it. But sediment cores taken from lakes in northern Australia reveal that fire took hold only after the megafauna vanished, when uneaten vegetation accumulated, creating a mass of dry tinder that was a magnet for fire. In the world of efficient marsupial stomachs, only spinifex, heathlands and some eucalypt-dominated forests were prone to fire.

Indigenous peoples tend to work the land of Australia not with the plough but with the firestick. Burning in specific patterns and at precise times, they unlock resources, promoting seeding of grasses and forbs, and attracting herbivores to fresh growth. Perhaps their ancestors set fires for similar purposes. The habitats that suffered most from the human practice of burning were without doubt the dry rainforests of the inland. Dominated by araucarias (of the hoop pine and monkey puzzle tree family), vines and dry-season deciduous trees like bottle trees, these forests were exceptionally diverse and widespread before the firestick. Today mere remnants survive, protected by thickets of fire-resistant brigalow or other fire inhibitors, like rocks. Today the last brigalow-protected remnants of the dry rainforest are threatened, for brigalow grows on fertile soils and poor law enforcement permits illegal land clearing on a horrendous scale.

The burning of the dry, seasonally deciduous rainforest that once covered northern Australia may have changed the climate. The forests transpired water vapour, allowing rains to reach further inland, filling Lake Eyre. But after the firestick, eucalypts, which transpire far less moisture, took over. A distinct boundary developed between the few surviving patches of wet rainforest and the fire-promoting eucalypt forests. Fire bared the soil, eroding it, filling the estuaries with mud and promoting the growth of mangroves.

Grasses benefited from the burning and spread rapidly. It's no accident that Australia's largest surviving marsupials are all grazers. Perhaps more surprising is that they are also considerably smaller than their ancestors. Two of the largest are the eastern and western grey kangaroos. Their remains, abundant in the fossil record, reveal that in megafaunal times the largest individuals were twice the size of a contemporary grey kangaroo. Male grey kangaroos only get to have sex, if they are lucky, in the last year of their life. By then the most well fed and genetically blessed have reached such a size that they can drive off other males, ensuring that their genes are passed on. But human hunters invariably focus on the largest individuals, and the relentless elimination of large male grey kangaroos before they could pass on their genes may have reversed this selective process, replacing it with selection for early-maturing dwarfs who managed to pass on their genes before becoming a meal for humans.

As Australia's ecosystems destabilise in the face of feral species and climate change, some scientists and landowners are asking what can be done. The issue of fire is becoming urgent, with the summer 2019–20 megafires burning 20 per cent of the nation's forests. It is very early days, but rewilding, as is practised in Europe, may be worth considering. This would involve restoring functional, complex ecosystems to Australia that include megafauna. But there is a great problem here because Australia's diprotodons, along with most of its megafauna, became extinct so long ago that not even fragments of their DNA remain. If Australia is to rewild – if it is to regenerate its dying landscape and stimulate biological complexity and dynamism again – it will have to focus on its few surviving megafauna, and perhaps species from other continents, to do so. This might include some carefully managed populations of feral species, like water buffalo, donkeys and camels, to remove combustible plant matter.

But what of the Komodo dragon? Australia's north is infested with feral pigs, donkeys and water buffalo – introduced species wreaking havoc on ecosystems. How would the impact of these pests alter if Komodo dragons were lurking in dense vegetation, keeping them away from delicate ecosystems like swamps and rocky knolls?

Perhaps more complex vegetation patterns – creating habitats for smaller species and limiting the opportunity for fire to spread – might be re-established. There might be risks to finding out whether the ecosystem would benefit from the introduction of Komodo dragons. They have an exaggerated reputation as a danger to humans. But Australians have become used to living with crocodiles and great white sharks, not to mention venomous snakes, spiders and jellyfish. I think we could cope.

But what of the impact on Australia's wildlife. After all, Komodo dragons have been absent from Australia for 45,000 years, and some native mammals might have lost their wariness of them. Having watched how cautious wallabies are around goannas and crocodiles, however, I don't think that this is a great risk. We must also ask whether Australia has everything Komodo dragons require to complete their life cycle. Komodos nest in the mounds of megapodes and Australia is home to three megapode species, whose mounds could be used by Komodo dragons to incubate their eggs.

After hatching, for the first two years of their life, young Komodos live in dead *Corypha* palms. These lofty trees fruit only once – a great inflorescence ejecting from the top of the trunk – and then they die. The upright trunks then rot and hollow out, providing both refuge and food for the baby dragons. Eventually, when they are large enough to avoid being eaten by their elders, the juveniles brave life on the ground. Fortunately, north-eastern Australia still has *Corypha* palms.

As I write, the last survivors of Australia's true megafauna lie lethargically in the shade on the islands off Flores, oblivious of their genetic significance and their potential for restoring ecological balance. And that is where many, I suspect, would argue they should remain. But I am being provocative here for a purpose. I think that long-lost natural processes could be rekindled by the return of this apex predator to its ancestral homeland of Australia. Were Australians willing, the Komodo dragons could instigate an experiment in rewilding that could result in the recovery of some of the lost ecology of Australia's glorious past. ■

Nate Duke

Projects Not Realized

Installation artists Christo and Jeanne-Claude
meant to cover miles of Arkansas headwaters
in silver canopies. Their axiomatic structure
would've dimmed sunlight in riparian biomes,
disrupted trout migrations, blocked the route
of wildlife to a high prairie's only water source,
eroded banks in parallel construction – the list
swells. In an alternate present, white rapids fade
as I float down the gorge on a blue plastic raft
and in the noon dark I miss my landing: a boulder
with a trailblaze and cairn on the beach. I'd meant
to camp there – with parachute cord and tarp
enough for shelter, I'd rest after the day's rowing
till the sunset melted on a lip of canyon. Instead,
I drift blind past that beach under one more
of the planet's smoke carpets. A parched cow elk
the artists didn't consult – practiced as she was
at scaling the canyon in a switchback of leaps –
lands on a canopy, rips its moorings, then falls
to the river in a silver-gray sack. I scull my raft
across the channel toward the sky museum
that's opened now above her grave, and pretend
I'm the docent – addressing tours of foam
with a drenched oar brandished at the sun.

© MATTHEW OATES
Purple emperor butterflies on fox scat, 2018

THE POSSIBILITY OF AN EMPEROR

Patrick Barkham

When I was growing up, the nearby wood loomed on the horizon, a domed, multi-tentacled thing, dropped upon an orderly patchwork of ploughed fields and tightly boxed hedgerows. It appeared to be an interloper in the English lowlands when the surrounding farmland was actually the conquering force.

Back then, Foxley was three miles from my boyhood home. It was our local wood, and another world. We used to go there in autumn for the fungi and falling leaves and in spring for the carpet of bluebells. But most exciting was high summer, when it drew a leaved curtain over itself and Dad and I would go in search of the purple emperor.

'[T]hat dark prince, the oakwood haunting thing / Dyed with blue burnish like the mallard's wing' – John Masefield's poem soared through my dreams as a boy. If I rested my pictorial guide to British butterflies on its spine, the pages fell open at the emperor. A photograph showed the male of the species, perched on a spray of oak, wings pointed like a shark's fin, shimmering iridescent purple. This spirit of the woods has captivated generations of naturalists but it bewitched me because *it was not there.*

The distribution map in my 1980s field guide showed blotches of red over Hampshire, Surrey, West Sussex, Oxfordshire and Buckinghamshire where the emperor flew. The rest of Britain, including our county, Norfolk, was white with the butterfly's absence. The purple emperor was understood to be a 'woodland' butterfly, and the red dots correlated with native broadleaved woodlands, places characterised by deciduous trees such as oak, ash, beech, elm and lime that had recolonised Britain after the last ice age. In most parts, such woods survived in pitiful fragments, remnants – it's widely believed – of the primordial forest that once covered our landscape. The emperor was rare, we thought then, because its kingdom had been decimated.

In the heart of Norfolk, Foxley had endured at just over 300 acres, the same size as a modest Norfolk family farm, for centuries. From the air, its square of forested land with a rectangular bite removed from one side was such an aberration – so dark and distinctive – that RAF pilots used it to navigate. This scrap was Norfolk's largest 'ancient woodland', defined as continually forested since at least 1600. But Foxley was far older than that. Its heavy clay soil was not easily cultivated and its trees had probably never been clear-felled. Certainly, by the Domesday Book of 1086 Foxley was a distinct wood, a place where domesticated pigs were released for 'pannage' to fatten up on fallen acorns. In the early Middle Ages it was managed as a deer park; later it was coppiced. Coppicing was first recorded in the Bronze Age, and involves the regular cutting back of trees and shrubs, such as oak, ash, willow, field maple, sweet chestnut and hazel, down to their base to stimulate the growth of multiple stems in place of a single large trunk – strong, flexible 'rods' that were used for making hurdles, stakes, tool handles, baskets and poles. Bigger 'standard' trees would be saved as timber for buildings and ships. As an indicator of its antiquity, Foxley contained both wild service trees and small-leaved limes, once-common native trees that became increasingly rare over the centuries because they were of no commercial value.

During the twentieth century, as the purple emperor vanished from East Anglia, Foxley became its last hiding place. One was spotted dashing through the wood in 1971. By my 80s childhood, the emperor was extinct in Norfolk. Or was it? I hoped, despite my field guide's pessimism, that it was possible the emperor could reside there.

In theory, Foxley offered this notoriously tricksy insect its ideal habitat: sallow (wild willow) and oak trees. Males took territorial positions high in prominent oaks like resting big cats, only emerging for percussive aerial engagements with fellow males for the possession of females but also with perceived 'rivals' such as dragonflies, blue tits and even passing kestrels or hobbies. Females, which lack the iridescent purple, skulked unseen in sallow, where they laid eggs and their caterpillars fed.

If such a creature was still hiding in Foxley, I knew it would be hard to spot. The emperor did not deign to descend from its ethereal realm to sip from flowers like an ordinary butterfly but, if undisturbed, might settle to probe for the minerals found in fox scat, muddy puddles and other execrable treats. Ordinarily, it moved so fast that most might only glimpse a dark silhouette as it flashed high across a forest ride.

Every July in the 80s, Dad and I parked on the lane outside the wood and entered via a new Forestry Commission ride, a broad grassy track that provided access to a recent conifer plantation. Foxley cocooned us from the outside world, swallowing all sight and sound of the conventional countryside. Dad, an environmental scientist, explained how this was once a bewilderingly diverse place. He had produced a diagram of Foxley's compartments in the 1970s: oak, bracken and bluebells; oak and larch; birch and brambles; alder coppice; lime coppice; aspen-ash-hazel coppice. Back then, each section had its own scent, he said, each its own distinctive sound. By the 1980s, however, Foxley had been corralled into two simplified woods: an old wood mostly made up of what foresters call 'derelict' coppice, and a new conifer plantation of tightly packed neatly rowed ranks of lodgepole pine from the American Northwest, grand fir from northern California, spruce from Norway and Scots pine from Europe. This global, industrial wood was dark and silent, and not just in midsummer. Its silence was not the cocooning of the trees but of obliteration – no birds singing, no insects humming, not even the clap of a wood pigeon's wings.

We would turn left, into the overgrown coppice, where the grassy ride narrowed. Hazel ballooned beneath larger oak 'standards' although even then grand oaks had long since been removed. In midsummer, the woodland floor was a gloomy carpet of dog's mercury: my dad had measured the light levels here and found them to be 3 per cent of those in the open air. Honeysuckle threw plaited ropes like Rapunzel's hair through the darkness, although its vitality was dwindling. It used to be so thick that a forester who worked in the wood told me it had once twined around the axle of a tractor being driven through the trees and held it fast. Coppicing had ceased in Foxley, the canopy had closed in, and we admired the white admirals that glided past, the only butterfly that tolerated such crepuscular summer conditions. Of the emperor, there was no trace.

Foxley Wood may have been at least 1,000 years old and the largest ancient woodland in Norfolk but it was a wholly unexceptional memorial to an age of extinction – its declining diversity a fate shared by almost all ancient woodlands in Britain.

I had always been told that the purple emperor was rare because old woods were rare. In the last century, they had vanished, alongside many other insects, plants and birds, because of the loss of the traditional coppicing practices that created light, dappled shade and complex, varied habitats. Before coppicing, however, how did all these species survive? What did the original 'wildwood' look like? The dark, enclosed forest of our imaginings may be far from the landscape that prevailed in Britain before humans made an impression. The idea that, say, a purple emperor could have once flown from Land's End to John o'Groats over an unceasing canopy of trees is debunked by Oliver Rackham, the pre-eminent chronicler of British woodlands. 'It is debatable whether "virgin forest" or "primaeval forest", unaffected by mankind, exists anywhere in the world, or whether it is one of those phantoms, like "primitive man", that haunt the scholarly imagination,' he wrote.

We no longer believe that dense woodland was once the natural state. Before humans reshaped the land, trees were constantly disrupted by storms, landslides on steep hillsides, diseases and insect infestations, as well as by the browsing and disturbance of wild herbivores. Dutch ecologist Frans Vera, the author of *Grazing Ecology and Forest History*, has repopulated historic landscapes with armies of aurochs (wild cattle), tarpans (wild horses), bison, boar, beavers and deer that would have browsed on leaves, shoots and emerging saplings, brought down mature trees by gnawing their bark, and snapped off their branches. These animals were the first to coppice our woods; their actions were why our native trees responded so well to our axes and billhooks. Their disturbance would have created a more open treescape, a mosaic of wood pasture with giant trees, grazing 'lawns', groves and thickets of scrub; where no clear boundary existed between wood and wider countryside.

That the purple emperor is traditionally viewed as a creature of ancient oak woodlands, is, according to Matthew Oates, a naturalist who has dedicated his life to the study of this confounding butterfly, because it was in old woodlands that we looked for them. He says the emperor is, essentially, a butterfly of damp clay lands, where grows both pedunculate oak and sallow, its foodplant. The oak requires sunlight, and cannot naturally regenerate in dark woods. Sallow, a fast-growing bushy tree, thrives in damp areas but is shaded out within mature woodland. According to Oates, the emperor's caterpillars seem to thrive on heterogeneity: of topography, microclimates, and complex varieties of sallow, and sunny and shady conditions. For centuries, this butterfly would have lived outside what we regard as woodland, along riverine landscapes, on commons and on wood pasture, a more open treescape, like the landscapes of the distant past, which combines mature open-grown trees and glades grazed, browsed and disturbed by either wild animals or domesticated livestock.

Old maps show Foxley's boundaries – fixed by humans – have remained unchanged over the centuries. Its shape on a 1797 map is almost identical to today. What has been transformed since then is the surrounding land. The 1797 map depicts vast commons and open field systems. Enclosure – consolidating village farmland into individual, private farms – caused the loss of huge areas of communal grazing. In earlier times, sallow branches had many uses, not only as rods in medieval wattle and daub walls but as spring fodder for cattle before the grass began to grow. As farming intensified following enclosure, overgrown hedges, boggy scraps of woodland and other sallow-rich habitats convivial for the emperor were excised. By the twentieth century, the butterfly had retreated to woods where oaks and remnants of sallow managed to cling on.

Once confined there, the emperor was further emasculated by the revolution within British woods. Surveying the sinking of ships importing timber during the First World War, politicians realised that even the coal-fired industrial age required timber for coal-mine pit props and, with barely 10 per cent tree cover, the country was perilously dependent on foreign imports. The Forestry Commission, founded in 1919, grew a strategic reserve of timber on cheap land – heaths, poor farmland and, after the Second World War, ancient woodland. In a rational world, argued Rackham, a woodland would be the last location for a new plantation, requiring the arduous removal of all competing natural trees. He called 1950 to 1975 the 'locust years', when native flora and fauna were devoured by politicians' and foresters' hunger for monocultures of non-native conifers. At that time, the emperor's foodplant, sallow, was considered a 'weed'. Meanwhile, over the same century, coppicing, mimicking the effect of browsing animals, almost died out. Surviving broadleaved woods became dark and denuded of species. Sallow, which had thrived on coppice edges, was shaded out as trees closed in. It was not just the emperor that suffered: sallow is our third most important tree for moths (after birch and oak), supporting 108 moth species.

During this period, Foxley, and most other old woodlands, saw biodiversity disappear. As well as the emperor, Foxley was once home to an abundance of fritillaries. The chequered golden brown butterflies were perfectly adapted to the chiaroscuro light of a woodland in midsummer, their caterpillars feeding on violets which flowered in profusion in the glades created by coppicing. Silver-washed, high brown, dark green, small pearl-bordered and pearl-bordered fritillaries all once bred in Foxley. The last of these was known as 'the woodman's friend' because it so rapidly colonised the sunny glades created by freshly cut coppice. All vanished from Foxley, and hundreds of other British woods, during the twentieth century.

While childhood walks in Foxley were an uncomplicated pleasure for me, for Dad and others who experienced the butterfly-filled glades of the 50s, it was a place of loss. The wood was given a national designation as a Site of Special Scientific Interest in 1954, in theory giving the Nature Conservancy, the government's conservation watchdog, the power to ensure that it was managed for wildlife. Despite this, Foxley was leased to the Forestry Commission and more than a third was cleared for conifers. Foxley's old trees were sprayed from the air with 245T, a now-banned herbicide related to the infamous Agent Orange of the Vietnam War. As there was no demand for firewood, all but the largest oaks were dragged into pyres and burned.

Dad moved to Norfolk in the aftermath of this tragedy. In the 1970s, Foxley became a research site for his students and Dad encouraged Norfolk Wildlife Trust (NWT) to buy Foxley. By the 80s, as the new conifers struggled on Foxley's heavy clays, the Forestry Commission's lease was returned to its previous owners, who used the wood as a pheasant shoot. NWT tried to acquire it, but the sale was a fraught process. I remember watching Dad on the local television news. He seemed flustered. The report suggested that the owners were being 'forced' by conservation bureaucrats to sell their treasured wood. That week at school, the son of Foxley's gamekeeper said my dad was pushing his dad out of a job; the land-labouring man's son versus the namby-pamby conservationist's son. I felt for the first time what most middle-class conservationists are often reminded of: we don't own the land, nor do we authentically inhabit it as the classes above and below say they do, so how dare we lay claim to it? Dad told me that NWT offered the gamekeeper a job as Foxley's warden but the gamekeeper decided that working for a conservation charity wasn't for him. The trust completed the purchase of Foxley in the early 1990s. During that decade, Dad moved away from deforested Norfolk for good. I relocated as well, to university and then to work in big cities. During our absence, over the next two decades, Foxley Wood was transformed.

Coniferisation may have given plantation forestry a bad name among conservationists but we live in a new age of tree planting. Placing a native tree in the soil is an act of beneficence, 'a ritual of atonement', wrote Richard Mabey, who is old enough to remember the government-sponsored 'Plant a Tree in '73' campaign. Planting trees is political catnip, an altruistic act and a declaration of faith in the future. Politicians and big businesses are keen to tell the world how many they are planting. Donald Trump shuns global climate accords but in 2020 the American president signed up to 1t.org, the World Economic Forum's campaign to plant a trillion trees. British prime minister Boris Johnson has been an enthusiastic tree planter since his London mayoral days, when he pledged 10,000 new street trees and planted one by wielding a spade from over his shoulder like a pickaxe. His government's commitment – to plant 30 million new trees each year – is outbid by every other political party. Labour has promised 2 billion by 2040. (In the year up to March 2019, the country managed approximately 22 million, many of them conifers, mostly in Scotland.) These aspirations are dwarfed by those of other nations. Ethiopia claims to have planted 353 million in one day in 2019. The Chinese government says it has planted more than 66 billion new trees in the country's north since its Great Green Wall programme to repel the Gobi Desert began in 1978. It wants billions more, aiming to increase forest cover from around 22 per cent to 30 per cent by 2050.

These grand afforestation targets are proceeding alongside their polar opposite: deforestation. The planet lost 3.8 million hectares of tropical primary forest in 2019, an area almost the size of Switzerland. This loss shows no sign of slowing: it has continued at a similar rate for every year this century, apart from an even greater spike in 2016 and 2017. In the first four months of 2020, Amazon deforestation increased by 55 per cent compared to the same period the previous year, as loggers and ranchers took advantage of the coronavirus crisis. In Britain, in 2020, the builders of HS2, the high-speed railway between London and Birmingham, are bulldozing fragments of the remaining fragments of thirty-two ancient woodlands. Meanwhile, many native saplings planted on surrounding fields in 'compensation' have died through want of watering. In a couple of woods, HS2 aims to relocate ancient woodland soils to new sites, but it is farcical to suggest this could replicate the character of an ancient woodland with its incredibly rich and undisturbed subterranean life of roots, bulbs, fungi, invertebrates and microorganisms. Planting a tree is more useful to late capitalism than leaving a wood alone, or allowing trees to regenerate naturally, because it is a more easily measurable act.

Trees are planted for many reasons: to collect grants, to make money, for greenwashing, landscaping, legacy building, vanity. But the prime motivation for the current planting frenzy is a conviction that trees are a balm for the climate emergency. Tropical deforestation has caused almost a third of anthropogenic warming, but the opposite is also true: add forest, and we can remove carbon from the atmosphere. This 'natural climate solution' is safe, proven and affordable. Trees do not pollute; they create sustainable jobs via timber and tourism, protect water supplies and combat desertification. Britain's Committee on Climate Change, an expert body that advises the government, calculates that the country requires an extra 32,000 hectares of woodland – roughly 50 million trees – every year for thirty years to meet its legally binding target of net zero carbon emissions by 2050. According to the Intergovernmental Panel on Climate Change, adding forests could store around one quarter of the atmospheric carbon required to limit global warming to 1.5°C. But this would require a lot of trees, right now: a new forest the size of the UK (or Uganda) planted every year this decade.

The science of counting trees, and calculating the carbon they sequester, is complicated. Simon Lewis, professor of global change science at University College London and the University of Leeds, examined the restoration commitments of forty-three countries pledging to reforest nearly 300 million hectares of degraded land under the Bonn Challenge. Lewis, a dynamic, mop-haired academic who spent his youth as a protester attempting to save trees and woods from being bulldozed by the Conservatives' 'Roads for Prosperity' building programme of the 1990s, found that if natural forests were grown across the entire Bonn Challenge target area, 42 billion tonnes of carbon would be sequestered; if plantation monocultures were grown instead, just 1 billion tonnes of carbon would be stored. Unfortunately, nearly half of the land pledged to trees is to be plantations such as eucalyptus or rubber, fast-growing trees that are likely to be harvested every decade or so.

'There's quite a bit of either self-delusion or saying one thing to the public and doing another,' Lewis told me. 'If these plantations have a time horizon of say twenty years and you're counting the carbon sequestration over the years the trees are growing and you're claiming a carbon credit for that but then chopping down trees at the end and most of that carbon is going back into the atmosphere, we've got a real problem. We think we're removing carbon from the atmosphere in perpetuity but actually we're just part of the usual carbon cycle.'

In Britain, the drive for carbon sequestration is focused on planting conifers, which are quicker to sequester carbon than broadleaved trees because they grow faster. Twentieth-century coniferisation used cheap land, such as ancient woodland, which was disastrous for biodiversity. For this next boom, new forests must go on better, more expensive farmland. Ideally, they would rise on low-quality fields around cities, enhancing access to nature for urbanites. But there are fears that the mistakes of the locust years will be repeated: a recent planting of saplings in Cumbria resulted in outcry when it turned out the chosen site was an important orchid habitat. The new trees will have to be uprooted.

Sticking a tree in the ground costs money. It is grown in a nursery and usually transported by vehicle and sometimes ship – burning carbon. Often encased in a protective plastic tube and attached with a plastic tie to a tanalised wooden stake, it is introduced into alien soil as a sapling, or 'whip', lacking any mycelium, the dense subterranean network of mycorrhizal fungi that transfer nutrients to plants in the wild. A study has calculated that the carbon absorption of naturally regenerating British forest began at 0.6 tonnes of carbon per hectare per year, rising to 4.1 tonnes per hectare per year in maturity. This is less than a coniferous plantation, but a regenerating wood left in perpetuity (for sequestration and biodiversity) does not add emissions via forest management nor release emissions when wood is harvested. Why is natural regeneration not a more widely used, or tested, method of carbon sequestration? 'There are no grants to do it,' said Lewis bluntly. 'It's apparently so left field that it's not being done in very many places so it isn't really well studied.'

I can imagine the caustic response of Oliver Rackham to tree planting as an act of atonement or carbon sequestration. He called saplings 'gateposts with leaves'. Planting trees 'is no substitute for woodland conservation', he wrote not long before he died. And he rather majestically dismissed the idea of planting to solve the climate crisis: 'Exhorting people to plant trees to sequester carbon dioxide is like telling them to drink more to hold down rising sea level.' Even with a global effort, 'it is hardly likely that growing timber, which lasts a few decades, will balance the release of carbon accumulated in fossil fuels over hundreds of millions of years.'

'The easiest way to create a wood is to do nothing,' is the gospel according to Rackham. I returned to live in Norfolk in 2011, when my twins were born. Half asleep, we pushed our double buggy between Foxley's bluebells, imbibing the great green calm. In midsummer, we were startled by a large golden butterfly landing on the mauve head of a marsh thistle. A silver-washed fritillary! It had been extinct from Norfolk for forty years; gone from Foxley for seventy. Its reappearance was a moment of delight but no fluke. It was later confirmed that the species had rapidly recolonised the county. Global warming had quickened its arrival but it stayed because the wood had been transformed.

The Ordnance Survey still showed conifers across much of Foxley's slab of green. But the map marks were wrong. The conifers were gone. In their place stood a lush native English woodland, roiling with life. I walked a narrow ride filled with flying insects, like motes of dust in the new morning sunshine. Two speckled woods tumbled together through the dappled light. A four-spotted chaser patrolled the upper airspace. Chiffchaffs, willow warblers and blackcaps sang from the thickets. I noted the trees as I walked: guelder rose, dog rose, dogwood, sallow, hazel, blackthorn, hazel, sallow, field maple, ash. It was like the native hedgerow I had planted in my garden. But it had not been planted. This new forest had arisen entirely by itself.

A newcomer would never imagine this tumult of new life had been anything other than native woodland. To someone like me, who had missed a couple of decades in Foxley's long life, these pop-up trees were so instantaneous that they appeared more film set than forest. A wood moves through spring like a slow motion firework. Buds pop open. The floor colours with wood anemones followed by bluebells, then fills with sallow fluff; foxgloves strain upwards, leaves surge to the sun, light flares, shadows deepen. But I had never before witnessed a wood moving through the years like a firework, heaving, teeming and then exploding with an overpowering kaleidoscope of green.

Foxley had undergone what Norfolk Wildlife Trust called restoration. In the old wood, untouched by coniferisation, many of Foxley's areas of coppice were being cut again, on their traditional ten-year cycle. Then new trees, growing where the conifers had been, were willed by the wood, its seeds and its soil, where roots linked to that supportive subterranean network of mycorrhizal fungi. The Great Storm of 1987, which felled an estimated 15 million trees, first awakened foresters to the power of natural regeneration. But allowing a cleared wood to grow back without planting was still a relatively new idea when NWT acquired Foxley. Some suggested that the conifers, which all conservationists agreed should be removed to promote a more diverse, species-rich wood, should be replanted with native saplings. NWT's first warden at Foxley, John Milton, noted previous foresters' inefficient weeding of broadleaved saplings from coniferous rows. Many of these young natives had clung on. They, and the soil and the mycorrhizal fungi that supported them, were a ghost wood, waiting to step into the light. The first conifers were removed in 1995; other compartments were not cleared until the early 2000s. Some fencing was required to stop the four burgeoning wild deer species found in Foxley from nibbling the regenerating trees. The Forestry Commission helped fund operations. So did Milton, labouring each December to cut and sell off Norway spruce as Christmas trees.

In Foxley, as the forest flew back, so did its flowers. More than 350 flowering plants have been recorded in the wood: adder's tongue, herb Paris, early purple and greater butterfly orchids, moschatel, self-heal. The resurgent diversity of Foxley was analogous to the resilience of a whole, indivisible organism. If the wood was challenged, it could often fix the problem. After the damp summer of 2012, Foxley's current warden, Steve Collin, acquired the dubious honour of being the first person to find ash dieback in the wild, a fungal disease that damages ash trees. He first discovered the fungus, which originated in Asia, at Ashwellthorpe, another ancient wood, but soon identified it at Foxley too. 'In these compartments that were cleared of conifers we were a little worried about the over-dominance of ash. We're a bit less worried now,' said Collin wryly. We are scared of novel tree diseases, which are thriving with climate change and are also delivered to our door because of our desire to plant up the planet with globally traded nursery trees. But death was rejuvenation, opportunity. Every bit of dead tree was being exploited and devoured by bats, birds, insects and fungi. Each tree's absence – new light in the forest – was used too. Foxley's dying ashes were swiftly swallowed up, just as the victims of Dutch elm disease had disappeared before them.

This Catherine wheel of life spun disconcertingly quickly. The pace of change was overwhelming. After watching my garden hedge grow from centimetre-high saplings, I believed I possessed a realistic sense of what five years of growth looked like. Returning to Foxley in recent summers, I saw that my five was Foxley's two. In one coppiced section, one-year-old oaks reached my waist. The regenerating woodland was also a thicket of sallow. This pioneer tree was billowing across the damp clay. One sallow put on seventeen feet in a single year. If sallow was booming, could the purple emperor return too?

Allowing woods to grow themselves is hardly a radical idea. But each time I've encountered regeneration it has revealed the radical power of wild plants in wild soil. Toys Hill, on the North Downs, lost 98 per cent of its trees during the 110 mph winds of the Great Storm. Unusually, parts of the wood were allowed to regenerate – 90 per cent of private woodlands toppled elsewhere were replanted. Fallen beech was supplanted by a birch thicket. Within the thickets, half hidden by holly, were enormous moss-covered fallen trunks. It resembled an overgrown cemetery except many of these fallen giants were still alive. They shot up robust vertical limbs from their horizontal trunks, competing for sky with the upstart birches. Wind-toppled trees die more rarely than we imagine. As Rackham wrote, such trees 'call in question the assumption that the "normal" state of a tree is upright.'

I saw a different kind of natural regeneration in Glen Feshie, in the Cairngorms National Park, where willows, dog rose and blaeberries grew, and baby Scots pines poked their tiny fluffy heads above the heather beside the river. This scrubby scene did not look very Scottish. Our vision of the 'wild' Highlands – treeless expanses of glen and mountainside – is derived from an unusually high population of red deer. Since Victorian times, the prevailing model for landowners in the Scottish uplands is what naturalist Sir John Lister-Kaye calls 'the Balmoral triad' – hunting salmon, grouse and red deer. High populations of the last of these prevent the regeneration of native trees, particularly the succulent young Scots pines. Ecologists calculate that capping the red deer population at five per square kilometre in the wider landscape will allow trees to regenerate naturally; in many Highland regions, it is twenty. The 17,000 hectares of Glen Feshie are returning to a scrubby, frizzy-wooded state analogous to uplands in geographically comparable Norway because its owner, the Danish billionaire Anders Holch Povlsen, has reduced deer numbers. Such new land management is, at last, challenging the Victorian version of the Highlands that was assumed to be the perpetual way of things.

Rather than simply expand the reach of our 'woodland', we need to expand our idea of what woodland is. The purple emperor is wrongly seen as a 'woodland' butterfly because our notion of it, and woodland, is as denuded and lifeless as most British woods became during the twentieth century.

Land shapes our thinking. Its transformation changes our minds. The land that has most vividly revealed our limitations in recent years is Knepp in West Sussex, a 3,500-acre dairy farm that was given over to wild nature by its owners, Charlie Burrell and Isabella Tree. For twenty years, it has been lowland England's only example of rewilding, or wilding, whereby human intervention has been minimised except for the careful introduction of free-living herbivores such as longhorn cattle, Exmoor ponies and Tamworth pigs to mimic the grazing of extinct wild animals, and red and fallow deer.

Encountering Knepp for the first time, or any time in midsummer, is to be confronted by the explosive power of plants in soil liberated from human dominion. Blackthorn hedges have marched into fields. Wet meadows are filled with sallow thickets where turtle doves purr. Sunny glades are a tangle of flowering plants, their germination assisted by the indefatigable rootling of wild pigs. It is not a wood, nor farmland, nor like any corner of lowland England except in the eyes of the oldest of rural residents who may recall the abandoned acres of the 1930s Depression. As well as white storks and nightingales, visitors may encounter a naturalist sporting a tatty sun hat with a jay's feather tucked in a band of purple: Matthew Oates, our purple emperor specialist. And then they are certain to meet a purple emperor. The emperor, already living almost unseen at low density in the area, rapidly colonised Knepp's diverse sallow thickets. Male purple emperors dash around veteran hedgerow oaks, becoming inebriated on their sap runs; females lay eggs in the ample shade of the regenerating sallow. Oates, who considers Knepp to be 'New Age wood pasture' – ancient hedgerow trees, groves of pioneer species and grazing – has crowned it Britain's emperor capital. Recent summers have seen records smashed for this elusive insect: Oates recorded 2,500 individual sightings at Knepp during the summer of 2018; an enthusiastic lepidopterist might typically tot up 250 over a lifetime.

As Tree shows in *Wilding*, her account of the open-ended, open-minded Knepp 'experiment', Britain's simplified countryside has imprisoned our thinking. Knepp's transformation has revealed the rigidity of many conservation orthodoxies. Turtle doves are not 'farmland' birds; how did they live before farmland? Purple emperors are not 'woodland' butterflies. They retreated to fragments of woodland because this was the last place they could survive. Knepp has shown us that they will thrive in rather different settings. Can this place liberate our conception of woodland too? Must woodland have an edge? Can a wood segue into wood pasture, a heterogeneous landscape of glades and groves running through a densely populated, intensively farmed landscape? Can British woods begin to resemble again the 'forests' of our Norman forebears – not dense woodland but a mosaic of trees and cultivated land, givers of life, diversity, resilience, employment, diversion, joy?

I returned to Foxley early one Sunday morning in July 2019. The wood was vibrating with the insects of midsummer and also with human life. Visitors were clambering out of cars, forcing up the rides at speed, necks craning, long lenses banging against chests, their energy like a walk to a vital football match; a sharing of nerves, hopes, dreams; a communal act of worship. Something momentous was unfolding. That week, a purple emperor had been spotted again in Foxley.

The early morning air was sweet and still. A buzzard cried, riding an unseen thermal overhead. My children and I took a luminous pathway through the trees, a river of waist-high grass flowing through meandering banks of hazel. At a corner filled with pendulous sedge, where plump large skippers busily patrolled hummocks of bramble, I plastered fermenting banana-and-spirits on a sprig of hazel. 'You can tell that the purple emperor has returned when rotten bananas start appearing on signposts,' warden Steve Collin had told me. Butterfly obsessives bait the emperor with rotten fruit or execrable fish paste, hoping to entice one down from the treetops.

As I waited by the lure, and my children fidgeted, there was a murmur from a group at the far end of the ride. A coalescing of lenses; a hush, solemnity; an indescribable pause. We abandoned our rotten banana and skipped towards the small throng. Pointing. There. A male emperor perched high on a spray of an oak, one of the 'weeds' that hadn't been evicted from between conifers four decades earlier. Wings of imperial purple tilted, ready for lift-off. The spirit of Foxley had returned. For a few seconds, multiple planes of existence seemed to join together. The wood, the trees, the air, the sky, this butterfly. The universe was united; me, it, them, us; all was well, everything was made whole. This moment in July.

The ecstasy could not last, nor should it. The emperor powered away, over great pillows of sallow, prospecting for newly emerged females. The world glowed as every participant in this moment slowly moved apart. We shared pleasure, looked at photographs, debated theories. I met David Ruthven, a retired print compositor now eighty-six, who had last seen a purple emperor here in 1971. 'I never expected to see it again in my lifetime,' he smiled. He had returned every summer to see if it was there, and enjoy Foxley.

In 2018, Ruthven said he had spotted an 'unusually large female peacock' butterfly high in the trees. He was now convinced this was an emperor. The last person to see it could have been the first, forty-seven summers later. It had returned because Foxley Wood was again typical of its era. Like many other recovering ex-conifer plantations, it was rampant with regenerated sallow and myriad other life forms. Change was possible. Good things, longed-for things, could happen. It wasn't exactly restoration, nor regime change, but a new spirit, bequeathing us a new sense of what woodland was, could be and might become. ∎

Hare, 2000
Courtesy of Galerie Peter Sillem

ALIENS AND US

Ken Thompson

Horse chestnut. Sycamore. Sweet chestnut. Apple trees.
Larch. Spruce. Snowdrop. Wild poppy. Cornflower. Corn
marigold. Snake's head fritillary. Burdock. White campion.
Shepherd's purse. Hemlock. Mayweed. Pheasant. Little owl.
Rainbow trout. Rabbit. Hare. Fallow deer. Edible dormouse.

E ach of the animals and plants on this list of species that Britons
are all familiar with was introduced to Britain by human agency,
either accidentally or on purpose, which, technically, makes them all
aliens. And yet, despite such aliens being (according to some reports)
one of the world's worst environmental problems, I doubt you've ever
felt particularly threatened by any of them.

The lesson I take from this commonplace observation is that
although a dislike or fear of alien species is widespread, it is not
automatic, and certainly not innate – it has to be learned. In fact we
can go further than that: the *knowledge* of nativeness, or alienness,
has to be learned – there is no operational definition of alienness.
By which I mean that if I took you to a wood consisting of, say, oak,
beech and sweet chestnut, there is nothing you could measure that
would tell you that one of those trees is an alien and the other two are
native. And I don't just mean that the measurement would be difficult

or expensive, I really do mean literally *nothing*. Given all the time in the world, and as many scientific resources as you like, up to and including the Large Hadron Collider, there is no way to distinguish a native species from an alien one. In fact for a long time many of the species mentioned at the outset – for example, sweet chestnut and snowdrop – were assumed to be native. Not only that, not being native is no barrier to being the object of active conservation efforts. The brown hare, for example, is a UK Biodiversity Action Plan priority species (one of the species 'identified as being the most threatened and requiring conservation action under the UK Biodiversity Action Plan'). Nor is the brown hare unique – the white-clawed crayfish (introduced from Europe in early medieval times) is also a UK BAP priority species, felt to be in need of protection from the more recently arrived American signal crayfish.

The logic behind decisions about which species need protection is clearly far from straightforward. Still, the overwhelming majority of professional biologists and conservationists have strong – and rigid – opinions about aliens and natives. Natives (animals and plants that evolved where they live now, or spread there without human assistance) belong, and thus merit our concern and, if necessary, our care. Aliens, introduced by humans, even if in the relatively remote past, do not belong, and thus deserve only indifference (at best) or active persecution. As an ecologist, I began my career feeling the same way. As an undergraduate, I was more or less obliged to regard the snowdrop (a classic 'nice' alien) as a UK native, because the then standard book on British flora, written by my taxonomy tutor, Professor Tom Tutin, said it was. Later, as a university ecologist, I began to look a bit more objectively at the published research on alien species, and I soon realised that much of it was, if not positively dishonest, at least being economical with the truth.

Many professional biologists and conservationists seemed happy to promote erroneous ideas about the relative value of native and alien species. Alien species that appear to have some kind of negative impact (often described as 'invasive') are obvious targets for research funding, and bad news is always more newsworthy than good news, so ecologists often choose to study the most damaging alien species we can find, even if they are atypical of alien species as a whole. And, not content with studying the relatively few species that are genuinely detrimental, we also start out by choosing to study the times and places where they appear to be having the largest effects, if only because dramatic effects are easier to notice and measure than small ones.

The result of all this is both predictable and well documented (in a 2013 paper in *Trends in Ecology & Evolution*). If we begin by studying an alien species where it appears to be having the most severe effects, it's inevitable that further work on the same species will reveal smaller impacts. Eventually, researchers get around to looking at places where it's having no effect at all, or even positive impacts. But this is all too late, because it's only the most alarming findings that make the headlines, or are worth reporting at all. Two well-studied European invaders in America, purple loosestrife and tamarisk, or salt cedar, both illustrate this pattern. And don't forget that the overwhelming majority of alien species that seemed to be just quietly minding their own business were never worth investigating in the first place.

Along the way, we (both ecologists and the public) adjust (consciously or otherwise) what we mean by 'negative impact', first by assuming our chosen alien is causing economic or environmental harm, and then looking for the evidence to support that view. So we often define the 'costs' of an alien species in a circular, question-begging way. For example, it's not easy to see how aliens 'harm' ecosystems, given that ecosystems do not feel pain, or have interests, hopes or ambitions that could possibly *be* harmed. But if we define any change to the state of an ecosystem as harmful, then aliens are often harmful by definition. Further, the cost of an alien routinely includes – and indeed sometimes consists entirely of – the price tag we put on its eradication. But the eradication of almost *any* species, native or alien, would be expensive, and that tells us nothing about the real cost of the economic or environmental harm it may be causing, if any.

Anything on the credit side of the balance sheet is routinely ignored. Drawing attention to any of this is not the way to make friends and influence people. A decade ago I was one of the authors of a short paper in the journal *Nature* that made the (I still think) modest proposal that we should stop worrying about where species come from and simply treat them on their merits. A swift rejoinder was entitled 'Non-natives: 141 scientists object' – in other words, 'We must be right because lots of people agree with us.' More recently, a whole new class of offence has been created specifically for those who think like me: 'invasive species denialism'. Unbelievably, calling for a less hysterical attitude to alien species is often lumped together with denying the evidence for climate change and evolution, downplaying the risks of tobacco smoking and exaggerating the risks of immunisation, and originates, apparently, from 'a vested interest in opposition to the scientific consensus', according to a paper published in *Trends in Ecology & Evolution* in 2017. And if you're curious about the nature of that vested interest, the same paper claims that 'deniers typically consistently reject scientific evidence on a range of different topics and there is a strong correlation with support of free-market ideologies such as *laissez-faire* regulation'. As someone with a lifelong and passionate belief in the primacy of scientific evidence, I find these accusations fairly ludicrous.

But before we go any further, do those who accuse me of 'invasive species denialism' have a point? *Am* I guilty of denying the negative impacts of alien species in *every* case? No, I'm not. I would be the first to admit that some alien species have had some very undesirable effects indeed. This is especially likely on remote islands, where specialised floras and faunas have evolved in the absence of the usual set of predators, herbivores and competitors. Guam would undoubtedly be better off without the brown tree snake, Australia without the cane toad, several Pacific islands without the predatory snail *Euglandina*, and a long list of oceanic islands without introduced rats, cats and goats. But extrapolating from these examples to the whole world is simply wrong; studies that claim to show big effects of aliens on native biodiversity are always heavily biased by data from remote islands.

To return to the question underlying all this discord: why do we think we disapprove of alien species when so many of them are familiar – even valued – parts of the landscape? I genuinely don't know, but if we are alarmed by some kind of environmental problem, it's a lot easier to blame any aliens we find hanging around the crime scene than it is to look for the real, underlying (and often intractable) cause of the problem. History teaches us that we love a convenient scapegoat. For example, it's increasingly apparent that American grey squirrels might never have become established in the wild in the UK if we had not driven their only serious predator, the pine marten, to the verge of extinction. But it's a lot easier to blame the squirrel than to admit our past mistakes.

And, of course, fear and alarm sell newspapers, and drive traffic to Facebook and other online sources of (mis)information. On these platforms, alien species are just one convenient source of fear and alarm, along with everything that might give you cancer, which, if you read enough online, eventually turns out to include every foodstuff you've ever heard of.

Only the brave, or foolhardy, swim against this powerful tide. For instance, as everyone knows, Japanese knotweed '[chews] through buildings, destroying walls and ripping up transport links', and 'tears through brickwork and concrete', according to one disturbing report from the *Daily Mail* in 2013. Paranoid insurance companies and banks, and companies that profit by controlling Japanese knotweed, are only too willing to promote such beliefs, leading to its presence on residential properties regularly being used as a reason to refuse mortgage applications – a response out of all proportion to the threat. In reality, reports of knotweed actually damaging buildings are rare, and even if we look at a genuine, worst-case-scenario Japanese knotweed disaster area, such as when the plant is growing among crumbling, derelict buildings, knotweed is only rarely associated with damage. And when it is, it's clearly an 'accessory after the fact', exploiting existing cracks or other damage. Trees, either by pushing walls over or simply by falling, are far more destructive. All this is documented in a 2018 paper in the journal *PeerJ*. It's also worth noting that Japanese knotweed in the UK is effectively sterile, and its only means of long-distance dispersal is human carelessness.

To complete our picture of Britain's favourite pantomime invasive alien villain, the latest research, published in *Biodiversity and Conservation* in 2018, reveals that Japanese knotweed is a terrific late-season source of nectar for both bees and hoverflies, but that's not much of a headline, is it?

Something else that makes it hard to think rationally about alien species is the issue of timescale. The most far-sighted among us struggle to look much beyond the next election, and our usual attention span is closer to that of a goldfish. And although the mills of natural selection eventually grind exceeding small, they do grind slowly, at least on a human timescale. Take, for example, giant hogweed, a plant so huge and apparently unstoppable that it even inspired its own hit pop song (although you do need to be of a certain age to recall 'The Return of the Giant Hogweed' by Genesis).

Given the right conditions, especially on riverbanks, giant hogweed does indeed start out by just steamrollering other plants into oblivion, and for the first thirty years or so these effects continue to increase. By which point you could be forgiven for assuming that they will last forever – but they don't. Careful work in the Czech Republic, published in *Ecology Letters* in 2013, shows that eventually hogweed goes into a gradual decline and the associated natives begin to recover. By fifty years this recovery process is well under way, but we don't know the eventual outcome because there just aren't enough really old hogweed populations to study. Experiments reveal that the likely cause of hogweed's decline is a build-up of soil pathogens.

In every case where data is available for a long enough time, the same pattern emerges: however invincible an alien appears at first, competitors, predators and diseases eventually catch up, as natural selection says they must, and as they always have throughout the history of life. This is as true for animals as it is for plants. For example, their high social and economic value means that brown trout have been introduced to practically all parts of the globe, starting with the European settlement of North America and Australasia in the mid-nineteenth century. The result is always the same: large negative impacts on native fish and other aquatic species, but gradually these effects decline, and after a century or more they can no longer be detected. Cynics among you will suspect that this is because a hundred years is how long it takes species sensitive to predation by trout to go extinct, but the evidence demonstrates that this is not the case, and the true cause appears to be adaptation by species that either eat trout or are eaten by them.

If you still think one hundred years is a long time to wait for the locals to catch up with a successful invader, remember that the biosphere has been around for hundreds of millions of years, and with any luck will be around for another few hundred. From that perspective a century is much less than the blink of an eye.

Does any of this matter? Should we care if most people believe, wrongly, that Japanese knotweed is both far worse than it is and typical of alien species in general? I think we should. On the most simple level, the world has enough real problems without worrying about imaginary ones. Resources devoted to a war against alien species (a war that is almost always unsuccessful and often counterproductive) are resources that are not available for dealing with anything else. In 2015, the UK government stated that invasive aliens cost at least £1.7 billion per year, while in 2017, the US government spent an estimated $3 billion across a range of federal agencies and activities in an effort to prevent, control and eradicate invasive alien species. Most of this expenditure is ineffective; for example, by 2009, Australia had spent more than twenty years and over AUS $500,000 trying to eradicate the Mexican weed *Martynia annua* from a single national park. It is, of course, still there.

There can also be subtle negative effects of worrying too much about potentially invasive aliens. Within the conservation community, a debate rumbles on about the advisability or otherwise of 'assisted translocation': moving species to new regions to allow them to keep pace with a changing climate (some species will manage this on their own, but a lot won't). The chief argument against assisted translocation is a misplaced fear of the translocated species becoming invasive.

Believing that alien species are all out to get you, or are at best useless, has other undesirable consequences. British gardeners have been happily growing thousands of species of alien plants for centuries, mostly without knowing or caring where they originally came from: for example, roses from Asia, fuchsias from South America and dahlias from Mexico. Fifty or more years ago, there was a widespread perception (among both gardeners and scientists) that those alien plants were unable to nurture and sustain native wildlife, and therefore that gardens were basically wildlife deserts. That perception has now been completely overturned, beginning with ecologist Jennifer Owen's monumental thirty-year study of her Leicester garden, which found an astonishing selection of diverse wildlife, including not only species previously unrecorded in Britain, but a handful of species new to science.

The transformation in our understanding of garden wildlife was continued by the Sheffield Biodiversity in Urban Gardens project and completed by the recent four-year-long Plants for Bugs project carried out by the Royal Horticultural Society. The lesson from all this work is that yes, the wildlife value of alien plants is inferior to that of natives, but only marginally, and the effect of plant origin is completely overwhelmed by the impact of vegetation quantity. In short, more flowers and more plants (of any sort) equal more wildlife, and *how* you garden is far more important than *what* you grow. Jennifer Owen, who made no particular effort to grow native plants, suggested at the end of her study that collectively Britain's private gardens may be our most important nature reserves, and indeed together the UK's gardens exceed the area of all of our National Nature Reserves combined.

You will not be surprised to learn that this discovery has gone down badly with those who never liked alien plants as a matter of principle, and especially with those for whom 'native plants for native wildlife' was essentially a religious belief, not susceptible to either confirmation or refutation by the normal rules of evidence. This belief shows every sign of being almost perfectly elastic, so that knocking it on the head in one place always leads to its popping up somewhere else, even in places where you were starting to hope people knew better.

For example, *Garden Birds*, published by the Royal Society for the Protection of Birds in 2019, chooses to ignore thirty years of evidence and issues a pretty stern injunction to those gardeners (virtually all of them, that is) who might have thought it was okay to grow alien plants: 'If you want plenty of birds in the garden you need plenty of insects, and for the insects you need native plants.' That this view stems from a straightforward dislike of aliens of any sort is confirmed by the fact that the book almost airbrushes out of existence altogether the non-native ring-necked parakeet (now a familiar bird in London, and spreading elsewhere in the UK), perhaps on the principle that if we ignore it, it will just go away?

But we know gardeners like to grow alien plants, so if they are told that filling their gardens with native plants is what it takes to attract wildlife, many will probably conclude that it's just not worth the effort. The most likely result of ordering gardeners who want to do their best for wildlife to grow native plants is to discourage them from engaging with wildlife gardening at all – surely the exact opposite of what anyone intended. Of course, many sterile, double-flowered cultivars have little to offer wildlife, but that's as true for native plants as it is for aliens.

In truth, pretending that the native–alien dichotomy has much practical value is lazy, out of date and pessimistic. Lazy because conservation is all about values, but there's surprisingly little debate about what those values are. 'Aliens are nasty, natives are nice' has been one of the very few things everyone thought they could agree on without having to think too hard, so a lot of practical conservation has involved digging up, poisoning, burning or shooting alien plants and animals. This military-industrial approach has rarely been successful, and has often simply created suitable conditions for the establishment of yet more aliens.

Losing sleep over aliens is out of date because trying to control or eradicate alien species frequently stems from a yearning to return to a pristine, alien-free state that was often a romantic illusion anyway. Today's wildlife managers, like it or not, have to recognise that the natural systems of the past have gone forever thanks to climate change, pollution and urbanisation, among other things. It can't be much of a surprise, when you stop and think about it, that in the face of such pressures, many natives are no longer the best-adapted species in any particular spot, and conservation of a functioning countryside in the face of climate change may even *require* introducing aliens, particularly trees from warmer climates to mitigate the failure of our native trees to respond quickly to rising temperatures and changing weather patterns. Much of the modern natural world now consists of a mixture of long-term residents and new arrivals, and ecosystems are emerging that never existed before, sometimes living in climates that never existed before either. Restoring such ecosystems to some 'rightful' historical state is no longer possible, even in theory, so we should stop trying, embrace such 'novel ecosystems' and determine to get the best out of them, for humanity and for the planet.

Finally, disparaging aliens is profoundly pessimistic. No one would dispute the fact that we have a global biodiversity crisis, but biodiversity means different things to different people, and as long as it means just 'native biodiversity', the only way is down; the very best that we can hope for is to prevent biodiversity in any specific habitat or region from declining. But once we allow aliens to contribute, then *local* biodiversity can – and does – increase. Of course every time a forest is converted to oil palm or soya beans, local diversity plummets. Nevertheless, there's plenty of evidence to show that *regional* biodiversity (that is the number of species per country, state or island) is increasing, as the number of introduced species establishing themselves exceeds the number of native species that die out. For example, introduced aliens have added nearly 2,000 established non-native species to the British flora (some of them in the list that opened this article), and there's no evidence that any native species has suffered as a direct result. Nor is Britain at all unusual; the total number of species on the planet may be declining, but all the evidence points to increases in the number of terrestrial species in most of the world's regions over recent decades and centuries.

It's even possible for introduced species to *add* to *global* biodiversity. In the British flora, over a hundred hybrids, either between a native and an alien plant, or between two aliens, are now widespread. History teaches us that such hybridisation is often a stepping stone to speciation, and half a dozen hybrids have taken that step and become new naturalised species (our commonest salt-marsh grass, for example, started out as a native-alien hybrid). Once you've put aside the alien-bashers' frothing at the mouth about 'genetic pollution', this is actually a profoundly hopeful development, and suggests that the trajectory of biodiversity in the Anthropocene might not be downhill all the way after all. But it's a crumb of comfort that, if you insisted on remaining behind the sandbags in the 'natives good, aliens bad' camp, would be denied you. ■

THE HIGH HOUSE

Jessie Greengrass

Caro

Ileft school for good at lunchtime on the day I turned eighteen. I
walked home. The house was empty. I had no plans, either for the
afternoon, or for the time beyond it – my life, which stretched empty
ahead. Or didn't. It was becoming clear to everyone, now, that things
were getting worse. The winter before, half of Gloucestershire had
been flooded, and the waters, refusing to recede, had made a new fen,
covering homes and fields, roads and schools. In York, the river had
burst its banks and the city centre was gone, walls which had stood for
nearly two millennia washed halfway down to Hull. People didn't say
these places were gone. They didn't say that there were families living in
caravans in service stations all along the M5, lined up in the car parks with
volunteers running aid stations out of the garage forecourts. People said,
– They must have known their homes were vulnerable –
We were protected by our houses and our educations and our
high-street shopping centres. We had the habit of luck and power,
and couldn't understand that they were not our right. We saw that the
situation was bad, elsewhere, but surely something would work out,
because didn't it always, for us? We were paralysed, unable to plan
either for a future in which all was well, or one in which it wasn't.

– I'm not going back, I said to father, when he came home from work because the school had called to tell him I had left.

–What will you do instead? he asked, and I shrugged one shoulder up and slid my eyes away. There had been daffodils in the park at Christmas. The coast path had been redrawn at six different places over the last three years.

– I have to go and pick Pauly up from nursery, I said, Unless you're going to do it, and I walked down the road to where Pauly was waiting, standing at the gate in his coat and hat and mittens.

That evening, Francesca came home. I don't know where she had been – which of the many places, savaged by weather, that might have needed her expertise, and her anger – but she smelled of mould and filthy water and she was exhausted. She looked thin. After Pauly was in bed I sat with her and father at the kitchen table.

– What will you do? father asked me again, and Francesca said, That's a pretty stupid question, under the circumstances.

Father let his breath hiss out between his teeth. He said, We can't just give up on everything.

– No, Francesca looked at me, Of course. But anyway, she said, We need you to look after Pauly.

And then I knew how absolutely she had given up herself.

Later, unable to sleep, I went downstairs to fetch a book, and, standing in the hall, I heard them talking, father and Francesca together. The door was slightly open and I watched them through the crack it made. They were still sitting at the kitchen table, just as I had left them, side by side, facing my empty chair. Father asked,

– Are you so sure?

–Yes, Francesca replied, I am. I think I am. We always knew a tipping point would come. It's a surprise, really, that it's taken so long.

–You could stop, father said. If there's no point. We could stay together, for a while at least. Caro is unhappy. Paul too, probably, although I agree it's harder to tell.

They were silent for a long time then, and I stood very still in the corridor and thought of Pauly, the way his body twitched in his sleep, the tense look he got when Francesca was there, and how it was not hard at all for me to tell if he was happy or not.

The next morning, when I went downstairs, father was in the kitchen drinking coffee, and Francesca was gone.

– She had an early flight, he told me. She said to say goodbye.

– To me? I asked, Or to Pauly?

– Both. Of course, both –

Pauly only went to nursery in the mornings now, to give me time to tidy, do the washing, get the shopping. I picked him up just before lunch and took him home, walking the short distance hand in hand, stopping to look at things that caught his interest, at leaves and beetles, car number plates, discarded crisp packets.

– Oh Pauly. Please don't pick that up. It's filthy.

– But Caro it's *green* –

For lunch, we ate sandwiches, then washed up together and went to the park. Played on the swings. Came home. Ate tea. Played. Bath. Stories. Bed. When he was asleep, the washing-up, ironing, hoovering. Every day the same. And, in the routine of it, I found that I had misplaced my fear. The future was only the weeks until half-term, when there would be planned trips to museums, city farms, the cinema, then back to nursery and all to do again. Things had a form and, carried along by it, the future ceased to seem important, although I knew that it would still happen to us, coming on while I was cutting carrots for snacks, while we fed oats to the ducks, played tag, stuck plasters to grazed knees. I fitted my life to Pauly's, because he needed me – or because I needed him, the way he looked me full in the face and smiled, the excuse he gave me: that I could not possibly be anywhere else, because I was here. This was the absurdity of it – that I couldn't forgive Francesca because she chose the world over Pauly, and now I can't forgive myself because I didn't. I'm no longer angry with Francesca. Somewhere in the miles and miles I ran between the high house and the river, the river and the sea, I found that I had come to understand what it was she had tried to do, but who is there left to do the same for me? What option is there, in the end, for those few of us who have survived, but to be the unforgivable, and the unforgiven? All those who might have lived instead of us are gone, or they are starving, while we stay on here at the high house, pulling potatoes from soft earth.

The spring before Pauly and I came to the high house, Francesca and father were away almost constantly and it was hot, from the last week of February right through March and April, into May, every day high and clear and bright like a remembered summer, except that it wasn't summer. In the afternoons, Pauly played naked in the garden, poking in the bushes to find insects, or pouring water on my feet from the watering can while I squealed and laughed at the cold. I wore Francesca's big sun hat, and when we went out, both of us in shorts and sandals, we ran through the sliver of shade the houses made on the pavement and felt the warmth come up from the ground to meet us. We knew that it was fever heat, a sign of illness, the air too thin and the cement on the ground too thick, the whole city a storage heater, but still we couldn't help but feel ourselves stretch up towards it, the sun, which reached into our bodies and softened them like wax. People stopped work early to lounge in parks. Children sat on doorsteps sucking Freeze Pops. On buses, passengers smiled at one another. There was such joy in it, the light and warmth, as though we had escaped the winter. Pauly and I went on day trips, into the forest to the east of the city to feel the trees make their own cool, or west, to swim in the river. Away from the pavements, the acres of concrete, the heat was less pronounced. Away from people, it was easier to maintain the fiction of normality – but in the long grass of a deer park we searched for grasshoppers and there were none. The hum of bees was missing. The birds were quiet. I took Pauly to a place I remembered going to with father, once, where there was a greengage tree. I remembered father lifting me up above his head so that I could pull the soft fruit from the branches, and I remembered how sweet it had tasted, juice running down my wrists – but now the tree was bare, its branches brittle, its leaves a brown carpet across the dry ground.

I lay in the big bed with Pauly curled up next to me, asleep. The window was open to let in what breeze there was and I heard the city sounds which came in with it, the hooting and the roaring of traffic, the wailing of sirens, the rattle of trains. Somewhere, a party was happening. I heard the steady thumping of the bass, an occasional bark of laughter. Someone shouted something indistinct. Beside me, my phone rang, an overseas number. I picked it up, climbing swiftly out of bed and leaving the room so that I didn't wake Pauly when I answered it – Hello?

– Caro? It's me. It's Dad.

It was five hours behind where he and Francesca were, on the east coast of the US, and so it must have been early afternoon for him, but I thought he sounded tired. Perhaps they had been up all night, sat round a table in a conference centre trying yet again to force understanding where it wasn't welcome. I said, Dad! and heard him sigh.

– I'm sorry, but we're going to be here longer than we thought. I –

I sat down at the top of the stairs and leaned my head against the wall.

– I'm sorry, he said, and he sounded it.

– What's happening, Dad? I asked, but instead of an answer, he said, I want you to take Pauly to the high house. Pack your bags now. Leave in the morning. Okay? First thing. Get the early train –

– What's happening?

From somewhere in the space behind him I heard a click, the sound of a door opening, a voice calling his name – Yes, soon, he said, to someone else, and then to me he said, I have to go. I love you, Caroline. I love Pauly, too. Tell him –

The line went dead. I stayed where I was, sitting on the staircase in the dark, until I was sure that he wouldn't call again, and then I went back into the bedroom where Pauly, fast asleep, had turned himself to lie in a star shape across the full width of the bed.

While Pauly slept, I packed a hiking rucksack, stuffing it with handfuls of pants, with T-shirts and socks, toothpaste, toothbrushes, soap. Pauly had his own suitcase, a ladybird on wheels which doubled as a kind of seat, and into that I packed his raincoat, his wellington boots, some toys. I made sandwiches for the journey and put them in a shoulder bag. I didn't pack a photograph of father. I didn't pack the necklace that had been my grandmother's, or the card that Pauly had made me for my birthday the year before – but then, what good would those things have been, even had I thought to bring them? I wish that I had packed the *Penguin Book of English Verse*. I wish that I had packed a garlic press. I wish I had the scissors that Francesca used to cut Pauly's hair.

Before I went back to bed, creeping quietly in beside Pauly, gently nudging his warm feet away from my side, I went downstairs and switched the television on. A hurricane that had been building in the Caribbean had veered west, suddenly, and was now projected to hit Florida sometime in the early hours of the next day at a strength so high that it lacked any current designation. Weather conditions in the area were already difficult, bordering on extreme. Evacuation was advised, but might be impossible.

– How is it, a man in a suit, sat in a television studio, asked, That so little warning has been given? and the woman opposite him, whose hair was not quite smooth, whose blouse was rumpled, as though she had dressed hurriedly, her mind elsewhere, answered, These conditions are unprecedented. We have no models appropriate to this situation.

– So are you saying, the man pressed her, That we are now looking at a future in which we no longer have fair warning of extreme weather events?

– Yes. The woman said, That is exactly what I am saying.

In the morning, I got Pauly dressed, ate breakfast. When Pauly went to wash his hands I checked the news, but could find out only that the storm had hit, with what seemed to be extraordinary violence, and that its epicentre had been near to where father and Francesca were staying. I had no message from them. Pauly had woken in a bad mood, contrary, bolshy, and so it was easy, as I fought to get him to eat his toast, to get dressed, to put his shoes on, to ignore my worry and think only about ourselves.

– But I don't want to go away, he said, his voice a whine.

– We have to, Pauly.

The concourse was very busy. I left Pauly standing with our bags by a pillar next to a sandwich shop and went to buy our tickets, trying hard, as I waited in the queue, not to look at the large screen above the departure boards where rolling news showed footage of trees bending in the wind, waves breaking across an esplanade. There were still three quarters of an hour left until our train was due to leave. I took Pauly to a cafe where we drank smoothies from plastic bottles and ate pain au chocolat that came in little bags and I can still feel it in my mouth, even now – the cheap, oily chocolate and the doughy pastry wrapped around it, packet-stale, familiar. Pauly didn't want to finish his, so we left it on the table when our platform was called, and it seems extraordinary to think how profligate we were. How careless. We were so unaware of all we had to lose, and how long has it been, now, since we had any bread except the flat, heavy loaves that Pauly makes, sometimes, from the wheat we grow and grind ourselves? How long has it been since we could leave even the worst food behind, uneaten?

Station by station the train emptied. We ran east into the tail end of the morning and then into the afternoon, rattling through the outskirts of the city, through its hinterland to what lay beyond, a succession of small towns with bunting strung across their streets giving out to fields, to woods, to the curve of a river and children standing on a white-painted bridge, a village with a fete, a farm with horses. Pink houses sat alone between hedges. Unfamiliar stations stood undisturbed. By the end there was only us and one other woman, who sat two seats in front of us and turned to stare at me. Pauly stood up on his seat.

– Sit down, I said, and he flopped back again, crossing his arms and sulking until he saw a white bird from the window.

– Look, Caro! An egret!

– Is that a good one? I asked, and he nodded.

The winter before, Pauly had found a bird spotter's guidebook on the shelves at home and since then he had spent hours looking at it, making me read out the names of the birds, their identifying features, the descriptions of their eggs – but where this information had left my mind, running out of it like water, Pauly had stored it, reproducing details at will.

– They're a kind of heron, he said, Oh, isn't it beautiful – and it was, pale as a ghost and tall and still at the edge of a lake. We watched it until it was out of sight.

The town was eight miles inland from the high house, another half from the village where the road ran, and I had thought that we would get a taxi, but it was early on a weekday afternoon and the station was empty and so was the street outside. There were no people, and no cars on the road. I checked my phone, but there was no internet connection. The station had no ticket office, only a machine to put your card in and a window with a blind drawn down. There was a note pinned to a board with the number of a cab firm, but when I called it there was only the steady monotone of a disconnected line. The air shivered with heat. There was a smell of dust and lavender.

– We can get a bus, I said to Pauly, my voice shrill with the effort of sounding unconcerned, but when I checked the timetable I found that the next bus wouldn't be until the following day. I made a heap of our bags in the shade of the awning above the station door and left Pauly sitting on them.

– Don't move, I told him, I'll try and find a cab office. I won't be long.

I walked as quickly as I could around the nearby streets but there was no cab office and I was afraid to leave Pauly too long in case he wandered off, or someone came and found him. I went into the post office, where a woman sat behind the counter, scrolling on her phone.

– Excuse me, I asked, But do you have the number for a taxi?

The woman shrugged, barely looking up, and gave me a number, different to the one I had found in the station, but when I called it, although the dial tone sounded and sounded, no one answered.

– No one's picking up, I said. What shall I do? I have a child with me.

The woman shrugged again. Try the pub, I would, she said. The landlord's son does lifts, sometimes.

In the street again, I found that I was close to crying. It was only the thought of Pauly waiting for me that made me swallow my humiliation and go inside the pub, where it was cool and dim and a handful of men sat round tables, glasses cupped in their hands, staring up at a television screen which showed footage of a hotel with its front wall ripped open. Through the hole I saw beds, wardrobes, sofas. The camera panned, and I saw twisted metal sticking out like bone from split concrete. Brown water, scummed with wreckage, swirled in and out of restaurant windows.

– Can I help you, love? someone asked, but he was very far away indeed, and anyway I had no answer. I turned, and went back into the street, back into the sunshine, back to the station where Pauly sat on his suitcase, kicking his heels against the pavement.

– I can't find a taxi, I said. We'll have to walk – and, trusting, uncomplaining, he looked at me, stood up, smiled.

– Is it a long way, Caro?

– Not too far.

I collected up the bags, and as I did so I found myself thinking of the television in the pub, its images of destruction, and all those who surely must have drowned. How quickly things can fall apart. That city which, a day earlier, had been impregnable, glinting bright with glass and power, was swallowed by the sea. Its land was forfeit, and with it the sense we'd always had that we would be, whatever happened, to some degree all right. I took Pauly's hand, and we started to walk.

We followed the river out towards the sea, first through the outskirts of the town, past the new-build housing estates and the playgrounds, the primary school, the supermarket with its car park, the drive-through fast-food restaurant and the petrol station. Pauly walked beside me, holding my hand.

– I'm thirsty, he said, and I gave him some of the water that was left in the bottle, tepid from lying in my bag in the sunshine. At first, the path was tarmacked, the river in its well-cut bed ran slow and brown, but soon we were out into fields, green beet tops and maize, and wheat. The river widened. There was an embankment, and we walked along the top of it, the path becoming narrower and runnelled. My rucksack was heavy. Pauly slowed to a trudge in front of me, his suitcase bouncing along behind him on its small wheels, sticking in the tufty grass. He stumbled, and stumbled again.

– You're doing really well, I said. It's not far now – but really I didn't know how far it was. The sun was hot. I thought that I could smell the sea. The fields ended and there was a heath, and then a wood. Pauly began to cry.

– I'm too tired, Caro. My feet are sore.

– Sit down here for a bit, then, I told him, Have a rest. I won't be long.

Leaving him cross-legged on the path I took the bags and walked with them away from the river, scrambling down the side of the embankment into the trees, pushing through the thicket of new growth at the wood's edge, whippy saplings rising out of brambles, to where the old oaks were, their trunks split low, their lichened branches growing long and hanging into one another. I stuffed my bag into the bowl of one so that it would be held off the ground and might, with luck, stay dry, and balanced Pauly's suitcase on the top of it. When that was done I stood for a moment, surrounded by the forest sounds, the rustlings and scurryings, the songs of innumerable birds, and wondered how I would go on – but what else could I do? I turned, and made my way back to the path, to Pauly with his tear-stained face, and I picked him up and set him on my back, his hands around my neck, mine beneath his legs. I walked again, one foot in front of the other, and I thought only of the burning in my legs and spine, the ache like heated wires in my arms, the sharp ground underneath my feet, and time was gone. The world was gone. There was only Pauly left, and me, and the path.

It was approaching dark by the time I saw the sea, a thin grey line on the horizon, and Pauly had fallen asleep, his head resting loose on my shoulder. The river was very slow, now, and on each side of it there was meadowland, green and empty, and above it the vast sky – and then, at last, there was the path I recognised, leading away from the river and down among the reeds, where wooden boards were slung across the many small channels which stood at intervals, cutting this way and that, their water still and dark and deep. The first stars were out. Each step made me wince with effort but finally we reached the tide pool, and then I saw for the first time that it had been cleared, no longer the scrub that I remembered. Beyond it, the yew hedge which marked the boundary of the orchard was neatly pruned. I was too tired to be surprised. I went through its arch, and found that where I had been expecting a garden run to seed and a house that was shuttered, dark, there was clipped grass between the apple trees and light spilling out through the windows of the house. A girl walked towards me. She had come out to meet me from the house, and when she reached us she lifted Pauly from my back, gently so she didn't wake him, and then she was walking on ahead, and I was following her, back through the garden, into the house – and that is how we came here, and we have never left. ∎

20 October 1897: Inuit returning from hunting caribou inland on board the SS *Diana* at Qanartalik (Douglas Harbour)
Left to right: Auvviq Taliqpik, his wife Irqumiak Igijuk, unknown man, Kauktungajaq, the author's great-great grandfather, and, with the headband, the author's great-grandfather, Davidie Qisaruassiaq, who was known to be a Shaman

UPIRNGASAQ
(ARCTIC SPRING)

Sheila Watt-Cloutier

I write this from my home in Kuujjuaq, an Inuit community in Nunavik, northern Quebec, Canada. We're located about 1,500 kilometres north of Montreal, on the tidal banks of the Kuujjuaq River, at a point where the northern extent of the treeline meets the Arctic tundra.

The remoteness of Nunavik has not entirely shielded us from the global reach of the current pandemic, and indeed outbreaks – although small in number – of infection have occurred in two of our communities. And so, for the past two months, I have been living in self-isolation, part of this time caring for my seven-year-old grandson, Inuapik. He's an extremely active little boy, always curious and observant. He has kept me on my toes from dawn to dusk.

It is now early June – the beginning of springtime in the Arctic, that brief period between winter and summer when life is miraculously renewed. The snow, apart from patches here and there, will soon vanish from the land. Our delicate plants, such as the purple saxifrage, fireweed and poppies, suddenly freed from their covering of snow, are quickly greening again. The snow buntings – *qupannuaq* – always the first to arrive, are being followed by flocks of other migratory birds, among them geese, ducks, loons and terns. The snow-white winter plumage of the ptarmigan – *aqiggiit*, our Arctic grouse – is taking on its summer camouflage. And our favourite fish, the Arctic char – *iqalukpik* – will soon begin their seaward migration from lakes connected to the upper reaches of the river, where they overwintered, to feed and replenish in the rich coastal waters of nearby Ungava Bay.

This is also a time when families look forward with intense joy to escaping community life for a while, heading to their traditional springtime camping spots near the mouth of the river or on the shores of Ungava Bay. Many of these sites have been occupied by the same Inuit families for generations, and being in any one of these places is to sense immediately the depth of history and connection they hold. In this way, year after year, families simultaneously renew their attachment to the land and to our ancestors. It is a time of storytelling, of remembering who we are. Here, our language, Inuktitut – ultimately a language of the land – reclaims its rightful place. And here our children, according to their age and gender, participate fully in traditional daily activities: learning and absorbing all the essential skills, aptitudes and attitudes required to survive and thrive on the land when their own time to be autonomous comes. In so many ways, the land never fails to invigorate and teach. Family and communal bonds are restored, and our spirits uplifted. We become healthier in mind and body, nourished by the 'country food' the land and sea provides. This includes a varied menu of goose and duck, fresh-run Arctic char and trout, and, of course, *natsiq*, the common seal, a staple food of Inuit coastal dwellers everywhere. This ample diet is inevitably supplemented by seagull, goose and eider duck eggs, gathered from islets just off the shore. At low tide we dig for shellfish, mostly mussels, or catch sculpins, a small, spiny fish we call *kanajuq*, stranded in rocky pools by the falling tide. Raw, crunchy seaweed, gathered from these same pools, occasionally complements the boiled *kanajuq*.

With the signs of spring all around me, and my dreams of soon being able to get out on the land again, in season to go berry picking with fellow Inuit women, it's perhaps not surprising that my thoughts have turned to the place of nature in Inuit life. In our language we have no word for 'nature', despite our deep affinity with the land, which teaches us how to live in harmony with the natural world. The division the Western world likes to make between 'man and nature' is both foreign and dangerous in the traditional Inuit view. In Western thinking, humans are set apart from nature; nature is something to strive against, to conquer, to tame, to exploit or, more benignly, to use for 'recreation'. By contrast, Inuit place themselves within, not apart from, nature. This 'in-ness' is perfectly symbolized in our traditional dwellings of the past: *illuvigait* (snow houses) in winter and *tupiit* (sealskin tents) in summer. What could be more within nature than living comfortably in dwellings made of snow and sealskin!

This is especially true of our relationships with the animals that sustain us: the *puijiit* – sea mammals – seals, whales and walruses; and the *pisuktiit*, the land animals, in particular caribou and polar bear. No other people have relied so exclusively on animals as my Inuit ancestors.

In one of the world's harshest environments, these Arctic animals provided everything needed to sustain human life. Their flesh supplied all the nutrition required for a healthy diet. From their skins, cut and worked as needed, clothing and shelter were sewn. The blubber of marine mammals fuelled the *qulliit* – our soapstone lamps – providing light and a little warmth for the snow houses in the depths of winter. From bones, ivory and caribou antler, tools, utensils and hunting equipment were expertly fashioned. Thread, strong and waterproof, used with the seamstresses' delicate bone and ivory needles, came from the sinews of caribou and beluga whales. The reliance on animals was total. Other than berries and roots, in some places available at the end of the Arctic's brief summer, there was no plant life, no agriculture, to fall back on should the hunt fail.

Our ancient beliefs held that the animals we relied upon had souls, just like ours, which needed to be treated with respect and dignity. In the early 1920s, Avva, an Inuit shaman from Igloolik, whose descendants I know well from my residential schooldays, as well as from the time I lived in Iqaluit, Nunavut, for almost twenty years, famously summed up these beliefs at the very core of our pre-Christian identity:

All the creatures that we have to kill and eat, all those that we have to strike down and destroy to make clothes for ourselves, have souls, like we have, souls that do not perish with the body, which must therefore be propitiated lest they should revenge themselves on us for taking away their bodies.

Founded on respect, our appeasement of the animals we harvested took many forms: for instance, giving a newly killed seal or walrus a mouthful of water, a practice based on the knowledge from a deep understanding of and connection to the animals we hunt that these mammals, having spent all their lives in the sea, craved a drink of fresh water. Taboos associated with particular animals were strictly observed. In this way, care was taken to avoid mingling creatures of the sea with those of the land, and so there were prohibitions against sewing caribou-skin clothing on the sea ice. Nor could the flesh of seal and caribou be boiled in the same pot. I remember my mother reminding me of this even when I would eat both frozen fish and frozen caribou together. Above all, the absolute bond between my ancestors and the animals they hunted (and, by extension, the land, sea and air) was founded on respect. Hunters never boasted about their prowess. Abusing animals in any way, or mocking them, or using them for 'sport', resulted in serious consequences for society, as did disputes over sharing. In response to maltreatment or insults, animals would withdraw from hunting grounds. Hunters were obliged to kill only animals who 'presented' themselves for the taking. This is exactly why, when I lived in the south and made visits home to Kuujjuaq in the early spring, and we hunted *aqiggiit*, my mother would say to me: 'Isn't it wonderful that the *aqiggiit* brought themselves to you so that you could take them back with you to eat in Montreal!' My mother always had that deep Inuit understanding of how life gives life.

There's an ancient tale that vividly illustrates the ethical imperative for Inuit of respecting animals when they 'present' themselves, a story that explains why walruses disappeared from a place called Allurilik, a large inlet on Ungava Bay, just over 200 kilometres north-east of my home in Kuujjuaq. It is said that here there was once a hunter out on his *qajaq* (kayak) looking for walruses. Suddenly, a small walrus surfaced in front of him and begged to be taken because it craved a drink of fresh water. Noticing that this little walrus had very small, deformed tusks, the hunter refused, saying: 'Go away . . . I don't want you. Your tusks are too small and deformed!' Hearing these words, the walrus was deeply offended and went away. Shortly after that incident, all the other walruses left the area and never came back. It is said that the caribou, after hearing about the insult, also abandoned the land around Allurilik. The lesson here is that all animals presenting, or in my mother's words 'bringing' themselves to the hunter, should be understood not as confirmation of death, but affirmation of life.

Indigenous communities and cultures everywhere have been ravaged by contact with the Western world. Introduced diseases, against which they had no resistance, decimated their populations. Christianity – usually the forerunner of colonialism – pushed aside Indigenous belief systems, altering the way they viewed the world, and endangering their mutual bonds with nature, with the land, animals and forests that sustained them.

Europeans first came into contact with my Inuit ancestors on the south shore of Ungava Bay just over 200 years ago. From that moment forward, our essential oneness with the natural world was challenged and would eventually change forever. Like the start of any infection, at first the symptoms were subtle. In those early days of contact, the Arctic, in the European imagination, offered nothing worth exploiting. Our land was dismissed as a barren wilderness, covered in snow and ice for most of the year, inexplicably inhabited by a few nomadic 'heathens'. Above all, the Arctic, with its ice-filled summer seas, was seen as a sort of adversary to be heroically conquered in Europe's futile efforts to find a north-west passage to the 'riches of the Orient'.

Regardless, wherever Europeans 'discovered' Indigenous peoples, commerce and Christianity were sure to follow and my Arctic homeland was no exception. In time, the inescapable reach of the Europeans extended to our shores. We named them 'Qallunaat'. Men of the Hudson's Bay Company were the first to arrive, setting up, in 1830, a trading post on the east side of the Kuujjuaq River, more or less across from the place where the modern community of Kuujjuaq now stands. Shortly after the turn of the century, an Anglican mission was also established there, joined by a Catholic mission in 1948.

We slowly began to accept these strangers in our land and over time we gained some understanding of their ways. But through coercion, when our own powerful spiritual beliefs, which included shamanism, drum dancing and throat singing, were forbidden and considered 'taboo', our people eventually converted. The traders' goods were an obvious convenience, especially metal items such as needles, knives, kettles, traps and firearms, joined later by an increasing selection of woven fabrics, sewing materials and basic foodstuffs, including flour, lard, sugar and tea. And, of course, tobacco. Although we could not have known it at the time, the seeds of consumerism, profound and dangerous changes to our diet and new diseases were unobtrusively planted among us. We distanced ourselves from the Qallunaat, and our interactions with them tended to be irregular and infrequent. We continued to live on the land, moving predictably from place to place in harmony with the animals, which had sustained us for countless generations. From time to time, usually travelling by dog team, visits were made to the post to trade furs, or to celebrate Christmas at the mission. Yet despite this distancing, our way of life, our unity with nature, was to change forever. Our traditional perception of time, for example, which had ticked to nature's clock – the rising and setting of the sun, the position of the stars, the cycle of the tides, the succession of the moon months – now needed to make room for the Christian calendar. Suddenly there was a unit of time called a 'week'; how very strange the idea must have seemed to my ancestors that one in every seven days was a special day when hunting and all other 'work' had to stop! Similarly, the traders' constant need for fur, especially white fox, began to alter our subsistence patterns as we spent increasingly more time on our traplines during winter.

Throughout this initial period, which lasted from the mid-1930s to the late 1950s, of coming to terms with the now permanent presence of traders and missionaries in our lands, our lives remained relatively unchanged. We continued to live in extended family groups, distributed along the coast of Ungava Bay. Our culture, values and traditions remained strong, as did our language, which easily incorporated new concepts and objects brought from the south. 'Sunday', for example, we called *allituqaq*, literally a time when we have to 'respect a taboo' – in this case the taboo against hunting on that particular day. And the kettles and pocketknives we bought from the traders were named *tiqtititsigutik* or *uujuliurutik* (that which is used to boil something) and *puuttajuuq* (that which regularly unfolds). So we slowly adapted to the newcomers, integrating their ideas and material things at our own pace. In the beginning we came to view this new relationship with the Qallunaat world as essentially balanced and sustainable. Above all, by continuing our life on the land, usually several days of dog-team travel away from the Qallunaat dwellings, we were able to retain our autonomy over the aspects of our lives that mattered most. This included our bonds with the land (including the sea ice) and its animals; and, most important of all, teaching our children the traditions, philosophies and skills needed to continue this land-based life.

Looking back on this period we certainly did not think that this way of life would last forever. And indeed, it didn't. In the 1950s and early 1960s the Canadian government suddenly took an interest in 'its territories' in the far north. Focus on the area first came from the construction of the so-called Distant Early Warning Line, a sort of necklace of defence radar stations built by the US military above the Arctic Circle, from Baffin Island, Canada, to Wainwright, Alaska. With advancing technology and increasing explorations by prospectors, mineral exploitation in the Arctic was becoming a real possibility. And there were also tragic reports of inland-dwelling Inuit in Canada's 'barren grounds' starving to death. The Canadian government decided it was time to act. Without any meaningful consultation, they instigated a policy to move Inuit from the land into settlements that, in most instances, would be built at sites previously established by the Hudson's Bay Company and the missionaries.

From the start, the government's policy to move us 'off the land' was misguided and paternalistic. The idea was to make the 'administration' of Canada's Eskimos (as we were then called) easier. We were seen as a problem needing to be fixed. This would be mended by gathering us into settlements, building houses for us and 'educating' our children in English with a 'Dick and Jane' curriculum, an education that had nothing to do with what we knew to be the real world. We would partake of the government's assistance programmes such as family allowances (which sometimes could be withheld if we didn't send our children to school) and, when needed, social assistance payments and subsidized housing. Along with the provision of health services, these seemingly positive enticements were difficult to resist. Nowadays we recognize these offerings as coercive, though strangely packaged in well-meaning wrappings.

In my case, our family's move into the settlement happened in 1957, earlier than for most Inuit then living in the Canadian Arctic. At the time, we were living at Old Fort Chimo, where I was born, and where the Hudson's Bay Company still ran a trading post. Across the river from us, the US military had built a weather station and landing strip during the Second World War, one of several airstrips on a northern route to Europe, along which the Americans used to ferry aircraft to Britain. After the war the US transferred the site's buildings and airstrip to the Canadian government and in time, under its 'ingathering of Inuit' policy, these became the present-day community of Kuujjuaq.

April 1956: In Old Fort Chimo, where the author was born, across the river from where Kuujjuaq is now. Back row, left to right: Maggie Gordon, Kitty Munick, Mary Simon and Bridget Watt, the author's sister; front row: Joanne Ploughman, Donna Ploughman and the author
Courtesy of the author

With the move, things happened very quickly. At first, we expected that this new world in which we suddenly found ourselves would be as wise as our own. But it wasn't. It turned out that our new world was deeply dependent on external political and economic concepts and forces utterly at odds with our ways of being. In particular its structures seemed to have nothing to do with the natural world. Almost immediately, we started to give away our power. For a while we thought that if we were patient – as the Inuit hunters necessarily are – that patience would pay off. But we soon lost that sense of control over our lives, especially over the upbringing of our children. They were brought into the classrooms of southern institutional schooling, a concept totally foreign to us, where they were given an 'education' that had nothing to do with the knowledge and skills we needed for life on the land. All our traditional character-building teachings went out the window, and our social values began to erode. When we surrender our personal autonomy, we also give away our sense of self-worth, we lose the ability to define ourselves and to navigate our own lives. Being brought into the settlements was the beginning of the end for our traditional way of life. In the settlements we lived in a kind of bubble, separated from the natural world, exchanging our independence for increasing dependency.

In this new, confusing life – which, at least on the surface, seemed to meet all our basic needs – we also lost, above all, our sense of purpose. In our attempts to replace this loss with something else, many of us drifted into addictions and self-destructive behaviours, made worse by unemployment and poverty. This downward trend has played out over several generations in the most horrific ways, seen most tragically in the current levels of suicide among Inuit youth.

I was in my late teens when we experienced our first suicide in Kuujjuaq, a young Inuit woman, though she was not actually from our community. Traditionally suicide, in Inuit society, was rare and affected mostly adults, so this was shocking and incomprehensible to us all. Nowadays it's a tragic fact that our Inuit youth suicide rates are among the highest in the world. I have no doubt whatsoever that this tragedy is rooted in our move from the land, and the subsequent erosion of our culture and values, not to mention the historical traumas of forced relocations, the slaughter of our sled dogs and abuse in many forms by those with authority. Whatever the underlying causes, these suicides can often be impulsive. In our traditional ways, impulsivity had no place. On the land, to act impulsively was to put yourself and everyone else around you at risk. Even under extreme pressure, decisions had to be weighed carefully. In our upbringing we were taught to develop that sense of holding back, of reflecting and being focused: our very lives depended on us avoiding any urges towards reckless behaviour.

Along with many others of my generation, I was fortunate enough to have spent my formative years deeply steeped in Inuit traditional ways and values that gave us our understanding of the world and our place in it and, importantly, our responsibilities to it. My age group still talk about this – that sense of training and the grounding we got, which have kept us going and made us resilient.

My early years in Kuujjuaq cocooned me in these traditions thanks, primarily, to two incredibly strong women: my mother and my grandmother. I also learned by observing my uncle, a skilled hunter and community leader with a lot of integrity and dignity, as well as my older brothers, who had been taught many skills by my uncle and other men in our community. Beyond these, teachers enough in themselves, were the always gently instructive social interactions I enjoyed with the small community around us. This supportive and caring circle was occasionally enriched by Inuit visitors from other parts of Ungava Bay, coming into Kuujjuaq to trade, travelling by dog team in the winter or canoe in the summer. To this day I can vividly recall their words as I sat, silent and wide-eyed with amazement, listening to them relate their news and stories to my mother and grandmother.

Of course, these occasions were always an opportunity to liberally share in whatever country food we had at hand. Depending on the season, this could be any combination of fish, ptarmigan, seal and the choice parts of caribou, raw, dry, frozen or cooked, according to preference. Most often these foods would be enhanced by our traditional condiment, a dipping sauce we called *misiraq*, made from fermented seal oil. Sharing the food our land provides is a deeply held Inuit tradition, indeed an imperative – there's no other word for it. Wherever we are, this practice is still at the core of our family and community life. In this unspoken ritual, sharing nature's bounty renews, again and again, our bonds with each other and the land that sustains us.

I have an early memory that brought all these strands together, underscoring our essential place within nature that I didn't fully understand it at the time. Inuit have many categories of relationships and relationship terms without an exact equivalent in the Western world. Traditionally, personal names given at birth were said to carry souls and they immediately established a wide network of relationships, even mutual responsibilities, often extending beyond the immediate family. Nor were personal names ever gendered. For instance, a baby boy named after, say, his maternal grandmother would be addressed by his own mother as *anaana* – meaning mother – and, in some cases, at least until puberty, would be dressed and even socialized as a girl. Family members would notice with delight how he took on some of his grandmother's personality traits and mannerisms. In this way, his grandmother continued to live through him.

A particularly significant relationship, in terms of linking community and nature, was initiated at birth with the person who cut the umbilical cord, usually a woman. If the baby was a girl, this woman would be known as her *sanajik*; if a boy, she would be his *arnaqutik*. The baby then became the *arnaliak* of her *sanajik*, or the *angusiak* of his *arnaqutik*.

Both my grandmother and mother were known for their midwifery skills, and so they had a good number of *angusiaks* and *arnaliaks*. One of the main obligations of their *angusiaks* was to present them with their first catch from the hunt – be it fish, seal, ptarmigan or caribou, a rite of passage, celebrating the very foundations of Inuit society: that is the sacred, interdependent relationship between the animals we hunt and our hunters. When I was a small girl, I saw this ritual played out many times as these budding hunters – my grandmother's *angusiaks* – honoured their obligations to her. One at a time, every other month or so, young men would come by our house to present their catch. In response my grandmother put on an amazing performance. This normally quiet, dignified elderly woman would suddenly turn into an animal-like person, rolling around and making animal noises on the floor. Sometimes she would nibble the young hunter's hand or wrist, acknowledging their power, encouraging him to become a great hunter. I watched this startling performance almost in embarrassment because then, as a child, I didn't fully grasp its deep ceremonial significance, beyond sensing it was a necessary part of our hunting culture.

Left to right: Daisy Watt (the author's mother), the author and their friend Pasha Simigaq in Kangirsuk, Nunavik, *c.* summer 1957
Courtesy of the author

For their part, the girls and young women who were my grandmother's and mother's *arnaliaks* would be similarly honoured and encouraged when they brought gifts demonstrating their increasing ability in sewing. Proper, well-made skin clothing, warm and watertight as needed, was an absolute necessity for the successful provider. Inevitably my grandmother's ritual would finish with the young men or women we had just celebrated leaving the house confident and reassured, knowing that their work or hunt had been well received, endorsed by the woman who had helped to bring them into this life.

Sadly, this ancient custom is not much practised now. Though from my early years working at the Kuujjuaq nursing station, I assisted at several births and therefore have my own set of *angusiaks* and *arnaliaks*. I do my best to keep up with them, encouraging them over the years as they successfully fulfil their varied roles in life. Some of the young men have brought me their first hunt; the young women, gifts of their picked berries, caught fish or first pieces of handiwork. My response was not as dramatic as my grandmother's, but it was no less full of delighted gratitude. I was humbled and honoured that they had thought to keep this tradition alive.

Despite the extensive damage done to Inuit society and culture when we moved from the land into the villages, there is, in most of these settlements, an essential core of families instinctively committed to maintaining our traditions. Individual members of these families, even while living within the semi-urban settings, strive to relate to the land and its resources in the same respectful way that sustained us prior to the move. They acquire an intimate knowledge of their local area and the various animal species it supports. The men employ many of the same hunting skills used in former times while the women prepare and soften the skins of seals and caribou for the clothing they make for themselves and their hunters, using techniques, patterns and stitches handed down by an endless succession of mothers, aunts and grandmothers. Most importantly, members of these families embody the essential philosophies and understandings of the land and animals that enabled us to thrive over countless generations before we suffered the consequences of European contact. In a real and substantial sense such Inuit keep the vital flame of our culture alive. They are an irreplaceable resource, in both practical and intellectual ways, and they need and deserve every possible means of support.

But beyond the challenges this already vulnerable way of being endures, in the face of the Arctic's rapidly increasing urbanization (and globalization), there is another imminent threat – no less insidious – that, unless checked, will end forever our unique attachment to the land and its life-giving resources: climate change.

Dramatic climate change caused by greenhouse gases has left no feature of our Arctic landscape, seascape or way of life untouched. Climate change now threatens our very culture, our ability to live off the land and eat our country foods. Nowhere else in the world are ice and snow so essential to transportation and mobility. And yet the snow and ice coverings over which we access our traditional foods are becoming more and more unreliable and therefore unsafe, leaving our hunters more prone than ever to breaking through unexpectedly thin ice or being swept out to sea when the floe-ice platform, on which they are hunting, breaks off from the land-fast ice.

Additionally, climate change is affecting the migration patterns and routes of the animals we rely upon. This means that our hunters have to travel further, often over unsafe and unfamiliar trails, to access our country food. So, when we can no longer count on our vital, long-established travel routes, and can no longer find the animals where they should be, the matter immediately becomes an issue of safety and security at several levels.

With less traditional food available, many families are forced to shift away from our traditional food to a far less healthy diet shipped from the south, consisting mainly of processed foods crammed with sugar, salt and carbohydrates. It is no surprise that in Canada our Arctic communities are experiencing rapidly rising rates of diabetes and other food-related illnesses, trends that will only continue as we move away from a country-food diet.

Hand in hand with climate change is the ongoing threat of Arctic resource development targeting our rich mineral and oil deposits. Our anxieties on this front are regularly dismissed by our own governments who see the Arctic as the next super-energy 'feeder' for the world. In the greater scheme of things, Inuit concerns over their livelihoods and environment are dismissed as unimportant.

As someone who has led pioneering global work on connecting climate change to human rights, I am convinced that the escalating pressures we now face regarding resource development will deepen the need for all parties to adopt a rights-based approach in the search for solutions to these problems.

Everyone benefits from a frozen Arctic. The future of the Arctic environment, and the Inuit it supports, is inextricably tied to the future of the planet. Our Arctic home is a barometer of the planet's health: if we cannot save the Arctic, can we really hope to save the forests, the rivers and the farmlands of other regions?

We can also no longer separate the importance and the value of the Arctic from the sustainable growth of economies around the world. In the international arenas, where I have personally been involved, the language of economics and technology is always calling for further delays on climate action. We are constantly reminded that making any significant efforts to tackle greenhouse gas emissions will negatively impact the economy. But I truly believe that we must reframe the terms of the debate regarding the implications of environmental degradation, resource development and climate change in the Arctic and move beyond relying solely on the language of economics and technology. What is needed is a debate emphasizing human and cultural rights. Focusing only on economics and technology separates the issues from one another as opposed to recognizing the close connections among rights, environmental change, health, economic development and society. Ultimately, addressing climate change in the language of human rights and building the protection of human rights into our global climate agreements are not just matters of strategy, but moral and ethical imperatives that require the world to take a principled and courageous path to solve this great challenge.

And I strongly believe that we need to reimagine and realign economic values with those of the Indigenous world, the Inuit world, rather than merely replicating what hasn't worked with the values of Western society. And who better than the Inuit themselves, who are natural conservationists, to be out there on the land and ice as paid guardians and sentinels? How deeply affirming that would be for our hunters, whose remarkable traditional knowledge is so undervalued. What better way to reclaim what was taken from us: our pride, our dignity, our resourcefulness, our wisdom. We don't want to just be victims of globalization. We can offer much more to this debate if we could be included on every level. We have lived through states of emergency for decades now and we have attempted to signal to the world the climate crisis looming in front of us. Sadly, many in other parts of the world who are now experiencing these states of emergency, with the loss of their homes and livelihoods to fires, floods and other unnatural disasters caused by climate change, are finally beginning to see the connections.

So my message to you is: look to, listen to and support morally, respectfully, openly and, yes, financially the Inuit world, the Indigenous world, which from a place of deep love for their culture and traditions is fighting for the protection of a sustainable way of life. Not just for themselves, but for all of us. Heed and support those voices and their aspirations. We will help guide you as we navigate through these precarious situations together. Don't be on a mission to save us: this is not what we want or need. But together in equal partnership, with an understanding of our common humanity, we can do this together.

Epilogue

I began writing this piece in my Arctic home in Kuujjuaq. I am still here; still following the recommended social distancing and self-isolation measures brought on by the pandemic, a grim reminder of how interconnected and interdependent we all are. The remoteness of the Arctic no longer sets us apart from the rest of the world. This pandemic has also helped to break open unresolved issues of social injustices and racism: North American and European countries that often tout their great human rights reputations are now being fully exposed for outdated racist policies and attitudes which undermine, and put at great risk, the health of those most vulnerable. Black communities, the American Indian nations and our own Indigenous populations here in the Arctic show clearly that the economic and health gaps are huge in comparison to the white populations of rich countries. The only difference that sets us in the Arctic apart from our Black and Navaho brothers and sisters with the human losses they have suffered is that to date, as I write this, the geographic distance we live in and the lockdown of flights coming in and out of our regions have thus far protected us. That could easily change overnight if and when there is a resurgence of the virus. History has shown us that many Inuit families were wiped out by past epidemics, so our leaders are extremely committed in their attempts to keep the virus out of our regions.

In many different ways, the pandemic has also given us pause. I have been taking the time to use this pause as a gift to reflect on new possibilities, new perspectives. The world should not, cannot, go back to business as usual without a clearer understanding and consciousness of how we live.

In my life's work, dealing with climate change and the protection of our Inuit way of life, I have often wondered what is going to eventually 'give'? What big event will finally wake us up to the realization that the reckless, damaging way in which we do business around the world is unsustainable? In my talks, I often ask: 'What will it take to get the health back into our atmosphere so the earth can start to heal?' The earth is a living, breathing entity. If we care for it, it will heal just as our bodies do when we are sick.

I have always sensed the earth would reach its limits soon enough, but I didn't realize it would be in the form of a deadly virus that would virtually halt (at least temporarily) so many of our unsustainable activities. Almost immediately, the air and the waters of the world's industrial cities began to clear. Animals, suddenly relieved from unwelcoming human activity, appeared in some deserted city streets, as if reclaiming their rightful space. Nature is resilient, if only given the chance. Let's pay heed to these lessons. Let's make this a time of seeing that human trauma and planet trauma are one and the same. Let's not wait for another virus, driven by climate change and environmental degradation, to terrify us, too late, into half-hearted action. There is no time for half measures. The values and knowledge of the Indigenous world, the survival of which utterly depends upon living within nature, not apart from nature, hold the answer to many of the global challenges we face today. Indigenous wisdom is the medicine we seek in healing our planet and creating a sustainable world. I truly believe this. ■

CONTRIBUTORS

Patrick Barkham is a natural history writer for the *Guardian*. He is the author of several books including *The Butterfly Isles* and *Wild Child*, both available from Granta Books.

Xavi Bou began his Ornithographies project in 2012. His photography has been exhibited across the globe and published in the *Guardian*, *National Geographic*, *Der Spiegel*, *Geo* and *Sonntag*.

Nick Caistor is a British translator of Spanish, French and Portuguese. He lived in Argentina for a number of years, where he was the BBC Latin America analyst.

Tim Dee has been a birdwatcher for more than fifty years; his most recent book is *Greenery: Journeys in Springtime*.

Nate Duke's work is forthcoming in the *Colorado Review*, *Southern Humanities Review* and the *Arkansas International*. He is a PhD candidate in Creative Writing at Florida State University.

Tim Flannery is the author of thirty-two books including *The Future Eaters* and *The Weather Makers*. He has published over 140 peer-reviewed scientific papers and has named twenty-five living and fifty fossil mammal species. He was the 2007 Australian of the Year, and in 2011 was appointed as Australia's first Climate Commissioner.

Cal Flyn's first book *Thicker than Water* was selected by *The Times* as one of the best books of 2016. Her second book *Islands of Abandonment* is expected in January 2021.

Jessie Greengrass's collection of short stories, *An Account of the Decline of the Great Auk, According to One Who Saw It*, won the Edge Hill Short Story Prize

2016 and a Somerset Maugham Award. Her debut novel, *Sight*, was shortlisted for the Women's Prize for Fiction 2018. 'The High House' is an extract from a novel of the same name, forthcoming from Swift Press in April 2021.

Caoilinn Hughes's first novel *Orchid & the Wasp* won the 2019 Collyer Bristow Prize. Her short fiction has been awarded the Moth Short Story Prize and an O. Henry Award. *The Wild Laughter*, her second novel, is out now.

John Kinsella's recent books of poetry include *The Wound*, *Insomnia* and *Brimstone: A Book of Villanelles*. He is a Fellow of Churchill College, Cambridge University, and Professor of Literature and Environment at Curtin University.

Amy Leach is the author of *Things That Are*. Her second book, *The Modern Moose*, will be published by Farrar, Straus & Giroux in 2021.

Dino J. Martins currently serves as the Executive Director of the Mpala Research Centre and Research Scholar and Lecturer in Ecology and Evolutionary Biology at Princeton University. He is the author of four books, including *Our Friends the Pollinators*.

Rod Mason, also known as Ibai Wumburra, is an Indigenous Senior Law Man and local rainmaker of the Ngarigo people of south-eastern New South Wales. He is a healer, trained by his grandfather, and his totems are the Kaua (echidna) and Ibai (eagle-hawk). He is of the Wolgal-Bemmergal clan.

Charles Massy manages his family's sheep and cattle property of 2,000 acres on the Monaro, New South Wales,

Australia. He is the author of *Call of the Reed Warbler: A New Agriculture, A New Earth*.

Rebecca Priestley is an associate professor at the Centre for Science in Society at Te Herenga Waka – Victoria University of Wellington. Her most recent book is a memoir, *Fifteen Million Years in Antarctica*.

Callum Roberts is Professor of Marine Conservation at the University of Exeter, Chief Scientific Adviser of the Blue Marine Foundation and the author of *Reef Life: An Underwater Memoir*.

Judith D. Schwartz is an environmental journalist based in Vermont. She is the author, most recently, of *The Reindeer Chronicles: and Other Inspiring Stories of Working with Nature to Heal the Earth*.

Merlin Sheldrake is a biologist and the author of *Entangled Life: How Fungi Make Our Worlds, Change Our Minds and Shape Our Futures*. He received a PhD in tropical ecology from Cambridge University for his work on underground fungal networks in tropical forests in Panama.

Samanth Subramanian's journalism has appeared in the *New Yorker*, the *New York Times Magazine*, *WIRED* and *Harper's*, among other publications. His latest book is *A Dominant Character: The Radical Science and Restless Politics of J.B.S. Haldane*.

Ken Thompson was for twenty-five years a lecturer in ecology at the University of Sheffield. He is the author of *Where Do Camels Belong? The Story and Science of Invasive Species*, among other books. He writes regularly on gardening for the *Telegraph*.

Isabella Tree is the award-winning author of five books, most recently *Wilding: The Return of Nature to a British Farm*, which charts the story of the pioneering rewilding project in Sussex, where she lives.

Zoë Tryon is an environmental and Indigenous rights activist and speaker. Since 2006 she has been working with Indigenous groups in the Ecuadorian Amazon and across the globe. She is an ambassador for the Achuar people, Fundación Pachamama and Amazon Watch, and has been active in the case against Chevron in the Northern Ecuadorian Amazon.

Manari Ushigua was instrumental in achieving recognition for the Sápara as a distinct ethnicity from the Ecuadorian government, and winning UNESCO recognition for the Sápara language. He currently serves as an environmental ambassador for Ecuador's Education Ministry. Previously, he was the elected leader of the Sápara and a representative of CONAIE, Ecuador's national Indigenous confederation.

Sheila Watt-Cloutier is an Inuit activist and the author of *The Right to Be Cold*. She has been nominated for the Nobel Peace Prize and has received the UN Champion of the Earth Award, the Sophie Prize, the Jack P. Blaney Award for Dialogue and the Right Livelihood Award.

Adam Weymouth is a writer and journalist. His first book, *The Kings of the Yukon: An Alaskan River Journey*, won the 2018 Sunday Times / Peters Fraser + Dunlop Young Writer of the Year Award and the 2019 Lonely Planet Adventure Travel Book of the Year.